TWENTIETH CENTURY VIEWS

The aim of this series is to present the best in contemporary critical opinion on major authors, providing a twentieth century perspective on their changing status in an era of profound revaluation.

Maynard Mack, *Series Editor*
Yale University

CONRAD

CONRAD

A COLLECTION OF CRITICAL ESSAYS

Edited by

Marvin Mudrick

Prentice-Hall, Inc.   A SPECTRUM BOOK   *Englewood Cliffs, N.J.*

Current printing (last number):
10 9 8 7 6

Contents

CONRAD

Introduction

by Marvin Mudrick

Joseph Conrad is a puzzle for both the critic and the biographer. His reputation, forty years after his death, remains as protean and unfixable as many of the incidents of his unprecedented life. Criticism, which agrees on the importance of his example and influence, has not yet managed the approximation of a consensus regarding the relative merits of his individual novels: one could, for instance, compile collections of essays by intelligent critics on *Chance* and *Victory,* proving with equal vigor that these books are either masterpieces or fluent botches. The biographer of Conrad finds himself still turning over and reconsidering the enigmatic and self-contradictory personal records that Conrad seems to have taken some trouble to rearrange, alter, or suppress in his letters and under the guise of candid reminiscence.

Conrad is at the same time one of the most and one of the least autobiographical of writers. His experiences—especially his nautical experiences—were admittedly, and often with astonishing directness, the material of his novels; whereas his memoirs, when they are not inaccurate and misleading, are as reticent as those of any writer who has undertaken the confidential mode at all. Certainly, his life appears to be the material of art—of bad art however: summarized, it gives the impression of a meretricious novel. He was born of patriotic Polish gentry in their landlocked captive fatherland; at the age of four, companion of his parents into political exile in Russia; orphaned at eleven; in his 'teens, abruptly self-exiled to western Europe, a sailor and Carlist gun-runner off the coasts of France and Spain; at twenty, beneficiary and (almost fatal) casualty of a grand passion; master mariner in the British merchant marine before he was thirty; voyager to the heart of black Africa; ultimately, the most celebrated living novelist in a language he did not begin to speak till he had reached manhood. Thus recapitulated, it is less a life than a romance; and Conrad was not above touching it up here and there with mysteries and misrepresentations. Like his friend and occasional collaborator, Ford Madox Ford (one of his collaborations with whom was a novel named *Romance*), he was a romancer and a rhetorician. As with Ford, so with Conrad it is sometimes hard to make out, or even to guess at, the resistant, independent contours of his material, the

substance of his life and of a world at large. The actual is swallowed up
by his insistence on dispensing with it; it may not even survive as the
smile on the face of the tiger. Jocelyn Baines, having tried to ascertain
and sort out the facts about an adventure of Conrad's youth, tactfully
discusses Conrad's habit of reticence and evasion, and offers the requisite
cautions:

> . . . there are aspects of Conrad's version which are hard to reconcile with
> the known facts or are directly contradicted by them; and, if this were not
> sufficient warning, it is always dangerous unreservedly to accept a person's
> own account of his past. Few people relate events with any semblance of
> accuracy, even if they try to do so immediately after they have occurred;
> whereas Conrad's inaccuracy of memory was notorious among those who
> knew him and he was writing about his life in Marseilles several decades
> later. Moreover, in his autobiographical writings it was Conrad's aim to
> recreate a true impression of events rather than accurately to reproduce
> the facts, while in his fiction his intention was, obviously enough, artistic
> and not autobiographical.

Plainly, Conrad is an extreme case, whether he conceals his youthful
attempt at suicide under the more acceptable crisis of a duel, or, the
author of Part First of *Under Western Eyes,* angrily disclaims any indebtedness to Dostoevsky; whether he supplies his docile French friend
and biographer with hopelessly jumbled and mistaken personal chronol-
ogies, or constructs the intricate enclosures of method within whose in-
nermost circle the "events" of *Chance* or *Victory, Lord Jim* or *Nostromo*
may more or less confidently be presumed to occur. E. M. Forster's judgment of Conrad, that "the secret casket of his genius contains a vapour
rather than a jewel," testifies to the aura of unseizability that much of
Conrad diffuses, an aura of indifference or hostility to the refractory and
specifiable actual. "Illusion" is one of Conrad's favorite words. The
writer for whom reality appears, characteristically, as a trick of the imagination does not scruple to modify it for his own artistic and private
purposes.

Conrad is the nearly perfect skeptic who happens also to be a novelist.
His rhetoric is the act of will that intends to certify what is not otherwise certifiable, perhaps not even intelligible, possibly not even there;
and the continuous problem for the critic of Conrad is to determine just
when this powerful unity of intention unexpectedly encounters a set of
external conditions as vexatious and intransigent as itself. The effect of
Conrad's very best work is obstruction and deadlock, an opposition of
matched and mutually paralyzed energies; the effect of his worst is manner without matter; and both effects are liable to be found (as in *Heart
of Darkness*) side by side in the same novel. Against those who wish to
ascertain and sort out the facts of his life or the qualities of his fiction,
Conrad the man defends himself with the ingenuity of the pyrrhonist
for whom both life and art are not—as they are for Conrad the novelist

—contests between will and the stubborn actual, but pure invention, the autonomous and unreflected will.

The set of external conditions that Conrad could least successfully wish away was the mariner's life that he lived for two decades of his youth and manhood. Conrad never tired of denying indignantly that he was a writer of sea-tales, nor was he so special and local a writer. Yet those of his works which most successfully challenge the nullifying blast of his temperament are tales of the sea, or of distant coasts and places— tales of adventure that a thoughtful man might pick up and mull over, or put together and develop, while on the job as a merchant seaman or off duty in some remote port or other. The obvious instance is *Typhoon,* a short novel which is, straightforwardly enough, an account of a typhoon and of a ship that weathers it. The language is as densely referential as a logbook's, except that no ship's captain (except Conrad) could ever have sustained its precision and sardonic humor, or—as when the boat-swain looks in on the tumbled coolies in the hold—could have roused it to the pitch of descriptive passages matching the perturbation and wonder of the mighty storm itself:

> He pulled back the bolt: the heavy iron plate turned on its hinges; and it was as though he had opened the door to the sounds of the tempest. A gust of hoarse yelling met him: the air was still; and the rushing of water overhead was covered by a tumult of strangled, throaty shrieks that pro- duced an effect of desperate confusion. He straddled his legs the whole width of the doorway and stretched his neck. And at first he perceived only what he had come to seek: six small yellow flames swinging volently on the great body of the dusk.
>
> It was stayed like the gallery of a mine, with a row of stanchions in the middle, and cross-beams overhead, penetrating into the gloom ahead—in- definitely. And to port there loomed, like the caving in of one of the sides, a bulky mass with a slanting outline. The whole place, with the shadows and the shapes, moved all the time. The boatswain glared: the ship lurched to starboard, and a great howl came from that mass that had the slant of fallen earth.
>
> Pieces of wood whizzed past. Planks, he thought, inexpressibly startled, and flinging back his head. At his feet a man went sliding over, open-eyed, on his back, straining with uplifted arms for nothing: and another came bounding like a detached stone with his head between his legs and his hands clenched. His pigtail whipped in the air; he made a grab at the boatswain's legs, and from his opened hand a bright white disc rolled against the boat- swain's foot. He recognized a silver dollar, and yelled at it with astonish- ment. With a precipitated sound of trampling and shuffling of bare feet, and with guttural cries, the mound of writhing bodies piled up to port de- tached itself from the ship's side and sliding, inert and struggling, shifted to starboard, with a dull, brutal thump. The cries ceased. The boatswain heard a long moan through the roar and whistling of the wind; he saw an inex- tricable confusion of heads and shoulders, naked soles kicking upwards, fists raised, tumbling backs, legs, pigtails, faces.

"Good Lord!" he cried, horrified, and banged-to the iron door upon this vision.

Conrad never quite overcame his tendency—as of an occasionally faulty foreigner's ear for English—toward platitude and clumsy repetitiveness ("effect of desperate confusion," "inextricable confusion"; "overhead" used twice in some half-dozen lines for jarringly different purposes; "ahead" closely following the second "overhead"); but the passage, taken as a whole, is as bizarre and energetic as it is uninterruptedly in touch with external conditions. It has the momentum of an almost absolute coincidence between manner and matter; it confirms the breadth of man's ambition by certifying the existence and magnitude of his adversary; it defines the gusto and terror of total engagement. Another, and still more impressive, example of what might be called Conrad's power of conjuration is the storm episode in *The Nigger of the "Narcissus."* And Conrad's greatest, his subtlest, his most extended and most richly detailed example —perhaps the greatest descriptive passage in English fiction—is the episode of the voyage upriver in *Heart of Darkness.*

In recent years it has become the critical fashion to depreciate such "set-pieces" ("descriptions of sunsets, exotic seas and the last plunge of flaming wrecks": so F. R. Leavis pigeonholes them in his impatience to bring to light the plain virtues of Conrad's psychological realism). Critics devote themselves to Conrad's political acumen (*Nostromo, The Secret Agent, Under Western Eyes*) or to his pre-Jungian intuitions (*Lord Jim,* "The Secret Sharer," "Amy Foster," the "unspeakable" and "inscrutable" aspects of *Heart of Darkness, The Shadow Line*). The political critic discovers that Conrad has uncannily prophesied the forms and impulses of modern totalitarianism (as Shakespeare was once praised for having anticipated modern psychotherapy). The Jungian critic, on the other hand, is likely to eschew public issues for coterie hallucinations: alert to register the interminable significances in the night journeys of Conrad's gloomier protagonists (Jim, the captain in "The Secret Sharer," Marlow in *Heart of Darkness*); or pondering, as in one notorious essay, the mystic phoneme that not only occupies the front of the secret sharer's name but names the shape of his room. Mr. Baines, forthright Englishman, dismisses the more absurd among these lay analysts under the term "alchemical critics": they "appear to have assumed the mantle of the alchemists or dabblers in the occult; to them literary texts are arcana offering knowledge to those who can find the key." [1] Not that some of the political and depth-psychology critics aren't, some of the time, capable of helpful commentary on Conrad. Morton Zabel's introduction to *Under Western Eyes* is informative about the political origins

[1] Conrad's friend and confidant, Richard Curle, has noted that "Conrad was a realist, who disapproved altogether of the type of symbolism represented by such a work as Herman Melville's *Moby Dick,* a book which he detested." Richard Curle, *Joseph Conrad and His Characters* (Fair Lawn: Essential Books, Inc., 1958), p. 171.

of that novel, and their assimilation into recurrent Conradian themes. Thomas Moser has written authoritatively on Conrad's misogyny and its part in the feeblenesses and oversimplifications of his later work. Even Albert Guerard, self-consecrated to the boldest literary-Jungian banalities, now and again breaks free for a persuasive examination of Conrad's text.

Whatever one's doubts about the strenuous political and symbolic stresses of much Conrad criticism, it would not do to imply that Conrad's choice of a maritime or exotic subject out of the solidities of his seafarer's life guarantees the attentiveness to fact, the unobstructed intensity of observation, that one finds in *Typhoon*. Both *Youth* and *The Shadow Line* are similar to *Typhoon* in the sailor's routine they are grounded in and the kinds of suspense they are intended to generate. But *Youth* is undermined by the yeasty apostrophizing that Conrad, through the voice of Marlow, is liable to offer as moral illumination:

> Oh, the glamour of youth! Oh, the fire of it, more dazzling than the flames of the burning ship, throwing a magic light on the wide earth, leaping audaciously to the sky, presently to be quenched by time, more cruel, more pitiless, more bitter than the sea—and like the flames of the burning ship surrounded by an impenetrable night.

The Shadow Line suffers from comparable leakages of facile skepticism ("an immensity that receives no impress, preserves no memories, and keeps no reckoning of lives"); and it takes an awkward, disingenuous fling at the quasi-supernatural. Its principal shortcoming, though, is what certain critics have regarded as its triumph—an unreserved endorsement of the idea of duty, whether through the stiff upper lip of the all too quietly noble Ransome ("'You think I ought to be on deck?' . . . 'I do, sir.'") or expressly by the narrator himself as he condemns the dead captain:

> . . . the end of . . . [the captain's] life was a complete act of treason, the betrayal of a tradition which seemed to me as imperative as any guide on earth could be.

The author of *Heart of Darkness* knows that life is not so readily reducible to this idea of peremptory routine honorably carried out, this simple prop for the complex man whose strongest memory from twenty years of sea-life was a harrowing boredom, and who in *Typhoon* understood that Captain MacWhirr could serenely ride out the storm—could indeed be heroic—because he lacked the treacherous gift of imagination: "skimming over the years of existence . . . , ignorant of life to the last."

As for the exotic Conrad, like Swinburne he is his own parodist. "The Lagoon" is as ludicrous as Max Beerbohm's parody of it; it pours out cataracts of the silliest and most narcissistic prose by any major writer in English:

The ever-ready suspicion of evil, the gnawing suspicion that lurks in our hearts, flowed out into the stillness round him—into the stillness profound and dumb, and made it appear untrustworthy and infamous, like the placid and impenetrable mask of an unjustifiable violence. In that fleeting and powerful disturbance of his being the earth enfolded in the starlight peace became a shadowy country of inhuman strife, a battle-field of phantoms terrible and charming, august or ignoble, struggling ardently for the possession of our helpless hearts. An unquiet and mysterious country of inextinguishable desires and fears.

Conrad's two earliest novels have exotic settings also; but in fact for the most part—barring the incontinent last hundred pages of *An Outcast of the Islands*—they are interestingly plotted and soberly written books that initiate into English fiction, and treat with some penetration, the theme of moral decay in an alien setting. The early Conrad does have stories to tell that survive his annihilating temperament; the drawback is that he has not yet learned or worked out adequate techniques for giving them room to move and grow in. Both *Almayer's Folly* and *An Outcast of the Islands* are disfigured not so much by self-admiring exoticisms as by a crippled and dragging pace, a reliance on endlessly summarizing flashbacks. Those moments which ought to be their most vivid are buried in pages of spasmodic and breathless catching up.

The point, at any rate, is not that *Typhoon* succeeds because it is about the sea, or *Heart of Darkness* because its setting is exotic, or either of them because it has numerous passages of magnificent descriptive prose. Conrad's descriptive power, in these persistently scenic tales as in *The Nigger of the "Narcissus,"* is striking in itself, it produces set-pieces for anthologies and excitement for those readers who enjoy scraps of charged prose, it reveals and vindicates Conrad's attachment to the places and occupations of his young manhood, it profits by the picaresque resonances of ships at sea and sojourns in strange, far places. Crucially, however, what it does is to mediate and dramatize the extreme and therefore isolating actions—a typhoon, a reversion to savagery, a mortal illness—that determine and disclose character. Conrad's solipsistic temperament solves the problem of morality by the doctrine of extremity; his descriptive power provides the exploratory and illustrative scenes of trial and definition.[2] Man proves his moral nature not socially, not by talk or love or daily living, but by solitary ordeal, by passing through circumstances catastrophic and lonely enough to wring out of him all possible insincerities, not least the insincerity of a consoling rhetoric. Failing such disciplinary circumstances and the power to dramatize them, Conrad's fiction is likely to dilate with conspicuous ease into politics or

[2] The language of "the earlier Conrad" is "important to us" because it is "struggling to digest and express new objects, new groups of objects, new feelings, new aspects." T. S. Eliot, *Selected Essays* (New York: Harcourt, Brace & World, 1950), p. 285.

symbology or the pneumatic ironies of the "Cosmic Joke," Conrad's term for the spectacle of the inexhaustibly contemptible human condition.

To discuss Conrad as if he were a unique and self-created phenomenon is, of course, to ignore the very literary ambiences of his Polish childhood and of his English writing career, his acknowledgments of obligation to various masters, his adaptation of modes of fictional statement inaugurated by others. Sometimes the influence is comical in its unaccommodated identifiability, as in the opening sentences of *An Outcast of the Islands*:

> When he stepped off the straight and narrow path of his peculiar honesty, it was with an inward assertion of unflinching resolve to fall back again into the monotonous but safe stride of virtue as soon as his little excursion into the wayside quagmires had produced the desired effect. It was going to be a short episode—a sentence in brackets, so to speak—in the flowing tale of his life: a thing of no moment, to be done unwillingly, yet neatly, and to be quickly forgotten. . . .

Usually, however, the influence, whether of James's magisterial obliquities or of the remote exactitudes of Flaubert and Maupassant, is absorbed into Conrad's own manner and preoccupations. An outstanding instance is the early story, "An Outpost of Progress," Conrad's first working of his Congo recollections. It is as Flaubertian as *L'Éducation Sentimentale,* and its two principal figures are transferred alive from *Bouvard et Pécuchet.* The wholly Conradian result is a comedy of squalid hubris which concludes in murder and self-crucifixion, and which by the unrelieved blackness of its humor makes Flaubert seem sunnily genial. Incidentally, Conrad takes this early occasion to make explicit, in an assertion that weakens the otherwise diabolic objectivity of the story, his doctrine of extremity:

> Few men realize that their life, the very essence of their character, their capabilities and their audacities, are only the expression of their belief in the safety of their surroundings. The courage, the composure, the confidence; the emotions and principles; every great and every insignificant thought belongs not to the individual but to the crowd: to the crowd that believes blindly in the irresistible force of its institutions and of its morals, in the power of its police and of its opinion. But the contact with pure unmitigated savagery, with primitive nature and primitive man, brings sudden and profound trouble into the heart. To the sentiment of being alone of one's kind, to the clear perception of the loneliness of one's thoughts, of one's sensations—to the negation of the habitual, which is safe, there is added the affirmation of the unusual, which is dangerous; a suggestion of things vague, uncontrollable, and repulsive, whose discomposing intrusion excites the imagination and tries the civilized nerves of the foolish and the wise alike.

The haranguing note is untypical. Mostly, Conrad's tone in this story is sardonically casual, flexible, almost colloquial; and it allows him to

modulate into remarkable effects that he can only portentously attempt in
later, more self-conscious works; for instance, Kayerts' hallucination afteɪ
he has murdered Carlier:

> . . . he reflected that the fellow dead there had been a noxious beast any-
> way; that men died every day in thousands; perhaps in hundreds of thou-
> sands—who could tell?—and that in the number, that one death could not
> possibly make any difference; couldn't have any importance, at least to a
> thinking creature. He, Kayerts, was a thinking creature. He had been all his
> life, till that moment, a believer in a lot of nonsense like the rest of man-
> kind—who are fools; but now he thought! He knew! He was at peace; he
> was familiar with the highest wisdom! Then he tried to imagine himself
> dead, and Carlier sitting in his chair watching him; and his attempt met
> with such unexpected success, that in a very few moments he became not at
> all sure who was dead and who was alive. This extraordinary achievement
> of his fancy startled him, however, and by a clever and timely effort of mind
> he saved himself just in time from becoming Carlier. His heart thumped,
> and he felt hot all over at the thought of that danger. Carlier! What a
> beastly thing! To compose his now disturbed nerves—and no wonder!—he
> tried to whistle a little. Then, suddenly, he fell asleep, or thought he had
> slept; but at any rate there was a fog, and somebody had whistled in the
> fog.
>   He stood up. The day had come, and a heavy mist had descended upon
> the land: the mist penetrating, enveloping, and silent; the morning mist of
> tropical lands; the mist that clings and kills; the mist white and deadly,
> immaculate and poisonous. He stood up, saw the body, and threw his arms
> above his head with a cry like that of a man who, waking from a trance,
> finds himself immured forever in a tomb. *"Help! . . . My God!"*

Comparing this passage (even the stigmatic clusters of postnominal adjectives in the last paragraph are not altogether unfunctional) with the
heavy-handed and repetitive business, in *Under Western Eyes,* of Razumov's delusion that he is walking over Haldin's body, one can better
judge when Conrad is simply a rationalistic copyist of Dostoevskian
mysteries, and when he composes a scene that, in its ambiguous tremor
between sleep and waking, is fit to stand with the Dostoevskian mysteries:
with, say, the hallucinatory episode in *Crime and Punishment* that culminates in Svidrigaïlov's suicide.

If *Under Western Eyes* is an accomplished and labored imitation of
Dostoevsky by a novelist who has stopped believing in ghosts, *The Secret
Agent* and *Nostromo* are Conrad's Flaubertian novels. *The Secret Agent*
has been "rediscovered" in recent years, along with the other political
novels of Conrad, by critics who marvel at Conrad's insight into the
psychology of revolution and the psychology of despotism. However
clairvoyant Conrad may have been in these matters, *The Secret Agent*
is a masterly, if somewhat fatigued, Flaubertian exercise in the form of a
thriller. The fact that the criminals are spies and bomb-carrying anarchists, rather than routine murderers, is not so noteworthy as it purports

to be; the spies, anarchists, policemen, and Russians could come out of any clever melodrama; Stevie is a maladroitly obvious, and undeveloped, cousin of Dostoevsky's saintly idiots. Only the Verlocs achieve a degree of pathos, though never with the inwardness that would make their plight the animating center of the novel.

Nostromo is something else again, a novel of large intentions and on a heroic scale. It is the rock on which most Conrad critics founder, shouting "Masterpiece!" while their misgivings gleam like eyes through the unexamined defects of their convictions. Mr. Baines interrupts his very sympathetic consideration to remark on "the weakness of Conrad's characterisation":

> It is evident that most of the characters, in particular the leading ones, exist for what they represent rather than for what they are. Although they play important roles in the development of the themes and are in that respect vivid and real, their psychology is on the whole crude, blurred, or even unconvincing.

Dr. Leavis calls *Nostromo* Conrad's "most considerable work" and "one of the great novels of the language," continues to praise it without qualification, and unexpectedly ends with what appears to be about as severe a qualification as one could make:

> At any rate, for all the rich variety of the interest and the tightness of the pattern, the reverberation of *Nostromo* has something hollow about it; with the colour and life there is a suggestion of a certain emptiness. And for explanation it is perhaps enough to point to this reflection of Mrs. Gould's:
>
> > It had come into her mind that for life to be large and full, it must contain the care of the past and of the future in every passing moment of the present.

That kind of self-sufficient day-to-dayness of living Conrad can convey, when writing from within the Merchant Service, where clearly he has known it. We are made aware of hostile natural forces threatening his seamen with extinction, but not of metaphysical gulfs opening under life and consciousness: reality on board ship is domestic, assured and substantial. "That feeling of life-emptiness which had made me so restless for the last few months," says the young captain of *The Shadow Line,* entering on his new command, "lost its bitter plausibility, its evil influence." For life in the Merchant Service there is no equivalent in *Nostromo*—no intimate sense conveyed of the day-by-day continuities of social living. And though we are given a confidential account of what lies behind Dr. Monygham's sardonic face, yet on the whole we see the characters from the outside, and only as they belong to the ironic pattern—figures in the futilities of a public drama, against a dwarfing background of mountain and gulf.

Dr. Leavis overestimates the tidiness and metaphysical comfort of Conrad's representations of life at sea; but the case he belatedly makes against *Nostromo* is just. *Nostromo* is a novel full of astute, even apho-

ristic observations; its subject is a related group of serious issues seriously
scrutinized and elaborated; it is brilliantly put together with the mature
skill of an extraordinary craftsman; and it is hollow. It is a prodigiously
ingenious waxworks museum, which in certain lights and to certain innocent minds appears to be an assemblage of live human beings.

What has happened by the time of *Nostromo* is that Conrad's rhetoric
has grown hard and polished, the painstakingly articulated exoskeleton
of suppressed and no longer acknowledgeable nightmares; the monocle
through which a formidable uncle surveys, from his languid position
by the fireplace mantel, the places, colors, and theatrical tableaux of
a safely emptied world:

> He laughed wildly and turned in the doorway towards the body of the
> late Senor Hirsch, an opaque long blotch in the semi-transparent obscurity
> of the room between the two tall parallelograms of the windows full of
> stars.
> "You man of fear!" he cried. "You shall be avenged by me—Nostromo.
> Out of my way, doctor! Stand aside—or, by the suffering soul of a woman
> dead without confession, I will strangle you with my two hands."

By the time of *Chance* and *Victory* (to say nothing of such fag-end ad-
venture-stuff as *The Arrow of Gold, The Rescue,* and *The Rover*), even
the rhetoric has lost its stately air, it is shabby and hurried; the familiar
technical devices—the time-shift; the plurality of narrators, of whom
Number One learns from Number Two what Number Two has learned
from Number Three about Characters Five and Seven—are flung with
a desperate hurly-burly into creaky plots which, if they lacked the name
of Conrad and his increasingly mechanical prestidigitations, would
plainly enough mark the abdication by the artist of any pretense to an
adult interest in human issues.

In any case, Conrad is not a novelist but a writer of novellas. His impulse exhausts, or only artificially protracts, itself beyond their length:
the length of a nightmare or of a moral test, not—as novels require—
of history or biography. The enduring Conrad is the Conrad who had
learned his scope and his method without having yet decided to evade
the force of his obsessions. His great and unprecedented works were all
written within a period of six years: "An Outpost of Progress" in 1896,
The Nigger of the "Narcissus" in 1897, *Heart of Darkness* in 1899, *Typhoon* in 1902. *Lord Jim,* the only other considerable work during this
period, is, as Conrad himself seems to have thought,[3] essentially a short
story expanded far beyond its proper limits; expanded, besides, by
Marlow's more than customarily confused and high-flown ruminations
(so dear to the Jungian critics that *Lord Jim* is the pet of their idolatry):

[3] In Richard Curle's copy of *Lord Jim* Conrad wrote: "When I began this story,
which some people think my best . . . —personally I don't—I formed the resolve to
cram as much character and episode into it as it could hold. This explains its great
length which the story itself does not justify."

as Mr. Baines has commented, "one may be tempted to wonder whether even Conrad himself was always quite clear as to what he was trying to say or, in this case, whether there was not some unresolved ambiguity in his own attitude to the events described." Conrad was never, even during this period, quite insusceptible to the promptings of his self-indulgent skepticism, whether translated into the deliquescent jargon of Marlow (a much overrated personage, whose only necessary and luminous incarnation is in *Heart of Darkness*) or served out as a sauce without meat: "The Lagoon," it is disconcerting to recall, was written within a month of "An Outpost of Progress" and published in the same volume.

The primary fact about Conrad criticism is the insensitivity with which it has performed its task of discrimination among the tales and novels of the most uneven of fiction-writers in English. Meanwhile, one may hazard one's own provisional formulation. Before 1896 Conrad was an exceptional novice, already an innovator with his own individual tone and theme; after 1902 he was a distinguished and, at last, deservedly famous professional writer writing novels; in his best fiction between those years he is doubtless the most original, and very likely the greatest, writer of novellas in English (his only rivals are Melville and James). His claim on our attention is profound and durable, but his reputation should not be permitted to base itself—as recent criticism has more and more aggressively encouraged it to do—on one combination or another of those of his books which most pretentiously repudiate the boundaries of his claim. His finest work is as irreplaceable as, after all, the present renown of some of his weakest books is a judgment on the more eccentric hobbies of modern criticism.

The Feast

by Max Beerbohm

The hut in which slept the white man was on a clearing between the forest and the river. Silence, the silence murmurous and unquiet of a tropical night, brooded over the hut that, baked through by the sun, sweated a vapour beneath the cynical light of the stars. Mahamo lay rigid and watchful at the hut's mouth. In his upturned eyes, and along the polished surface of his lean body black and immobile, the stars were reflected, creating an illusion of themselves who are illusions.

The roofs of the congested trees, writhing in some kind of agony private and eternal, made tenebrous and shifty silhouettes against the sky, like shapes cut out of black paper by a maniac who pushes them with his thumb this way and that, irritably, on a concave surface of blue steel. Resin oozed unseen from the upper branches to the trunks swathed in creepers that clutched and interlocked with tendrils venomous, frantic and faint. Down below, by force of habit, the lush herbage went through the farce of growth—that farce old and screaming, whose trite end is decomposition.

Within the hut the form of the white man, corpulent and pale, was covered with a mosquito-net that was itself illusory like everything else, only more so. Flying squadrons of mosquitoes inside its meshes flickered and darted over him, working hard, but keeping silence so as not to excite him from sleep. Cohorts of yellow ants disputed him against cohorts of purple ants, the two kinds slaying one another in thousands. The battle was undecided when suddenly, with no such warning as it gives in some parts of the world, the sun blazed up over the horizon, turning night into day, and the insects vanished back into their camps.

The white man ground his knuckles into the corners of his eyes, emitting that snore final and querulous of a middle-aged man awakened rudely. With a gesture brusque but flaccid he plucked aside the net and peered around. The bales of cotton cloth, the beads, the brass wire, the bottles of rum, had not been spirited away in the night. So far so good.

The faithful servant of his employers was now at liberty to care for his own interests. He regarded himself, passing his hands over his skin.

"Hi! Mahamo!" he shouted. "I've been eaten up."

The islander, with one sinuous motion, sprang from the ground, through the mouth of the hut. Then, after a glance, he threw high his hands in thanks to such good and evil spirits as had charge of his concerns. In a tone half of reproach, half of apology, he murmured—

"You white men sometimes say strange things that deceive the heart."

"Reach me that ammonia bottle, d'you hear?" answered the white man. "This is a pretty place you've brought me to!" He took a draught. "Christmas Day, too! Of all the—— But I suppose it seems all right to you, you funny blackamoor, to be here on Christmas Day?"

"We are here on the day appointed, Mr. Williams. It is a feast-day of your people?"

Mr. Williams had lain back, with closed eyes, on his mat. Nostalgia was doing duty to him for imagination. He was wafted to a bedroom in Marylebone, where in honour of the Day he lay late dozing, with great contentment; outside, a slush of snow in the street, the sound of church-bells; from below a savour of especial cookery. "Yes," he said, "it's a feast-day of my people."

"Of mine also," said the islander humbly.

"Is it though? But they'll do business first?"

"They must first do that."

"And they'll bring their ivory with them?"

"Every man will bring ivory," answered the islander, with a smile gleaming and wide.

"How soon'll they be here?"

"Has not the sun risen? They are on their way."

"Well, I hope they'll hurry. The sooner we're off this cursed island of yours the better. Take all those things out," Mr. Williams added, pointing to the merchandise, "and arrange them—neatly, mind you!"

In certain circumstances it is right that a man be humoured in trifles. Mahamo, having borne out the merchandise, arranged it very neatly.

While Mr. Williams made his toilet, the sun and the forest, careless of the doings of white and black men alike, waged their warfare implacable and daily. The forest from its inmost depths sent forth perpetually its legions of shadows that fell dead in the instant of exposure to the enemy whose rays heroic and absurd its outposts annihilated. There came from those inilluminable depths the equable rumour of myriads of winged things and crawling things newly roused to the task of killing and being killed. Thence detached itself, little by little, an insidious sound of a drum beaten. This sound drew more near.

Mr. Williams, issuing from the hut, heard it, and stood gaping towards it.

"Is that them?" he asked.

"That is they," the islander murmured, moving away towards the edge of the forest.

Sounds of chanting were a now audible accompaniment to the drum.

"What's that they're singing?" asked Mr. Williams.

"They sing of their business," said Mahamo.

"Oh!" Mr. Williams was slightly shocked. "I'd have thought they'd be singing of their feast."

"It is of their feast they sing."

It has been stated that Mr. Williams was not imaginative. But a few years of life in climates alien and intemperate had disordered his nerves. There was that in the rhythms of the hymn which made bristle his flesh.

Suddenly, when they were very near, the voices ceased, leaving a legacy of silence more sinister than themselves. And now the black spaces between the trees were relieved by bits of white that were the eyeballs and teeth of Mahamo's brethren.

"It was of their feast, it was of you, they sang," said Mahamo.

"Look here," cried Mr. Williams in his voice of a man not to be trifled with. "Look here, if you've——"

He was silenced by sight of what seemed to be a young sapling sprung up from the ground within a yard of him—a young sapling tremulous, with a root of steel. Then a thread-like shadow skimmed the air, and another spear came impinging the ground within an inch of his feet.

As he turned in his flight he saw the goods so neatly arranged at his orders, and there flashed through him, even in the thick of the spears, the thought that he would be a grave loss to his employers. This—for Mr. Williams was, not less than the goods, of a kind easily replaced— was an illusion. It was the last of Mr. Williams' illusions.

On *The Nigger of the "Narcissus"*

by Albert Guerard

The complexities of *Almayer's Folly* are those of a man learning—and with what a perverse instinct for the hardest way!—the language of the novelist. *The Nigger of the "Narcissus"* is the first of the books to carry deliberately and with care the burden of several major interests and various minor ones. The one interest which existed for most readers in 1897 remains a real one today: the faithful document of life and adventure at sea. The story is indeed the tribute to the "children of the sea" that Conrad wanted it to be: a memorial to a masculine society and the successful seizing of a "passing phase of life from the remorseless rush of time." [1] It is certainly a tribute to this particular ship on which (for her beauty) Conrad chose to sail in 1884. But it is also a study in collective psychology; and also, frankly, a symbolic comment on man's nature and destiny; and also, less openly, a prose-poem carrying overtones of myth. No small burden, and one which Conrad carried with more care than usual: one passage exists in as many as seven versions. [2] "It is the book by which, not as a novelist perhaps, but as an artist striving for the utmost sincerity of expression, I am willing to stand or fall." [3]

A rich personal novel can hardly be overinterpreted, but it can be misinterpreted easily enough. The dangers of imbalance are suggested by three other masculine narratives which similarly combine faithful reporting and large symbolic suggestion. *The Red Badge of Courage* may well present a sacramental vision and still another of the ubiquitous Christ figures which bemuse criticism; the patterns of imagery are challenging. But it is also, importantly, a record of military life. So too I would allow that "The Bear" contains primitive pageant-rites, initiation ritual, the Jungian descent into the unconscious, perhaps even the Jungian mandala. These matters put the critic on his mettle. But he

[1] Preface, *The Nigger of the "Narcissus."*

[2] John D. Gordan, *Joseph Conrad: The Making of a Novelist* (Cambridge, Mass.: Harvard University Press, 1941), pp. 141-144.

[3] "To My Readers in America" (Preface of 1914), *The Nigger of the "Narcissus."*

should acknowledge that some of the story's best pages concern hunting in the big woods and the vanishing of these woods before commercial encroachment. The dangers of imbalance are even more serious when provoked by a slighter work, such as *The Old Man and the Sea*. To say that the novel is about growing old, or about the aging artist's need to substitute skill for strength, is plausible. But can a critic be satisfied with so little? One has gone so far as to find a parable of the decline of the British Empire. This, I submit, takes us too far from the boat and the marlin attached to its side; from the small greatness of a story whose first strength lies in its faithful recording of sensations, of fishing and the sea.

The Nigger of the "Narcissus" (sixty years after the event) is peculiarly beset with dangers for the critic. For Conrad has become fashionable rather suddenly, and comment on this story has passed almost without pause from naïve recapitulation to highly sophisticated analysis of "cabalistic intent." The older innocence is suggested by Arthur Symons' complaint that the story had no idea behind it, or by a journeyman reviewer's remark that James Wait had no place in this record of life at sea.[4] An example of recent sophistication is Vernon Young's important essay "Trial by Water," in the Spring 1952 issue of *Accent*. A single sentence will suggest its bias: "Fearful of overstressing the subaqueous world of the underconsciousness, the symbol-producing level of the psyche which, in fact, was the most dependable source of his inspiration, Conrad overloaded his mundane treatment of the crew." The comment is provocative; it leads us to wonder whether the crew isn't, for this fiction, too numerous. Yet we must rejoin that the crew is very important, and that many of the book's greatest pages have little to do with this subaqueous world. There remains the vulgar charge, yet real menace, that the critic may oversimplify a novel by oversubtilizing and overintellectualizing it—not merely by intruding beyond the author's conscious intention (which he is fully privileged to do) but by suggesting patterns of unconscious combination which do not and cannot operate for the reasonably alert common reader. Much of any serious story works on the fringes of the reader's consciousness: a darkness to be illumined by the critic's insight. But that insight remains irrelevant which can never become aesthetic enjoyment, or which takes a story too far out of its own area of discourse. I say this with the uneasy conviction that criticism should expose itself to as many as possible of a novel's suasions, and that it is only too easy (above all with a Conrad or a Faulkner) to stress the abstract and symbolic at the expense of everything else. One might begin by saying that *The Nigger of the "Narcissus"* recasts the story of Jonah and anticipates "The Secret Sharer" 's drama

[4] Gordan, *Joseph Conrad*, pp. 286, 289.

of identification. This is a truth but a partial truth. And how many partial truths would be needed to render or even evoke such a mobile as this one? Touch one wire, merely breathe on the lovely thing and it wavers to a new form! In the pursuit of structured meaning—of obvious purpose and overtone of conviction and "cabalistic intent" and unconscious content; of stark symbol and subtle cluster of metaphor—one is tempted to ignore the obvious essentials of technique and style. One may even never get around to mentioning what are, irrespective of structure or concealed meaning, the best-written pages in the book. They are these: the arrival of James Wait on board, the onset of the storm, the overturning of the ship, the righting of the ship, old Singleton at the wheel, the quelling of the mutiny, the death of Wait and his burial, the docking of the ship, the dispersal of the crew.

It seems proper for once to begin with the end: with that large personal impression which an embarrassed criticism often omits altogether. *The Nigger of the "Narcissus"* is the most generalized of Conrad's novels in its cutting of a cross section, though one of the least comprehensive. It is a version of our dark human pilgrimage, a vision of disaster illumined by grace. The microcosmic ship is defined early in the second chapter with an almost Victorian obviousness: "On her lived truth and audacious lies; and, like the earth, she was unconscious, fair to see—and condemned by men to an ignoble fate. The august loneliness of her path lent dignity to the sordid inspiration of her pilgrimage. She drove foaming to the south as if guided by the courage of a high endeavour." Or we can narrow the vision to a single sentence near the end: "The dark knot of seamen drifted in sunshine." The interplay of light and dark images throughout conveys the sense of a destiny both good and evil, heroic and foolish, blundered out under a soulless sky. If I were further to reduce the novel to a single key-word, as some critics like to do, I should choose the word *grace*. In thematic terms not the sea but life at sea is pure and life on earth sordid. Yet the pessimism of *The Nigger of the "Narcissus"* is (unlike that of *The Secret Agent*) a modified pessimism, and the gift of grace can circumvent thematic terms. Thus England herself is once imaged as a great ship. The convention of the novel is that the gift of grace may fall anywhere, or anywhere except on the Donkins. The story really ends with the men clinging for a last moment to their solidarity and standing near the Mint, that most representative object of the sordid earth:

The sunshine of heaven fell like a gift of grace on the mud of the earth, on the remembering and mute stones, on greed, selfishness; on the anxious faces of forgetful men. And to the right of the dark group the stained front of the Mint, cleansed by the flood of light, stood out for a moment dazzling and white like a marble palace in a fairy tale. The crew of the *Narcissus* drifted out of sight.[5]

So the novel's vision is one of man's dignity but also of his "irremediable littleness"—a conclusion reached, to be sure, by most great works in the Christian tradition. In *Heart of Darkness, Lord Jim,* and "The Secret Sharer" we have the initiatory or expiatory descents within the self of individual and almost lost souls; in *Nostromo* we shall see the vast proliferation of good and evil in history and political institution. But *The Nigger of the "Narcissus"* presents the classic human contradiction (and the archetypal descent into self) in collective terms, reduced to the simplicities of shipboard life. The storm tests and brings out the solidarity, courage, and endurance of men banded together in a desperate cause. And the Negro James Wait tests and brings out their egoism, solitude, laziness, anarchy, fear. The structural obligation of the story is to see to it that the two tests do not, for the reader, cancel out.

Presented so schematically, Conrad's vision may seem truly Christian. But this is indeed a soulless sky. In the restless life of symbols sunlight is converted, at one point, to that inhuman Nature which Man must oppose. The Norwegian sailor who chatters at the sun has lost his saving separateness from Nature, and when the sun sets his voice goes out "together with the light." The "completed wisdom" of old Singleton (one of the first Conrad extroverts to achieve some of his own skepticism) sees "an immensity tormented and blind, moaning and furious. . . ." And in one of the novel's central intellectual statements (the first paragraph of the fourth chapter) the indifferent sea is metaphorically equated with God, and the gift of grace is defined as labor, which prevents man from meditating "at ease upon the complicated and acrid savour of existence." The dignity of man lies in his vast silence and endurance: a dignity tainted by those who clamor for the reward of another life. The message is rather like Faulkner's, and these good seamen are like "good Negroes." But here too, as in other novels of Conrad, man's works and institutions must prepare him to profit from even such grace as this. From our human weakness and from the eternal indifference of things we may yet be saved . . . by authority, tradition, obedience. Thus the only true grace is purely human and even traditional. There are certain men (specifically Donkin) who remain untouched. But such men exist outside: outside our moral universe which is both dark and light but not inextricably both. And James Wait, as sailor and person rather than symbol? I am not sure. He seems to suffer from that "emptiness" which would be Kurtz's ruin: "only a cold black skin loosely stuffed with soft cotton wool . . . a doll that had lost half its sawdust."

This, speaking neither in terms of gross obvious intentions and themes nor of unconscious symbolic content but of generalized human meaning

[5] *The Nigger of the "Narcissus,"* p. 172.

metallic, hollow, and tremendously loud," resounding "like two explosions in a vault."

I would insist, in other words, that Old Ben is also a real bear, and Babo a fleshly slave, and Moby Dick a real whale, and James Wait (though his name was "all a smudge" on the ship's list) a proud, consumptive Negro. It is truly the critic's function to suggest potentialities and even whole areas of discourse that a hasty reading might overlook. But the natural impulse to find single meanings, and so convert symbolism into allegory, must be resisted. James's classic comment on *The Turn of the Screw* is relevant here: "Only make the reader's general vision of evil intense enough, I said to myself—and that already is a charming job—and his own experience, his own imagination, his own sympathy (with the children) and horror (of their false friends) will supply him quite sufficiently with all the particulars. Make him *think* the evil, make him think it for himself, and you are released from weak specifications." [11] Or, as Robert Penn Warren remarks, every man has shot his own special albatross. I am willing with Vernon Young to accept that Wait suggests the subconscious, the instinctual, the regressive; or, with Morton D. Zabel, to see him as the secret sharer and "man all men must finally know"; or, with Belfast more curtly, to know that Satan is abroad. This is neither evasion nor a defense of solipsism, I trust, but mere insistence that no rich work of art and no complex human experience has a single meaning. Wait is, let us say, a force; an X. But it is his role to elicit certain responses from the crew, and, through them, from the reader.

Thus our task is not to discover what Wait precisely "means" but to observe a human relationship. And the clue to any larger meanings must be found, I think, in the pattern of Wait's presences and absences. He is virtually forgotten (after that first dramatic appearance) while the men get to know each other and the voyage begins; he is something they are too busy to be concerned with. We return to him only when they have little work to do; when "the cleared decks had a reposeful aspect, resembling the autumn of the earth" and the soft breeze is "like an indulgent caress." And he is literally forgotten (by crew as well as reader) during the worst of the storm. After he is rescued, he is again neglected for some thirty pages, and returns only with the sinister calm of a hot night and beshrouded ocean. In the two major instances, the lazy Donkin is the agent who takes us back to him, the Mephistopheles for this Satan. The menace of Wait is greatest when men have time to meditate. Thus Conrad's practical ethic of a master-mariner (seamen must be kept busy) may not be so very different from the ethic of the stoic pessimist who wrote psychological novels. The soul left to its own devices scarcely bears examination, though examine it we must.

[11] Henry James, Preface to the *Aspen Papers*.

The pages of Wait's rescue are central, and manage brilliantly their double allegiance to the real and to the symbolic. Here more than anywhere else, even on a quite naturalistic level, the two sides of the seamen coexist: the heroic and the loathsome. "Indignation and doubt grappled within us in a scuffle that trampled upon our finest feelings." They risk their lives unquestioningly to rescue a trapped "chum." Yet these men scrambling in the carpenter's shop, tearing at the planks of the bulkhead "with the eagerness of men trying to get at a mortal enemy," are compulsive, crazed, and full of hatred for the man they are trying to save. "A rage to fling things overboard possessed us." The entire scene is written with vividness and intensity: the hazardous progress over the half submerged deck, the descent into the shop with its layer of nails "more inabordable than a hedgehog," the smashing of the bulkhead and tearing out of Wait, the slow return to a relative safety. Everything is as real and as substantial as that sharp adze sticking up with a shining edge from the clutter of saws, chisels, wire rods, axes, crowbars. At a first experiencing the scene may seem merely to dramatize the novel's stated psychology: these men have irrationally identified their own survival with Wait's and are therefore compelled to rescue him. Ironically, they risk their lives to save a man who has already damaged their fellowship, and who will damage it again.

But the exciting real scene seems to say more than this. And in fact it is doing an important preparatory work, in those fringes of the reader's consciousness, for Wait's burial and for the immediate responding wind which at last defines him as "symbol." On later readings (and we must never forget that every complex novel becomes a different one on later readings) the resonance of these pages is deeper, more puzzling, more sinister. We observe that the men remember the trapped Wait only when the gale is ending, and they are free at last to return to their normal desires. Thereupon they rush to extricate what has been locked away. The actual rescue is presented as a difficult childbirth: the exploratory tappings and faint response; Wait crouched behind the bulkhead and beating with his fists; the head thrust at a tiny hole, then stuck between splitting planks; the "blooming short wool" that eludes Belfast's grasp, and at last the stuffed black doll emerging, "mute as a fish," before emitting its first reproach. At least we can say, roughly, that the men have assisted at the rebirth of evil on the ship.

It may well be that Conrad intended only this (and conceivably less), or to insist again that men are accomplices in their own ruin. But the larger terms and very geography of the scene suggest rather a compulsive effort to descend beneath full consciousness to something "lower." The men let themselves fall heavily and sprawl in a corridor where all doors have become trap doors; they look down into the carpenter's shop devastated as by an earthquake. And beyond its chaos (beneath all the tools, nails, and other instruments of human reason they *must* fling over-

board) lies the solid bulkhead dividing them from Wait.[12] The imagery
of this solid barrier between the conscious and the unconscious may seem
rather Victorian. But the Jungians too tell us that the unconscious is not
easily accessible. In such terms the carpenter's shop would suggest the
messy preconscious, with Wait trapped in the deeper lying unconscious.

This is plausible enough, but does not account for the curious primitive figure of Wamibo glaring above them: "all shining eyes, gleaming
fangs, tumbled hair; resembling an amazed and half-witted fiend gloating
over the extraordinary agitation of the damned." Wamibo could, if we
wished, take his obvious place in the Freudian triad (as savage super
ego)—which would convert Wait into the id and the whole area (carpenter's shop and cabin) into all that lies below full consciousness. But
such literalism of reading, of psychic geography, is not very rewarding.
It could as usefully be argued that Wamibo is the primitive figure who
must be present and involved in any attempt to reach a figure still more
primitive, as the half savage Sam Fathers and half savage Lion must be
present at the death of Old Ben. Is it not more profitable to say, very
generally, that the scene powerfully dramatizes the compulsive psychic
descent of *Heart of Darkness* and "The Secret Sharer"? In any event the
men emerge as from such an experience. "The return on the poop was
like the return of wanderers after many years amongst people marked by
the desolation of time." (As for the rescued Wait, he presents the same
contradictions as the rescued Kurtz. Wait locked in his cabin and the
Kurtz of unspeakable lusts and rites suggest evil as savage energy. But
the rescued Wait and the rescued Kurtz are "hollow men," closer to the
Thomist conception of evil as vacancy.)[13]

So the night journey into self is, I think, one of the experiences this
scene is likely to evoke, even for readers who do not recognize it con-

---

[12] "Then the mariners were afraid, and cried every man unto his god, and cast forth
the wares that were in the ship into the sea, to lighten it of them. But Jonah was gone
down into the sides of the ship; and he lay, and was fast asleep" (Jonah 1:5). It is
Jonah who must be cast out. But he has *already* had an experience of descent: "The
waters compassed me about, even to the soul: the depth closed me round about, the
weeds were wrapped about my head. I went down to the bottom of the mountains; the
earth was about me for ever: yet hast thou brought my life from corruption, O Lord
my God" (2:5, 6).

[13] One is reminded of the surrealist disorder of the cuddy on the *San Domenick,*
where Babo shaves Don Benito: the room an effective image of the unconscious, whatever Melville intended. And, more distantly, of Isaac McCaslin's discarding of gun,
watch, compass (comparable to the tools thrown overboard) as he moves toward his
archetypal confrontation of the unconscious and primitive. To the few intentionalists
who may have consented to read this far: a great intuitive novelist is by definition
capable of dramatizing the descent into the unconscious with some "geographical" ac-
curacy, and even without realizing precisely what he is doing. If he is capable of
dreaming powerfully he will dream what exists (the "furniture" of the mind) as he
will dream archetypal stories. The more he realizes what he is doing in fact, the greater
becomes the temptation to mechanical explanation and rigid consistency to received
theory.

ceptually as such. But it may evoke further and different responses. It is so with any true rendering of any large human situation, be it outward or inward; life never means one thing. What I want to emphasize is not the scene's structuring of abstract or psychic meaning only, but its masterful interpenetration of the realistic and symbolist modes. Its strangeness and audacity (together with its actuality) prepare us for the symbolic burial which is the climax of the novel.

"We fastened up James Wait in a safe place." It is time to return to technical matters, and specifically to the art of modulation that was one of Conrad's strengths.

The ambiguous episode of a suspect heroism is over, Wait is again forgotten, and the chapter returns to its record of a genuine not specious courage. The impression left by the storm test must finally be affirmative, and we move toward that impression at once. Podmore madly offers to make hot coffee; and succeeds. "As long as she swims I will cook." And already the *Narcissus* herself has shown a tendency to stand up a little more. In the final pages of the third chapter the white virginal ship with her one known weakness is the human protagonist exerting a puny stubborn will; old Singleton is the indestructible machine. But the ship's heroism rubs off on the men. Captain Allistoun gives the command to "wear ship," the men do their work, but their eyes and ours are fixed on the wounded, still living *Narcissus*. "Suddenly a small white piece of canvas fluttered amongst them, grew larger, beating." The ship makes several distinct attempts to stand up, goes off as though "weary and disheartened," but at last with an unexpected jerk and violent swing to windward throws off her immense load of water. And now she runs "disheveled" and "as if fleeing for her life," spouting streams of water through her wounds, her torn canvas and broken gear streaming "like wisps of hair." The chapter ends with old Singleton still at the wheel after thirty hours, his white beard tucked under his coat. "In front of his erect figure only the two arms moved crosswise with a swift and sudden readiness, to check or urge again the rapid stir of circling spokes. He steered with care."

This is the end of the first great test. But this is also and only, and almost exactly, the middle of the novel. These men united by crisis must return again to the egoism of their several lives, and hence face again that other test of their selfish allegiance to Wait. The return to Wait (i.e., to the Wait theme) posed one of the sharpest of the novel's many tactical problems: how to modulate downward from the heroic to the everyday, then upward again to the symbolic death and burial. Such "modulations" (for they are much more than transitions) take us close to Conrad's technical art at its best; they show an exceptional sense of how language can manipulate the reader's sensibility.

The end of the storm was grand enough to break such a novel in two. What sentence, to be precise, what particular level of language could succeed such a stroke as "He steered with care"? In *Typhoon* Conrad solves, with one laconic sentence, the whole problem of transition: "He was spared that annoyance." In *Lord Jim* we are told, a little more evasively, "These sleeping pilgrims were destined to accomplish their whole pilgrimage to the bitterness of some other end." The one fact to be communicated is that the ships did not sink; that these men were reprieved. But in *The Nigger of the "Narcissus"* the reader's feelings and beyond them his attitude toward the crew must be handled with extreme care.

Here is the way it is done. I submit the paragraph not as an example of supreme prose but rather to suggest that Conrad's evasiveness and difficulty, his grandiloquence even, may serve at times a dramatic end and solve a tactical problem:

> On men reprieved by its disdainful mercy, the immortal sea confers in its justice the full privilege of desired unrest. Through the perfect wisdom of its grace they are not permitted to meditate at ease upon the complicated and acrid savour of existence, *lest they should remember and, perchance, regret the reward of a cup of inspiriting bitterness, tasted so often, and so often withdrawn from before their stiffening but reluctant lips.* They must without pause justify their life to the eternal pity that commands toil to be hard and unceasing, from sunrise to sunset, from sunset to sunrise; till the weary succession of nights and days tainted by the obstinate clamour of sages, demanding bliss and an empty heaven, is redeemed at last by the vast silence of pain and labour, by the dumb fear and dumb courage of men obscure, forgetful, and enduring.[14]

The paragraph does tell us something: these men were reprieved, and had no chance to rest from their labors. Everything else might seem to belong to that rhythmed and global moralizing that enrages certain lovers of the plain style. And in fact the lines I have italicized do border on double talk. Is the "cup of inspiriting bitterness" life itself? And if so, how can it be withdrawn "so often"? We seem to have a passage as suspect, logically, as the famous one on the "destructive element." And even Conrad must have come to wonder what these lines meant, for he removed them from the definitive edition.

The rest of the paragraph offers, most obviously, its dignity of tone. We move from the elevation of Singleton steering with care to the austere elevation of a narrator's statement on man and destiny, before returning to the drenched decks and exhausted swearing crew. But the language is more highly charged than it might seem at a first glance. The double metaphor (*sea–indifferent justice–God*) is obvious enough, un-

[14] *The Nigger of the "Narcissus,"* p. 90. Uniform Edition of the Works of Joseph Conrad (London: J. M. Dent and Sons Ltd., 1923-1928). My italics.

derlined as it is by so much irony: *reprieved, disdainful mercy, immortal, in its justice, the perfect wisdom, grace, justify, the eternal pity, commands toil to be hard, redeemed.* The paragraph expresses an ultimate skepticism; or, a conviction that man's dignity lies in his courage, labor and endurance. But the particular Conradian difficulty (or "tension") comes from the suddenness of the narrator's subversive intrusions. Thus the men desire life; it is the narrator who reminds us that life is unrest. And the sages who tarnish man's dignity by their references to an afterlife demand only the bliss of heaven. It is the narrator who remarks (a parenthesis within a parenthesis) that this heaven is empty. There is much more to say about the passage, and it would be interesting to know whether such flowing rhythms do not carry most readers, unnoticing, past these ironies. In general, however, not merely the austerity of tone and dignity of rhythm but the very difficulty of the language help to manipulate the reader's feelings, chill them even, in a way quite necessary at this point in the story.

This fine management of the reader through tone, style, and structure is the largest achievement, in 1897, of Conrad's technique. It would require a comment as long as Conrad's fourth chapter to describe and analyze the tact with which it leads us through the hard work of the storm's aftermath, through the desolation of the forecastle, through Singleton's physical collapse and also his collapse into skepticism, through Donkin's mutinous talk—back to Wait's cabin as the source of contagion. "The little place, repainted white, had, in the night, the brilliance of a silver shrine where a black idol, reclining stiffly under a blanket, blinked its weary eyes and received our homage. Donkin officiated." Only through many careful modulations (the gray human mixture a little darker after each) can we be made to accept the fact that such a brave crew would be capable of mutiny. The chapter is certainly more flawed than any of the others. But the transitional task it had to accomplish, and modulative task, was much the most difficult.

"A heavy atmosphere of oppressive quietude pervaded the ship." Thus begins the fifth and last chapter. The threat of mutiny has been broken; we are nearing the end of the voyage; ultimate meanings must be achieved now or not at all; and James Wait must die. Like Melville in *Benito Cereno* Conrad has prepared us early in the story for the themes of ambiguity and death by mortuary images:

> Over the white rims of berths stuck out heads with blinking eyes; but the bodies were lost in the gloom of those places, that resembled narrow niches for coffins in a whitewashed and lighted mortuary.

> The double row of berths yawned black, like graves tenanted by uneasy corpses.

> And alone in the dim emptiness of the sleeping forecastle he appeared bigger, colossal, very old; old as Father Time himself, who should have come

there into this place as quiet as a sepulchre to contemplate with patient eyes the short victory of sleep, the consoler.[15]

Beyond this Conrad has more than once asked us to regard the ship as a microcosm, and (in the rescue scene) has appealed darkly to the fringes of consciousness. But the hardest task remains, and this is to bring the symbolic possibilities of the ship and of Wait into full awareness. To put matters crudely: we must be directly prepared for the occult circumstance of a wind rising the moment Wait's body reaches the sea.

Singleton's prediction—his Ancient Mariner's knowledge that "Jimmy was the cause of the head winds" and must die in the first sight of land —accomplishes something. But the somber rhythms and Coleridgean distracted movement of the ship accomplish more. And there is at last the critical moment itself, a moment requiring audacity. How convince the reader that *anything* can happen on this more than ordinary ship? One way would be to use such words as "illusive," or frankly to say that nothing in the ship is "real." But more than flat statement is required to make us accept Coleridge's phantom ship. One could further suggest death through allusions to the moon, or *evoke a magic ship and transnatural night by imposing images of snow and cold and ice upon a hot night.* One could, indeed, appeal to the reader's recollection of *The Ancient Mariner.* And all this occurs, is done, in the last modulative paragraph:

On clear evenings the silent ship, under the cold sheen of the dead moon, took on a false aspect of passionless repose resembling the winter of the earth. Under her a long band of gold barred the black disc of the sea. Footsteps echoed on her quiet decks. The moonlight clung to her like a frosted mist, and the white sails stood out in dazzling cones as of stainless snow. In the magnificence of the phantom rays the ship appeared pure like a vision of ideal beauty, illusive like a tender dream of serene peace. And nothing in her was real, nothing was distinct and solid but the heavy shadows that filled her decks with their unceasing and noiseless stir: the shadows darker than the night and more restless than the thoughts of men.

Donkin prowled spiteful and alone amongst the shadows, thinking that Jimmy too long delayed to die. That evening land had been reported from aloft . . .[16]

These are matters of style: style as temperament, style as meaning, style as suasion and manipulation of the reader. And in *The Nigger of the "Narcissus"* we are watching the formation of a great style in which meditation beomes dramatic. We are dealing with a temperament chronically addicted to approach and withdrawal, and which can make the very ebb and flow of generalizing intellect an element of suspense. Thus a scene of action may be suddenly broken off and the reader

[15] *Ibid.,* pp. 8, 22, 24.
[16] *Ibid.,* p. 145.

alienated, *removed*, by the act of meditative withdrawal. And this removal
intensifies the drama:

> He shrieked in the deepening gloom, he blubbered and sobbed, screaming:
> " 'It 'im! 'It 'im!" *The rage and fear of his disregarded right to live tried*
> *the steadfastness of hearts more than the menacing shadows of the night that*
> *advanced through the unceasing clamour of the gale.* From aft Mr. Baker was
> heard:—"Is one of you men going to stop him—must I come along?" "Shut
> up!" . . . "Keep quiet!" cried various voices, exasperated, trembling with
> cold.[17]

This sudden deliberate distancing of narrator and reader will give *Lord
Jim* and *Nostromo* some of their richest effects.

The writing of *The Nigger of the "Narcissus"* remains uneven, though
vastly superior to that of the earlier stories. But the Conradian richness,
it must be admitted again, is built out of initial excess. "The Lagoon" and
its parody have shown us what Conradese could be, with its pervasive
melodrama of language and landscape and its monotonies of sentence
structure. The most monotonous paragraph in *The Nigger of the "Narcissus"* occurs in the first chapter, before the narrator has begun to speak
in his own right and voice. We have instead a writer methodically block-
ing out and methodically enriching a static scene and mood. The passage
suggests some of the indulgences which could, chastened, become
strengths:

> Outside the glare of the steaming forecastle the serene purity of the night
> enveloped the seamen with its soothing breath, with its tepid breath flow-
> ing under the stars that hung countless above the mastheads in a thin cloud
> of luminous dust. On the town side the blackness of the water was streaked
> with trails of light which undulated gently on slight ripples, *similar to* fila-
> ments that float rooted to the shore. Rows of other lights stood away in
> straight lines *as if* drawn up on parade between towering buildings; but on
> the other side of the harbour sombre hills arched high their black spines,
> on which, here and there, the point of a star *resembled* a spark fallen from
> the sky. Far off, Byculla way, the electric lamps at the dock gates shone on
> the end of lofty standards with a glow blinding and frigid *like* captive
> ghosts of some evil moons. Scattered all over the dark polish of the road-
> stead, the ships at anchor floated in perfect stillness under the feeble gleam
> of their riding-lights, looming up, opaque and bulky, *like* strange and monu-
> mental structures abandoned by men to an everlasting repose.[18]

The paragraph is unmistakably Conradian, and has its genuine felicities; the rhythm of any one of the overextended periods is lovely. But the
passage fails by attempting too many felicities; analogy becomes a weary
obligation, to be met once or twice each sentence. And yet, the captive
ghosts and monumental abandoned structures operate in a characteristic

[17] *Ibid.*, p. 76. My italics.
[18] *Ibid.*, pp. 14-15. My italics.

manner: taking the reader on far meditative journeys from their banal tenors, to "evil moons" and "everlasting repose." We are invited to dream and are being imposed upon by a temperament. A doubtful procedure, if the object is to clarify the tenor. But that is not Conrad's object, which is to create a tone and bemusing impression. Far more conducive to monotony are certain repetitions: the regular assignment of one adjective and one only to approximately half the nouns (the French "glow blinding and frigid" comes as a relief); the almost identical length of the first three flowing periods and of the second, fourth, and fifth sentences; and the predictable positioning of the subject in four sentences out of the five. This is, one detects, the prose of a writer even more devoted to cadence than to evil moons; who must (for the moment) externalize rhythms rather than visions; who enjoys expending to its fullest each long drawn in breath. The first sentence is in fact the most Conradian of all, since it pushes past no less than five natural stopping places. The style (as in certain other novels the plot and over-all structure) refuses the reader's reasonable expectations, and hence—if it does not merely lull— excites a certain strain. This impulse to frustrate the reader's ear will presently, and even in this novel, produce great prose.

Another reader, less conscious of rhythms, would be irritated by the fact that the night's purity is "serene" and repose "everlasting." Let us acknowledge at once that Conrad, early or late, could stock a sizable dictionary of bromidic clichés. Another way to put it is that some of his best pages are built with exceedingly obvious blocks. Most readers would agree (unless they are compiling dictionaries) that the first five pages of the second chapter, the sailing of the *Narcissus* and its first days at sea, are successful. But if one is compiling a dictionary! The water sparkles *like* a floor of jewels, and is as empty *as* the sky; the upper canvas *resembles* small white clouds; the tug *resembles* a black beetle (this analogy extended for twelve lines), a ship on the horizon lingers and hovers *like* an illusion; stars people the emptiness of the sky, are *as if* alive, are *more intense than* the eyes of a staring crowd, and *as inscrutable as* the souls of men; the ship is a microcosm of the earth (extended for a full paragraph) and is a high and lonely pyramid; the days are *like* flashes of a lighthouse and the nights *resemble* fleeting dreams; the Captain is "such *as* a phantom above a grave," his nightshirt flutters *like* a flag; and his gray eyes are still and cold *like* the loom of ice. He seldom descends from the Olympian heights of his poop.

How does Conrad get away with so much obviousness, as by and large he does? For one thing, the elaborate rhythms are both more varied and more "spoken" than in the first chapter, and this emerging meditative voice gives us, along the way, a good deal of authenticating nautical detail. Further, some of these analogies work visually and morally at the same time. The high and lonely pyramid is also lovely: "gliding, all shining and white, through the sunlit mist." But the tug, stained by land and stream, leaves a memorable round black patch of soot on the water, "an unclean mark of the creature's rest." The analogies taken together have begun to establish two of the novel's secondary meanings: its contrast between life at sea and life on land, its contrast between sail and steam. And even the captain as a phantom above a grave has its place in a novel depending upon much mortuary imagery to prepare us for the occult death of Wait. As for the studied and Victorian analogy of the ship and the earth, it can well be argued that Conrad should have permitted the readers so to generalize his ship. But we would be the poorer if we censored all Conrad's deeply meant skeptic's comments on our human lot. "The august loneliness of her path lent dignity to the sordid inspiration of her pilgrimage." We would be the poorer without that sentence and its several considered judgments.

In the best pages of *The Nigger of the "Narcissus,"* the storm action in Chapter III, the elaborate prose conveys action, motion, as well as a trembling and menaced beauty of sound.[19] But some of the striking Conradian effects are based on insistences which turn out to be obvious, and on a certain lack of inhibition. In context the docking of the *Narcissus* is very moving. It sums up the differences of sea and land, high endeavor and commerce, the beautiful and the sordid; it is the violation of the virgin by the soiled and practical; it brings the great adventure to an end. Only by underlining our text do we discover how obvious the insistences have been, in this devaluation of the land: "the steaming brows of millions of men," "drifts of smoky vapours," "an immense and lamentable murmur," "the anxious earth," "the shadows deepened," "barges drifted stealthily on the murky stream," "begrimed walls," "a vision of disaster," "a mysterious and unholy spell," and— horror of horrors in this story of masculine integrity and weakness—"two bareheaded women." "The *Narcissus* came gently into her berth; the shadows of soulless walls fell upon her, the dust of all the continents leaped upon her deck, and a swarm of strange men, clambering up her sides, took possession of her in the name of the sordid earth. She had ceased to live."

"My Lord in his discourse discovered a great deal of love to this ship." Conrad began with the ship, and it is with the *Narcissus* that the critic is well advised to end. And not only because the sea story as sea story is one of the greatest in English fiction. For the ship reminds us of the

[19] Consider the imitative rhythms of these lines, and the dramatic change of the sentence from passive to active force, ending in a dying close: "The hard gust of wind came brutal like the blow of a fist. The ship relieved of her canvas in time received it pluckily; she yielded reluctantly to the violent onset; then, coming up with a stately and irresistible motion, brought her spars to windward in the teeth of a screeching squall. Out of the abysmal darkness of the black cloud overhead white hail streamed on her, rattled on the rigging, leaped in handfuls off the yards, rebounded on the deck —round and gleaming in the murky turmoil like a shower of pearls. It passed away."

novel's over-all structural problem, which I have neglected to discuss.
This structural problem, and even Conrad's solution of it, can be simply
stated. It is only in the doing, only in the demands for sensitive modulation made by every paragraph, that such matters become truly difficult!
The problem was simply to avoid writing two distinct short novels, one
optimistic and the other pessimistic. The two tests and two impressions
of human nature must not be allowed to cancel out; we must forget
neither the men's sentimentality and egoism nor their heroic endurance;
at the last, the dark knot of seamen must drift in sunshine.

Conrad's tact becomes evident once we conceive any other structure
than the one he actually presents. Had the near mutiny and Wait's death
occurred before the storm, we would have had the two short novels,
and been left with a more affirmative statement than Conrad wanted to
make. Had Wait's demoralizing effect begun only after the storm, we
would have been left with no affirmation at all. The first necessity, then,
was to introduce the Wait story (tentatively, on the whole realistically)
before the storm, return to it briefly during the storm, but give it major
symbolic import only afterward. We are introduced to dim potentialities
of anarchy and fear before knowing, through much of the third chapter,
a magnificent courage and endurance. So much is simple indeed, in the
describing. But having the near mutiny and symbolic death occur after
the storm still threatened, of course, to leave an impression essentially
negative and, it may be, excessively symbolic. What is to remind us,
after Wait's burial, that these men were also, had also been, true ex-
trovert children of the sea? How could the story redress its balance?
The obvious answer would be to show them reacting heroically to another
great storm. But this too would have left an imbalance, and invited
further circular movements.

What Conrad does, instead, is to give up any close view of the men;
to focus attention on the ship rather than on them; to make *her* swift
homeward progress heroic; to distance the reader from human perils
either outward or inward and so confer on the crew, by association, some
of the ship's glamour. The individuals on board give way to the ship as
microcosm and finally to the ship as ship. Thus the object that unifies the
two stories is not really an object at all, but the white female ship,
which had left the stained land and now returns to it. What connects
nearly every page is the *Narcissus* herself. At the very end the seamen are
revalued by our distaste for the children of commerce, who can dismiss
Singleton as a disgusting old brute; and the *Narcissus* is consecrated by
the land that stains her. Crew and ship become part of history:

> The dark knot of seamen drifted in sunshine. To the left of them the trees
> in Tower Gardens sighed, the stones of the Tower gleaming, seemed to stir
> in the play of light, as if remembering suddenly all the great joys and sor-
> rows of the past, the fighting prototypes of these men; press-gangs; mutinous
> cries; the wailing of women by the riverside, and the shouts of men wel-

coming victories. The sunshine of heaven fell like a gift of grace on the mud of the earth, on the remembering and mute stones, on greed, selfishness; on the anxious faces of forgetful men. And to the right of the dark group the stained front of the Mint, cleansed by the flood of light, stood out for a moment dazzling and white like a marble palace in a fairy tale. The crew of the *Narcissus* drifted out of sight.[20]

"I disengaged myself gently." And by the same token the reader disengages himself from an adventure both extraordinary and intimate. There are novels whose endings suggest a continuation of the lives we have watched. But *The Nigger of the "Narcissus"* is a completed experience, recorded of a dead time; the voyage becomes at last the book we have just read.

In mere outline the matter is as simple as that. But there are novelists who in all their calculating careers never achieve such a triumphant simplicity and rightness of structure.

[20] *Ibid.*, p. 172.

The Originality of Conrad

by Marvin Mudrick

Conrad offers himself from the first as a dogged innovator of fictional techniques, like his own Kurtz one of the first thorough explorers of a rather dark continent; and it is tempting to read him for the sophisticated pleasure one takes in recognizing novel and schematizable, if not necessarily expressive, method. A teacher once worked out for his students a chronological chart of the events in *Victory*. The chart proved, of course, Conrad's creative cleverness at mixing up the events and the teacher's critical astuteness at setting them right again. This is one pattern of Conrad criticism. That it is a seductive pattern appears from Henry James's professional admiration for the multiple viewpoints intruding, in *Chance,* between the reader and the events (James placed Conrad "absolutely alone as a votary of the way to do a thing that shall make it undergo most doing"): the only residual doubt being whether, at a fifth or even a second remove, the events of *Chance* have any interest in themselves; whether, for example, once we have pushed through layers of Marlow's gruff archness to arrive at Conrad's inevitable sweet silent slip of a girl and what Mr. Zabel notes as Captain Anthony's "touch of inscrutable sanctimony," [1] our long attention seems worthwhile.

Length is usually, indeed, no advantage to Conrad. Albert Guerard has asserted that "Conrad's long stories and short novels are far more experimental and more 'modern' than his full-length novels" [2]; and, though it is an assertion that requires reservations, it points to the comparative economy and tact of Conrad's method in pieces like *Typhoon* and *The Nigger of the "Narcissus,"* to the unfailing grim power of Part First of *Under Western Eyes* (before the novel falls apart in a compulsion to extend itself beyond its normal novella length), as well as to the inert and wilful complications characteristic of such larger works as *Chance, Lord Jim, Victory, Nostromo,* and *The Secret Agent.* Everything Conrad wrote recalls everything else he wrote, in a pervasive melancholy

[1] M. D. Zabel, ed., *The Portable Conrad* (New York: The Viking Press, 1952), pp. 40-41.

[2] Conrad, *Heart of Darkness* and *The Secret Sharer,* introd. Albert Guerard (New York: Signet, 1950), p. 8.

of outlook, a persistency of theme ("the plight of the man on whom life closes down inexorably, divesting him of the supports and illusory protection of friendship, social privilege, or love" [3]), and a conscientious manipulation of innovational method; yet what marks Conrad as not a mere experimentalist or entertainer but a genuine innovator occurs only sporadically in his full-length novels, with discretion and sustained impulse only in several long stories or short novels: in *The Nigger of the "Narcissus,"* in *Typhoon,* in Part First of *Under Western Eyes,* and—with most impressive rich immediacy—in *Heart of Darkness.*

Conrad's innovation—or, in any case, the fictional technique that he exploited with unprecedented thoroughness—is the double plot: neither allegory (where surface is something teasing, to be got through), nor catch-all symbolism (where every knowing particular signifies some universal or other), but a developing order of actions so lucidly symbolic of a developing state of spirit—from moment to moment, so morally identifiable—as to suggest the conditions of allegory without forfeiting or even subordinating the realistic "superficial" claim of the actions and their actors.

Heart of Darkness—at least until we reach Kurtz and the end of the journey—is a remarkable instance of such order: details intensely present, evocatively characteristic of the situations in which they happen, and prefiguring from moment to moment an unevadable moral reality. The equatorial incubus of inefficiency, for example, is created and consolidated by a set of details memorable in their direct sensuous impact, almost farcical in the situations whose absurd disproportions they discover, and wholly dreadful as a cumulative cosmic denial of mind: the warship (" 'It appears the French had one of their wars going on thereabouts' "), its men dying of fever at the rate of three a day, " 'firing into a continent' "; the forsaken railway truck, looking " 'as dead as the carcass of some animal,' " rusting in the grass " 'on its back with its wheels in the air' "; the fat man with the moustaches trying to put out a blaze in a grass shed with a quart of water in a leaking pail; the brickmaker idling for a year with no bricks and no hope of materials for making them; the " 'wanton smashup' " of drainage pipes abandoned in a ravine; burst, piled up cases of rivets at the Outer Station, and no way of getting them to the damaged steamboat at the Central Station; the " 'vast artificial hole somebody had been digging on the slope, the purpose of which I found it impossible to divine. It wasn't a quarry or a sandpit, anyhow. It was just a hole' "; the blasting on the cliff—

"A horn tooted to the right, and I saw the black people run. A heavy and dull detonation shook the ground, a puff of smoke came out of the cliff, and that was all. No change appeared in the face of the rock. They were building a railway. The cliff was not in the way or anything, but the objectless blasting was all the work going on."

[3] Zabel, *The Portable Conrad,* p. 26.

In this world of the fortuitous, acutely realized details of nightmare, such efficiency as can survive will be of a very special kind; like the accountant's—

"Hair parted, brushed, oiled, under a green-lined parasol held in a big white hand. He was amazing, and had a penholder behind his ear. . . . His appearance was certainly that of a hairdresser's dummy; but in the great demoralization of the land he kept up his appearance. That's backbone. His starched collars and got-up shirtfronts were achievements of character. . . . I sat generally on the floor, while, of faultless appearance (and even slightly scented), perching on a high stool, he wrote, he wrote, he wrote. Sometimes he stood up for exercise. When a truckle bed with a sick man (some invalid agent from upcountry) was put in there, he exhibited a gentle annoyance. 'The groans of the sick person,' he said, 'distract my attention. And without that it is extremely difficult to guard against clerical errors in this climate.' "

In this climate, where life for a clot of exasperated foreigners contracts itself to the exploitation of the hopelessly alien, it is also difficult to guard against certain explicit moral errors; among them, a cruelty as ordained and unimpassioned as in " 'the gloomy circle of some inferno' ":

"Black shapes crouched, lay, sat between the trees leaning against the trunks, clinging to the earth, half coming out, half effaced within the dim light, in all the attitudes of pain, abandonment, and despair. Another mine on the cliff went off, followed by a slight shudder of the soil under my feet. The work was going on. The work! And this was the place where some of the helpers had withdrawn to die."

The work defines and embodies itself in its reluctant functionaries, starched accountant as well as dying natives; it has its particular countersign and gleaming talisman (" 'The word "ivory" rang in the air, was whispered, was sighed. You would think they were praying to it. A taint of imbecile rapacity blew through it all, like a whiff from some corpse' "); in its tangible promise of easy gratifications, it indifferently victimizes both the unwilling natives and their incompetent overseers, it prescribes the tableau of cruelty in the grove of death, it provides its own corresponding niche for every stage of opportunism from the novice exploiter (weight 224 pounds) who keeps fainting, to the manager of the Central Station, the man with the single talent and the essential defect—

"He was obeyed, yet he inspired neither love nor fear, nor even respect. He inspired uneasiness. That was it! Uneasiness. Not a definite mistrust— just uneasiness—nothing more. You have no idea how effective such a . . . a . . . faculty can be. . . . Once when various tropical diseases had laid low almost every 'agent' in the station, he was heard to say, 'Men who come out here should have no entrails.' "

The general blight and demoralization are inextricable, they do not detach themselves for scrutiny, from the developing order of actions that

intensely brings them to mind; they have no independent symbolic
existence, nor do any other of the spreading abstractions and big ideas
in the narrative. Even the journey into the heart of darkness—the more
obvious broad symbolic provocations of which have given joy to so many
literary amateurs—insofar as it has artistic (rather than merely psy-
choanalytic) force, is finely coincident with its network of details; its
moral nature steadily reveals itself not in the rather predictable grand
gestures of Conradian rhetoric (" 'Going upriver was like going back to
beginnings, when vegetation rioted and the big trees were kings' "), but
in the unavoidable facts of suspense, strangeness, vigilance, danger, and
fear: the difficulties of piloting the patched fragile steamer past hidden
banks, snags, sunken stones upriver; the sudden " 'glimpse of rush walls,
of peaked grass roofs, a burst of yells, a whirl of black limbs, a mass of
hands clapping, of feet stamping, of bodies swaying, of eyes rolling, under the droop of heavy and motionless foliage' "; the honest, " 'unmistakably real' " book mysteriously discovered in the abandoned hut;
the terrified savage tending the boiler, who " 'squinted at the steam
gauge with an evident effort of intrepidity' "; the arrows from nowhere;
the death of the black helmsman (" 'The man had rolled on his back
and stared straight up at me; both his hands clutched that cane. It was
the shaft of a spear that, either thrown or lunged through the opening,
had caught him in the side just below the ribs; the blade had gone in
out of sight, after making a frightful gash; my shoes were full; a pool
of blood lay very still, gleaming dark-red under the wheel; his eyes
shone with an amazing luster' "); and, most shocking of all in its evoca-
tion of mind at an intolerable extremity, the climactic farcical detail of
Marlow's panic to get rid of his shoes and socks overflowing with a dead
man's blood—

> "To tell you the truth, I was morbidly anxious to change my shoes and
> socks. 'He is dead,' murmured the fellow, immensely impressed. 'No doubt
> about it,' said I, tugging like mad at the shoelaces."

When Conrad is called, with a clear confidence that the judgment is
general and will not be challenged, "perhaps the finest prose stylist" [4]
among the English novelists, it is doubtless such passages as these that
the critic has in mind. One wonders, then, what the critic makes of such
equally representative Conradian passages as the following:

> "It was the stillness of an implacable force brooding over an inscrutable
> intention."

> "I tried to break the spell—the heavy, mute spell of the wilderness—that
> seemed to draw him to its pitiless breast by the awakening of forgotten and
> brutal instincts, by the memory of gratified and monstrous passions."

"I heard a light sigh and then my heart stood still, stopped dead short by an exulting and terrible cry, by the cry of inconceivable triumph and of unspeakable pain. 'I knew it—I was sure!' . . . She knew. She was sure."

Qualifying his account of Conrad as one of the four masters of English fiction, Dr. Leavis makes the definitive comment on this sort of thing: "Conrad must here stand convicted of borrowing the arts of the magazine-writer (who has borrowed his, shall we say, from Kipling and Poe) in order to impose on his readers and on himself, for thrilled response, a 'significance' that is merely an emotional insistence on the presence of what he can't produce. The insistence betrays the absence, the willed 'intensity' the nullity. He is intent on making a virtue out of not knowing what he means." [5]

Qualification, however, is not enough. Conrad's lapses of this sort are not rare or incidental, they do not merely weaken his master style but schismatically parallel it in a style of their own. The "finest prose stylist" in English fiction has in fact two styles: the narrative-descriptive, in which explicit details triumphantly cohere with implicit moral moments in an accumulating point-to-point correspondence (a style whose purest, if not most imposingly complex, manifestation may be examined in *Typhoon*); and the oracular-ruminative, which dotes on abstractions, exclamations, unexpressive indirections, pat ironies ("the arts of the magazine-writer"), a style which takes over, especially in the large scale works, whenever Conrad loses faith in the power of his details to enforce both their own reality and the symbolic substructure whose contours they are intended to suggest—so Marlow cries out as he and his author signalize, in a joint loss of faith, their drift from master to meretricious style, " 'I've been telling you what we said—repeating the phrases we pronounced—but what's the good? ' "

Conrad's symbolism, and his moral imagination, are, after all, as un-allegorical as possible. When they function and have effect they are severely realistic: they nourish themselves on voices heard and solid objects seen and touched in the natural world, they contract into rhetoric as soon as the voices and objects begin to appear less than independently present; when Conrad is not describing, with direct sensuous impact, a developing sequence of distinct actions, he is liable to drift into the mooning or glooming that for some critics passes as Conrad's "philosophy" and for others as his style in its full tropical luxuriance.

Moreover, to assume, as Dr. Leavis seems to assume, that all symbolism works *only* as it is anchored to a record of immediate sensations, that it must totally coincide with "the concrete presentment of incident, setting and image," is to transform Conrad's limitation (and gift) into a condition of fiction. To compare Conrad's symbolic method, his two-ply plot, with the methods of, say, Dostoevsky and Kafka is to become aware

[5] F. R. Leavis, *The Great Tradition* (New York: Anchor, 1954), p. 219.

of radically different possibilities: on the one hand, Conrad's realistic mode; on the other, moral imaginations not necessarily anchored to objects and places, symbolic means capable of producing, for example, those vibrations of clairvoyant hallucination in Dostoevsky, and of meaningful enigma in Kafka, which move through and beyond immediate sensations into a world of moral meanings almost as independent as, and far more densely populated than, the other side of the mirror of traditional allegory. Of such effects, beyond the capacities of even the most evocative realism, Conrad is innocent; yet when, in *Heart of Darkness,* he approaches the center of a difficult moral situation (desperately more troublesome than the simple choices permitted the characters in *Typhoon*), when facts and details begin to appear inadequate as figurations of the moral problem, it is just such effects that he is at length driven to attempt.

The problem is, of course, Kurtz. It is when we are on the verge of meeting Kurtz that Marlow's "inconceivables" and "impenetrables" begin to multiply at an alarming rate; it is when we have already met him that we are urged to observe "smiles of indefinable meaning" and to hear about "unspeakable rites" and "gratified and monstrous passions" and "subtle horrors"—words to hound the reader into a sense of enigmatic awfulness that he would somehow be the better for not trying to find a way through:

> "Everything belonged to him—but that was a trifle. The thing was to know what he belonged to, how many powers of darkness claimed him for their own. That was the reflection that made you creepy all over. It was impossible —it was not good for one either—trying to imagine."

The problem, as Conrad sets it up, is to persuade the reader—by epithets, exclamations, ironies, by every technical obliquity—into an hallucinated awareness of the unplumbable depravity, the primal unanalyzable evil, implicit in Kurtz's reversion to the jungle from the high moral sentiments of his report:

> "The peroration was magnificent, though difficult to remember, you know. It gave me the notion of an exotic Immensity ruled by an august Benevolence."

Unhappily, though, the effect of even this minor irony is to bring to mind and penetrate Conrad's magazine-writer style as well as the hollowness of Kurtz's sentiments. Besides, Kurtz's sentiments must, to help justify the fuss Conrad makes about their author, radiate at least a rhetorical energy; yet all Conrad gives us of the report is a phrase or two of mealy-mouthed reformist exhortation that would not do credit to a Maugham missionary let alone the "extraordinary man" Kurtz is supposed by all accounts to be, so that the "irony" of the scrawled outcry at the end of the report—"Exterminate all the brutes!"—is about as subtle and unexpected as the missionary's falling for the local call-girl.

In the effort to establish for Kurtz an opaque and terrifying magnitude, Conrad tends to rely more and more oppressively on these pat ironies. The very existence of the incredibly naïve young Russian is another such irony: the disciple who responds to Kurtz's abundant proofs of cruelty and mean obsession with the steadfast conviction—and no evidence for the reader—that Kurtz is a great man (" ' "he's enlarged my mind" ' "—another irony that cuts more ways than Conrad must have intended). And if the culminating irony of the narrative, Marlow's interview with Kurtz's Intended, is expertly anticipated long before, when Marlow remarks—

> "You know I hate, detest, and can't bear a lie, not because I am straighter than the rest of us, but simply because it appalls me. There is a taint of death, a flavor of mortality in lies—which is exactly what I hate and detest in the world—what I want to forget. It makes me miserable and sick, like biting something rotten would do."

—it is all the more disheartening, after such anticipation, to encounter in that interview sighs, heart stoppings, chill grips in the chest, exultations, the cheaply ironic double-talk (" 'She said suddenly very low, "He died as he lived." "His end," said I, with dull anger stirring in me, "was in every way worthy of his life" ' ") as well as the sentimental lie that provokes not only her " 'cry of inconceivable triumph and of unspeakable pain' " but the final cheap irony (" ' "I knew it—I was sure!" She knew. She was sure' ")—a jumble of melodramatic tricks so unabashed and so strategic that in any less reputable writer they might well be critically regarded as earning for the work an instant oblivion.

Still, in *Heart of Darkness* at least, Conrad is neither cynical nor laxly sentimental in his failure of imagination and corresponding failure of technique. The theme itself is too much for him, too much for perhaps any but the very greatest dramatists and novelists. The sense of evil he must somehow project exceeds his capacity for imagining it; he strains into badness while reaching for verifications of a great and somber theme that is beyond his own very considerable powers.

One instructive comparison is with James's *The Turn of the Screw*, another short novel that builds toward a vision of absolute unspecifiable evil. To be thrilled by the "unspecified 'horrors' " [6] of this Jamesian virtuoso exercise is to react just as James prescribes. Both *Heart of Darkness* and *The Turn of the Screw* aim at conjuring up—the former, in the pages devoted to Kurtz, by incantation; the latter, throughout, by a sophisticated choice among the stock devices of the ghost story—sequences of unspecified horrors that produce a moment-to-moment disquiet, and that will at length converge into a sense of smothering evil. But both works are eventually too willed, too consciously literary, too

[6] As many critics have been, including Leon Edel (*Henry James: The Untried Years* [Philadelphia: J. B. Lippincott Co., 1953], p. 175.)

gentlemanly almost: Conrad's incantation and James's ingenuity begin
to obtrude from the text, to disengage themselves even from their momentary effects. (And neither work shows any capacity for achieving that
almost independent sustained atmosphere of universal disquiet which—
in Dostoevsky or in Kafka, for example—*is* the sense of evil.) The *coup
de grâce* in both, however, is administered by their uneasy tendency to
go beyond techniques that merely suggest and, after ineffectual or
spurious indirectness, to fall into a disastrous specification: to attempt
a particular embodiment of the idea of evil. In *The Turn of the Screw,*
evil tends to specify itself dramatically—with hand over gaping mouth
—as casual coupling among the servants, and beautiful children uttering
naughty words (the trivially prurient Puritan reduction of the big idea
of evil); in *Heart of Darkness,* for Conrad, the simple, honorable, civilized
sailor, Kurtz's vision of "the horror" tends to dissolve at last into a wide
screen panorama of "unimaginable" orgies at "midnight dances" with
hordes of Hollywood natives howling round pyres of human sacrifice.
Ultimately, as both authors lose faith in all their contrived implicitnesses,
the horrors are only too plainly and justly specified.

    Heart of Darkness is, of course, as serious as *The Turn of the Screw*
is not. Even in its failure it does not trifle, rather it anxiously falls short,
it has its own intermittent costume jewelry glitter but nothing like the
uninterrupted cynical dilettantism of James's deliberate hair-raiser. It
is in fact one of those mixed structures whose partial success (not so
neatly separable as, for example, Part First of *Under Western Eyes*) is so
profound, so unprecedented, and so strikingly irreplaceable as to survive
a proportion and gravity of failure that would sink forever any other
work.

    It is one of the great originals of literature. After *Heart of Darkness*
the craftsman in fiction could never again be unaware of the moral re-
sources inherent in every recorded sensation, or insensitive to the need
of making the most precise record possible of every sensation: what
now appears an immemorial cliché of the craft of fiction has a date as
recent as the turn of the century. If Conrad was never quite equal to
his own originality, he was at least the first to designate it as a new
province of possibilities for the novelist; and, in *Heart of Darkness,* the
first to suggest, by large and compelling partial proof, the intensity of
moral illumination that a devoted attention to its demands might
generate. The suggestion was an historical event: for good and bad
novelists alike, irreversible. After *Heart of Darkness,* the recorded moment—the word—was irrecoverably symbol.

The "Unspeakable Rites"
in *Heart of Darkness*

by Stephen A. Reid

It is difficult to dispute the assumption that, for the particular emotions generated by *Heart of Darkness,* Kurtz's rites and secrets should, in the story, remain unspoken. But the critics have usually equated Conrad's election in this matter with the desirability of leaving them shrouded in uncertainty. Albert Guerard feels not only that "a confrontation with . . . the unconscious cannot be reported through realistic dialogue" but that "when Marlow finds it hard to define the moral shock he received on seeing the empty cabin . . . I think we can take him literally . . . and in a sense be thankful for his uncertainty." [1] Surely, however, the critical function need not stop where Conrad does. The fact that Marlow refuses to examine the rites and secrets is hardly a reason for the critic also to refuse. Insofar as we consider the story at all on the "realistic," non-symbolic level (and I think we must), we must try to understand what those rites were. And, a proper understanding of them will throw significant light on Kurtz's life and on Marlow's reactions.

I suggest that Kurtz's unspeakable rites and secrets concern (with whatever attendant bestiality) human sacrifice and Kurtz's consuming a portion of the sacrificial victim. Further, these sacrifices were established in the interest of perpetuating Kurtz's position as a man-god. My assumptions rest upon Sir George James Frazer's analysis of primitive man's anxiety about the continuance of the world and about the mortality of the man-god, and of the methods used by him to allay the anxiety and to circumvent the inevitability of the man-god's aging and dying. A relatively long passage from Frazer is required here:

> If the high gods, who dwell remote from the fret and fever of this earthly life, are yet believed to die at last, it is not to be expected that a god who lodges in a frail tabernacle of flesh should escape the same fate, though we

"The 'Unspeakable Rites' in *Heart of Darkness*" by Stephen A. Reid. From *Modern Fiction Studies,* IX, No. 4 (Winter 1963-1964), 347-356. Copyright © 1964 by the Purdue Research Foundation and reprinted with its permission.

[1] *Conrad the Novelist* (Cambridge, Mass.: Harvard University Press, 1958), p. 42.

hear of African kings who have imagined themselves immortal by virtue of
their sorceries. Now primitive peoples, as we have seen, sometimes believe
that their safety and even that of the world is bound up with the life of one
of these god-men or human incarnations of the divinity. Naturally, therefore, they take the utmost care of his life, out of a regard for their own. But
no amount of care and precaution will prevent the man-god from growing
old and feeble and at last dying. His worshippers have to lay their account
with this sad necessity and to meet it as best they can. The danger is a
formidable one; for if the course of nature is dependent on the man-god's
life, what catastrophes may not be expected from the gradual enfeeblement
of his powers and their final extinction in death. There is only one way of
averting these dangers. The man-god must be killed as soon as he shows
symptoms that his powers are beginning to fail, and his soul must be transferred to a vigorous successor before it has been seriously impaired by the
threatened decay. The advantages of thus putting the man-god to death instead of allowing him to die of old age and disease are, to the savage, obvious
enough. For if the man-god dies what we call a natural death, it means,
according to the savage, that his soul has either voluntarily departed from his
body and refuses to return, or more commonly that it has been extracted, or
at least detained in its wanderings, by a demon or sorcerer. In any of these
cases the soul of the man-god is lost to his worshippers, and with it their
prosperity is gone and their very existence endangered. Even if they could
arrange to catch the soul of the dying god as it left his lips or his nostrils
and so transfer it to a successor, this would not effect their purpose; for, dying
of disease, his soul would necessarily leave his body in the last stage of weakness and exhaustion, and so enfeebled it would continue to drag out a
languid, inert existence in the body to which it might be transferred.
Whereas by slaying him his worshippers could, in the first place, make sure
of catching his soul as it escaped and transferring it to a suitable successor;
and, in the second place, by putting him to death before his natural force
was abated, they would secure that the world should not fall into decay with
the decay of the man-god. Every purpose, therefore, was answered, and all
dangers averted by thus killing the man-god, and transferring his soul, while
yet at its prime, to a vigorous successor.[2]

Following this, Frazer discusses briefly the situation in the Congo:

The people of Congo believed, as we have seen, that if their pontiff the
Chitomé were to die a natural death, the world would perish, and the earth,
which he alone sustained by his power and merit, would immediately be
annihilated. Accordingly when he fell ill and seemed likely to die, the man
who was destined to be his successor entered the pontiff's house with a rope
or a club and strangled or clubbed him to death. (p. 343)

Kurtz's ascendancy to the position of a man-god needs no demonstra-
tion. Our concerns, in the light of Frazer's analysis, will center on the
susceptibility of the natives to Kurtz's domination, and their intense
concern for him. In the person of Kurtz, as in the person of the Chitomé,

[2] Sir George James Frazer, *The Golden Bough* (New York: The Macmillan Company, 1960), pp. 309-310.

lay the security of the earth. The most pressing question for them is his mortality and the need for a mortal successor. The awe of the natives toward the death of a man-god—the death of a man-god for whom no successor has been provided—is clearly seen in the brief passage about Fresleven:

> "He [Fresleven] whacked the old nigger mercilessly, while a big crowd of his people watched him, thunderstruck, till some man—I was told the chief's son—in desperation at hearing the old chap yell, made a tentative' jab with a spear at the white man—and of course it went quite easy between the shoulder-blades. Then the whole population cleared into the forest, expecting all kinds of calamities to happen, while, on the other hand, the steamer Fresleven commanded left also in a panic. . . . Afterwards nobody seemed to trouble much about Fresleven's remains, till I got out and stepped into his shoes. I couldn't let it rest, though; but when an opportunity offered at last to meet my predecessor, the grass growing through his ribs was tall enough to hide his bones. They were all there. The supernatural being had not been touched after he fell. And the village was deserted. . . . A calamity had come to it, sure enough. The people had vanished. Mad terror had scattered them." [3]

It is obvious that the gentle Fresleven had been regarded as a man-god by the natives. His sudden death destroys the group.

The poignant concern of the natives about the possible death or departure of Kurtz is one of the most striking things in the story. As Marlow's boat approaches the Inner Station, he hears a cry from the shore—"a cry, a very loud cry, as of infinite desolation." In the skirmish, very close to the Station, Marlowe blows the steam whistle:

> "The tumult of angry and warlike yells was checked instantly, and then from the depths of the woods went out such a tremulous and prolonged wail of mournful fear and utter despair as may be imagined to follow the flight of the last hope from the earth." (pp. 40-41)

There is no doubt whatever that the natives' mournful fear concerns the fact that the steamer may remove Kurtz. The Russian makes this explicit:

> " 'Why did they attack us?' I pursued. He [the Russian] hesitated, then said shame-facedly, 'They don't want him to go.' " (p. 48)

Kurtz's position as man-god, however, is significantly different from the usual one described by Frazer. That is, he comes from the outside, and is, naturally, unwilling to play the game of submitting to death when his strength fails. And thus we have the anomalous situation of the prolonged and acute anxieties of the natives (as Kurtz grows older and

---

[3] Bruce Harkness, ed., *Conrad's Heart of Darkness and the Critics* (San Francisco: Wadsworth, 1960), p. 6. All subsequent citations from this edition are given in parentheses.

suffers severe illnesses), and of Kurtz's continued power. To account for this anomalous situation, I believe that Kurtz had been able to establish the ritual which would allay the anxieties of the natives and therefore maintain his own position. This ritual—the sacrifice of a young and vigorous man, and the consuming of a portion of his body—has sufficient precedence, as Frazer demonstrates, to give it credence. There is first the question of the acceptability of the death of a proxy:

> When the king first succeeded in getting the life of another accepted as a sacrifice instead of his own, he would have to show that the death of that other would serve the purpose quite as well as his own would have done. Now it was as a god or demigod that the king had to die; therefore the substitute who died for him had to be invested, at least for the occasion, with the divine attributes of the king. (p. 337)

There is then the question of how it might be believed that the aging and infirm Kurtz should become strong and vigorous:

> When the Alake or king of Abeokuta in West Africa dies, the principal men decapitate his body, and placing the head in a large earthen vessel deliver it to the new sovereign; it becomes his fetish and he is bound to pay it honours. Sometimes, in order apparently that the new sovereign may inherit more surely the magical and other virtues of the royal line, he is required to eat a piece of his dead predecessor. Thus, at Abeokuta not only was the head of the late king presented to his successor, but the tongue was cut out and given him to eat. Hence, when the natives wish to signify that the sovereign reigns, they say, "He has eaten the king." A custom of the same sort is still practiced at Ibadan, a large town in the interior of Lagos, West Africa. When the king dies . . . his heart is eaten by his successor.
> Taking the whole of the preceding evidence into account, we may fairly suppose that when the divine king or priest is put to death his spirit is believed to pass into his successor. In point of fact, among the Shilluk of the White Nile, who regularly kill their divine kings, every king on his accession has to perform a ceremony which appears designed to convey to him the same sacred and worshipful spirit which animated all his predecessors. (pp. 343-344)

I suggest that Kurtz, at the midnight rituals, had been able to have the natives accept the most temporary of man-gods in the form of a young and vigorous man, invest him with all the trappings of his position, worship him, and finally slay him. Kurtz would succeed, once again, to the high position, but having partaken of the body of the newly slain man-god, succeed reinvigorated and revived. These rites were perhaps annual, or, as I feel, were instituted with increasing frequency as Kurtz's illnesses became more frequent and pronounced. The heads on the poles were those of the victims; they faced Kurtz's hut. The head of the dead king, says Frazer, "becomes his fetish and he is bound to pay it honours." (p. 343).

Marlow, as I have said, refuses to hear details. But the text is clear enough about this:

> "But this [Kurtz's report] must have been before his—let us say—nerves went wrong, and caused him to preside at certain midnight dances ending with unspeakable rites, which—as far as I reluctantly gathered from what I heard at various times—were offered up to him—do you understand?—to Mr. Kurtz himself." (p. 44)

There can be no quarrel with the generally accepted notion that Kurtz's bestiality involved an "exploitation" of the natives. But no critic, to my knowledge, has attempted to describe the precise nature of the relationship between the bestiality and the exploitation. The impression one has from criticism of *Heart of Darkness* is simply that Kurtz had, in effect, enslaved the natives, and was then free to practice upon them "unspeakable" acts of lust and brutality. This, however, is too simple as well as too vague. It betrays a wish to have Kurtz's behavior monstrous beyond belief, and therefore genuinely inaccessible to imagination. But it is necessary, psychologically, that Kurtz's rites have a particular content and a particular purpose. (This, of course, is not meant in any way to under-value the generalized fund of destructiveness in human beings. However, the expression of this destructiveness is never a "general" thing. Each expression is tied, irrevocably, to a specific motive and functions in a specific context.) Is there, then, a more plausible explanation of Kurtz's unspeakable rites than the one I have adduced?

The assumption that Kurtz's rites involved human sacrifice, and that they were for the purpose of maintaining Kurtz's power as a man-god, clarifies several otherwise inexplicable passages. Two such passages are those concerning the agitation of the proud native woman in Kurtz's hut, and Marlow's blank horror at seeing the empty cabin. The Russian, who relates the story of the native woman's agitation, himself a puzzling figure, is at the center of that agitation. He has attached himself to Kurtz, and has been faithful to him. He has nursed Kurtz through two serious illnesses, and Marlow notes that "he alluded to it [the nursing] as you would to some risky feat" (p. 49). Indeed, Kurtz (so the Russian informs Marlow) had more than once threatened to kill him. Why should the Russian's kindness invite murderous thoughts in Kurtz? I suggest that the Russian was seen by the natives as an ultimate successor to the dying Kurtz. A white man, younger than Kurtz, who looks up to Kurtz as if he were a god, would more than reasonably suggest to the natives the proper ultimate "replacement." But the Russian (as we learn) knows nothing of this, nor of the heads on the poles. This is the scene he relates to Marlow:

> "She [the proud native woman] got in one day and kicked up a row about those miserable rags I picked up in the storeroom to mend my clothes with.

I wasn't decent. At least it must have been that, for she talked like a fury to Kurtz for an hour, pointing at me now and then. I don't understand the dialect of this tribe. Luckily for me, I fancy Kurtz felt too ill that day to care, or there would have been mischief. I don't understand. . . . No—it's too much for me." (pp. 54-55)

The Russian's explanation (the woman's concern with his clothing) is on the same level as his explanation for the heads on the posts. From this incident, and from the fact that Kurtz had more than once during his illnesses threatened to kill the Russian, it seems plausible that the conversation between the woman and the seriously ill Kurtz concerns the Russian as a successor. The woman is urging Kurtz to sacrifice himself for the good of the tribe. And, as the Russian says, "luckily for me, I fancy Kurtz was too ill that day to care, or there would have been mischief." Kurtz would prefer to murder the Russian lest the natives take things into their own hands. Frazer's statement concerning the Congo pontiff, the Chitomé, is suggestive of this point. "Accordingly, when he [the Chitomé] fell ill and seemed likely to die, the man who was destined to be his successor entered the pontiff's house with a rope or a club and strangled or clubbed him to death." (p. 343)

Guerard would prefer to leave the question of Marlow's "pure abstract terror" at the sight of the empty cabin as Marlow leaves it. But it certainly should (if it can) be answered; and an answer will possibly clarify the story and Conrad's intent.

"I think I would have raised an outcry if I had believed my eyes. But I didn't believe them at first—the thing seemed so impossible. The fact is I was completely unnerved by a sheer blank fright, pure abstract terror, unconnected with any distinct shape of physical danger. What made this emotion so overpowering was—how shall I define it?—the moral shock I received, as if something altogether monstrous, intolerable to thought and odious to the soul, had been thrust upon me unexpectedly." (p. 57)

It is obvious that Marlow realizes, first of all, that Kurtz's disappearance means that he has gone to the acting of another midnight ritual. In the previous paragraph, Marlow had quite clearly noted the preparations of the natives. It is therefore possible that the "moral shock" is the result of an awareness, not yet brought to articulation, that he will be in close proximity to the "unspeakable" rites. But, I believe, there is a further significance in the situation for Marlow, one that he only dimly senses, and which accounts for the full shock. This is in the fact that Kurtz is mortally ill. ("He can't walk—he is crawling on all-fours" [p. 57].) Why would Kurtz, in such condition, go *voluntarily* to "attend" the rites? It is unreasonable to believe that, abstractly considered, Kurtz would have driven himself to gratify his "monstrous passions" (p. 59) when he was so ill. If not, then, the only possible alternative reason for Kurtz's disappearance is that he felt he had no choice: the rites were the demands of the natives. Marlow knows that the preparation of the natives is a result of the presence of the steamer, and therefore of Marlow himself. Marlow's "moral shock," then, comes from the realization that Kurtz is being forced into the rites, and that he, Marlow, is in some way responsible. (It may be argued that all of this is too complex for any man to have understood in an instant, and that, in any case, Marlow left the whole question of the shock unexplained. Such an argument ignores the mind's ability to register the most complex things, and instantly to repress what is too painful to confront.)

Marlow overtakes Kurtz. Kurtz says:

> " 'Go away—hide yourself,' . . . It was very awful. I glanced back. We were within thirty yards from the nearest fire. A black figure stood up, strode on long black legs, waving long black arms, across the glow. It had horns— antelope horns, I think—on its head. Some sorcerer, . . . it looked fiend-like enough. 'Do you know what you are doing?' I whispered. 'Perfectly,' he answered, raising his voice for that single word. . . . If he makes a row we are lost, I thought to myself. This clearly was not a case for fisticuffs, even apart from the very natural aversion I had to beat that Shadow—this wandering and tormented thing. 'You will be lost,' I said—'utterly lost.' One gets sometimes such a flash of inspiration, you know. I did say the right thing. . . .
>
> " 'I had immense plans,' he muttered irresolutely. . . . 'And now for this stupid scoundrel—' " (p. 58)

I think it is clear that Kurtz's rites had been for him essentially the means for his immense plans. He had, to an extent, kept them separated. Marlow's inspired words—"You will be lost—utterly lost"—strike home. Marlow does not *know* what possessed him to utter these words. For our understanding, however, they cannot have proceeded from anything but a vague sense of a *change* in Kurtz's situation. If, as the usual interpretation has it, Marlow understands that Kurtz's rites were voluntary, why would there be any question of hope left? Kurtz realizes that his means are becoming ends: he cannot hope for anything but the briefest reprieve by going through with the ritual. He says, sincerely, "I had immense plans," . . . "And now for this stupid scoundrel—" That is, the manager, who wishes to take him away, has caused the natives to panic, and him, Kurtz, to make another sacrifice. It is, I think, to be expected that Kurtz, even toward the end, would attempt to blame someone else, and not his own age and physical frailty, as the deepest cause of the natives' anxiety.

What are Kurtz's "immense plans"? Once again, criticism has failed to aim at explicitness. The reason for the failure is to be found in the very extravagance and absurdity of Kurtz's "plans." It is difficult to comprehend, I think, but Kurtz's plans cannot have been other than dominion over the world. The ivory was the means to that end, just as the sacrifices were the means to the continued flow of the ivory. We can say, also, what type of domination Kurtz hoped to exercise: a benevolent tyranny. We know, in general, of Kurtz's accomplishments in the arts ("he [a cousin] gave me to understand that Kurtz had been essentially a great musician" [p. 64]), and we know in particular Kurtz's extraordinary public magnetism. At the end, a journalist,

". . . anxious to know something of the fate of his 'dear colleague' turned up. This visitor informed me Kurtz's proper sphere ought to have been politics 'on the popular side.' He . . . confessed his opinion that Kurtz really couldn't write a bit—'but heavens! how that man could talk! He electrified large meetings. He had faith—don't you see?—he had the faith. He could get himself to believe anything—anything.' " (pp. 64-65)

As Kurtz lies dying on the steamer, his sense of omnipotence is still intact:

"He desired to have kings meet him at railway stations on his return. . . . 'You show them you have in you something that is really profitable, and then there will be no limits to the recognition of your ability,' he would say." (p. 61)

Any precise plans, Kurtz of course could not have. The precise plans centered on the ivory, and on the means for obtaining the ivory.

Kurtz descended into bestiality, but always with an awareness of what to him was the high purpose of his return to Europe. Throughout the story Conrad provides us with a sense of pity for the exploited natives. (We are here not concerned with the economic exploitation.) Kurtz is not untouched by this:

"We had carried Kurtz into the pilot-house. . . . Lying on the couch he stared through the open shutter. There was an eddy in the mass of human bodies, and the woman with helmeted head and tawny cheeks rushed out to the very brink of the stream. She put out her hands, shouted something, and all that wild mob took up the shout in a roaring chorus of articulated, rapid, breathless utterance.
" 'Do you understand this?' I asked.
"He kept on looking out past me with fiery, longing eyes, with a mingled expression of wistfulness and hate. He made no answer, but I saw a smile, a smile of indefinable meaning, appear on his colourless lips that a moment after twitched convulsively. 'Do I not?' he said slowly, gasping, as if the words had been torn out of him by a supernatural power." (p. 60)

And, at the very end:

" 'Close the shutter,' said Kurtz suddenly one day; 'I can't bear to look at this.' I did so. There was a silence. 'Oh, but I will wring your heart yet!' he cried at the invisible wilderness." (p. 61)

Kurtz is at this time sharply aware of two things: the natives' helpless dependency on him, and the methods he employed to maintain his ascendancy. It is ironic but true that both the natives and Kurtz were at one in wishing Kurtz's domination to continue. It is on the question only of the sacrifices that the natives and Kurtz differed. To the natives, the sacrifices were necessary and proper acts: without them, the world would be annihilated. Therefore, they felt no moral repugnance; these acts were no more bestial to them, say, than the bombing of cities in war is to some "civilized" minds. To Kurtz, however, these acts cannot have remained anything but morally reprehensible, because he could never feel the particular necessity for them felt by the natives. For him, they were only tricks to maintain his power. I do not, of course, intend to deny the sadistic satisfactions Kurtz obtained from them. Plainly, he could not have carried them through had he not derived intense pleasure from them. But, this pleasure only intensified his moral awareness. That Kurtz remains morally aware of his actions is certainly the case. He remains sharply aware of his cold-blooded exploitation of the natives' trust. What other meaning can his desperate cry—"Oh, but I will wring your heart yet!"—have but this? It is an expression of extreme guilt. Kurtz is saying to the natives, "When you will understand that I *had* to exploit you—when you understand the unequaled cause (the 'immense plans') that necessitated my actions—you will forgive and pity me."

It is, however, possible to speak of Kurtz's having originally been *forced* into the "unspeakable" rites as the only method of maintaining his ascendancy. Not only was he forced originally into the rites, but he was forced to continue them. Whatever sadistic satisfaction Kurtz derived from the bestiality, it is clear that the *involuntary* acts would become repugnant. And, most ironically, we see him, near death, crawling to the midnight ritual. It is this that lies behind his vicious statement, "Exterminate all the brutes!" (p. 44). Kurtz has made himself a prisoner of the natives. Insofar, then, as he is concerned with the natives' tyranny over him, it is "Exterminate all the brutes!" But, insofar as he is aware of his tyranny over them (a calculating use he sees as the necessary means to a morally high purpose), it is "Oh, but I will wring your heart yet!" Holding these two awarenesses together, as he does only once before he dies, it is "The horror! The horror!" (p. 62).

The civilized European Kurtz went to the Congo. After he had been there some time, we learn that he had given himself over to "unspeakable rites," had descended into bestiality. What had happened? The simple "giving in" to "uncontrolled lusts"—the usual explanation of Kurtz's disintegration—seems to me a psychologically unsound way of describing the case—especially when a more precise explanation is available. We know the relative ease with which a white man may become a god to the natives. Fresleven became one unwittingly. The difficulty (as Frazer makes clear) is the maintaining of the role. If we realize that Kurtz's essential problem was not to gain ascendancy, but to maintain it, what more likely situation—the instituting of the rite of sacrifice and the attendant cannibalism—can be imagined? Kurtz's descent into bestiality becomes psychologically plausible. He becomes more "human," and less a "hero of the spirit."

It is exactly this which has caused the critics (following Conrad) to avoid naming the rites. It is all very well to speak, as Lionel Trilling does,[4] of our attraction to the man who "goes down into that hell which is the historical beginning of the human soul," but we become something more than uncomfortable when the possibility of *our* doing so presents itself. Conrad left unstated the specific (and therefore possible) acts of bestiality that Kurtz sinks to. It is easier, then, for Marlow to announce his admiration of Kurtz:

> "Better his cry—much better. It was an affirmation, a moral victory paid for by innumerable defeats, by abominable terrors, by abominable satisfactions. But it was a victory!" (p. 63)

It is not only that Marlow does not know specifically what the rites are —he will not learn. The point is simply that if one is going to admire the bestial in man, it is safer not to know too much about it. If the bestial is specific, it is possible; if it remains abstract ("abominable terrors," "abominable satisfactions"), it is really only an idea.

Marlow, then, in his refusal to look deeply into Kurtz's depravity, is quite true to his own image of himself. The critical point is that not only does Marlow not "go ashore for a howl and a dance" (it is fitting that when Marlow contemplates *his* performing "unspeakable rites," they materialize safely enough as a "howl" and a "dance"), but that he will not (by refusing to hear the details of Kurtz's rites) dare face the possibility that a knowledge of them will find an echo in himself. He has, indeed, "peeped over the edge," and the dramatic situation for him at the end is that he remains fixed in the middle. He dare go no further in discovering within himself the kinds of bestiality he vaguely understands to have been in Kurtz. If, however, we do not find a fault, dramatically, in Marlow's overuse of strained adjectives ("It was the stillness of an implacable force brooding over an inscrutable intention" [p. 29]), we may yet wonder at *Conrad's* predilection for what F. R. Leavis calls "the same adjectival insistence upon inexpressible and incomprehensible mystery." [5] And the conclusion suggested by this is that Conrad's frequent and irritating indulgence in such vocabulary stems from the same source as Marlow's. He too has peeped only over the edge. But he has reported accurately enough what he did see, and we can reconstruct the rest. This will account for the fact that elsewhere—outside of *Heart of Darkness*—Conrad is silent about Kurtz's unspeakable rites.

---

[4] "The Modern Element in Modern Literature," *Partisan Review*, XXVII (January-February, 1961), p. 26.
[5] *The Great Tradition* (New York: G. W. Stewart, 1948), p. 177.

Lord Jim:
Conrad and the "Few Simple Notions"

by Douglas Hewitt

Lord Jim was begun immediately after Conrad had finished writing
"Youth" in the summer of 1898, dropped for a time, taken up again
after he had written *Heart of Darkness,* and finished in the summer of
1900. "My first thought," he says in the "Author's Note" to the Collected Edition, "was of a short story, concerned only with the pilgrim
ship episode; nothing more." But later he perceived that

> the pilgrim ship episode was a good starting-point for a free and wandering
> tale; that it was an event, too, which could conceivably colour the whole
> 'sentiment of existence' in a simple and sensitive character.

Signs of this change in conception may be discerned, though not where
we might expect to find them—in a thinness of material or an untidy
linking of an illogical second part. Rather are they apparent in a certain muddlement throughout, an uncertainty of the final impression intended by Conrad.

In terms of plot there are undoubtedly two parts to the story: the de-
fection of Jim and the disaster after he seems to have rehabilitated himself; certainly the second part has been added. But . . . they are intimately connected. It is, indeed, difficult to imagine the first part alone
as a satisfactory story—certainly as a story by Conrad; the account of a
cowardly leap for safety alone could hardly be enough; it demands
development.

The general lines of the story are given in miniature in the first chapter. Jim, having developed a romantic view of himself as one who will
meet crises with calmness and determination, is not shaken in this faith
by his failure to reach the cutter of his training ship when it puts out to
effect a rescue. In the main crisis of the first part of the novel the failure
is repeated under circumstances where he offends most unequivocally
against "the obscure body of men held together by a community of in-

glorious toil and by fidelity to a certain standard of conduct." His crime
is described in terms which are reminiscent of some passages of *Heart of
Darkness*—in terms of what, in that story, is called "sordid farce."

> It was part of the burlesque meanness pervading that particular disaster
> at sea that they did not come to blows. It was all threats, all a terribly ef-
> fective feint, a sham from beginning to end. . . .

There is a flavour of shameless farce about all the weaknesses and crimes
of which Conrad writes at this time; his mean characters are all horribly
comic.

Jim's offence is one upon which the Court of Enquiry can have no
mercy. But he insists on what, to many of the spectators, seems like trying to brazen it out. Brierly's question: "Why eat all that dirt?" sums up
the feeling of most of them. His hope, however, is that he can rehabili-
tate himself; as in his first failure in the training ship, he is still sure
that at bottom he is ready for any emergency, that he has only been betrayed by circumstances. He will not accept his weakness and stay in a
place where men knew his story, and so he is driven farther and farther
eastwards in the search for a refuge where he can start with a clean
sheet and establish himself as a trustworthy man.

Finally, in the jungle settlement of Patusan, he rises to be "Lord Jim,"
one whose authority and honour are never questioned and on whom all
the natives are dependent. It seems that he has successfully isolated himself from his past, in a place where

> The stream of civilization, as if divided on a headland a hundred miles
> north of Patusan, branches east and south-west, leaving its plains and val-
> leys, its old trees and its old mankind, neglected and isolated.

But, despite the fact that he has achieved "the conquest of love,
honour, men's confidence," his past comes in search of him. Gentleman
Brown and his crew of cut-throats penetrate the "wall of forests" which
shuts Jim in his isolation. Physically the people of Patusan are more
than a match for Brown, but mentally Jim is helpless before this man
who combines with his ferocity "a vehement scorn for mankind at large
and for his victims in particular" and who "would rob a man as if only
to demonstrate his poor opinion of the creature." Everything that
Brown says recalls Jim's past weakness, undermines his certainty that he
has put behind him a cowardice that was only momentary.

> He asked Jim whether he had nothing fishy in his life to remember that
> he was so damnedly hard upon a man trying to get out of a deadly hole by
> the first means that came to hand—and so on and so on. And there ran
> through the rough talk a vein of subtle reference to their common blood,
> an assumption of common experience; a sickening suggestion of common
> guilt, of secret knowledge that was like a bond of their minds and of their
> hearts.

Jim finds that "his fate, revolted, was forcing his hand." We remember the "unforeseen partnership" with Kurtz which Marlow accepts in *Heart of Darkness;* but here there is an explicit weakness in Jim to which the partner appeals, and he confronts this appeal under circumstances which make his actions of vital importance for all the inhabitants of Patusan. He speaks no more than the truth when he says: "I am responsible for every life in the land." Unable to disown Brown, he brings disaster on the village, takes the death of the chief's son on his own head, and is killed as punishment.

In enlarging the simple story of the pilgrim ship episode, however, Conrad makes a more significant addition than the second half of the story; he introduces Marlow, who, although he does not appear as story-teller until the fifth chapter, is the person to whom we naturally look for commentary and judgment. Judgment we find in plenty—but, far from clarifying the moral issues, Marlow's reflections only succeed in making them more confused.

We remain at the end, I believe, uncertain as to what our verdict on Jim is meant to be. Many views are put before us. The elderly French lieutenant's is clear:

> But the honour—the honour, monsieur! . . . The honour . . . that is real—that is! And what life may be worth when . . . when the honour is gone—*ah ça! par exemple*—I can offer no opinion.

This discourages Marlow; he feels that the lieutenant has "pricked the bubble." Yet at times he seems to see Jim as expiating his fault by taking on himself the punishment for the disaster to the village, finally re-establishing his honour. At other times a totally different verdict seems to be presented, as in the conclusion:

> But we can see him, an obscure conqueror of fame, tearing himself out of the arms of a jealous love at the sign, at the call of his exalted egoism. He goes away from a living woman to celebrate his pitiless wedding with a shadowy ideal of conduct.

We remain uncertain whether Jim's moment of panic is one which can be expiated or whether, in the judgment of Marlow the seaman, it has placed him for ever beyond the possibility of forgiveness, uncertain, indeed, whether he is to be blamed for hoping that his weakness can be forgotten or for being so morbidly conscious of it.

The reason for this uncertainty is clear; it is because Marlow, Conrad's mouthpiece, is himself bewildered. As in *Heart of Darkness,* which Conrad wrote while recasting the novel, Marlow plays a greater part than might at first be thought. We may reasonably wonder whether the feelings which brought *Heart of Darkness* to birth may not be the chief cause why *Lord Jim* developed from a simple short story into a complex novel, for there are many resemblances between the relationship of Marlow and Kurtz and that of Marlow and Jim.

There is an "unforeseen partnership" not only between Jim and Gentleman Brown but also between Jim and Marlow. "Why I longed to go grubbing into the deplorable details . . . I can't explain," Marlow says, and wonders:

> Was it for my own sake that I wished to find some shadow of an excuse for that young fellow whom I had never seen before?

A relationship is quickly established between them. When Jim explains his hopes of regaining the respect that he has lost, Marlow says:

> . . . it was I . . . who a moment ago had been so sure of the power of words, and now was afraid to speak, in the same way one dares not move for fear of losing a slippery hold. . . . It was the fear of losing him that kept me silent, for it was borne upon me that should I let him slip away into the darkness I would never forgive myself.

Just as in *Heart of Darkness* Marlow feels the power of nightmares which his previous experience and standards have not made him ready to understand, so here he is appealed to by Jim in ways for which he is not prepared.

> I was made to look at the convention that lurks in all truth [Marlow says] and on the essential sincerity of falsehood. He appealed to all sides at once— to the side turned perpetually to the light of day, and to that side of us which, like the other hemisphere of the moon, exists stealthily in perpetual darkness, with only a fearful ashy light falling at times on the edge. He swayed me. I own to it, I own up.

It is his own security for which Marlow fears; when he goes for information to one of Jim's fellow officers, it is because he hopes to learn of a redeeming motive for his offense.

> I see well enough now [he says of this incident] that I hoped for the impossible—for the laying of what is the most obstinate ghost of man's creation, of the uneasy doubt uprising like a mist, secret and gnawing like a worm, and more chilling than the certitude of death—the doubt of the sovereign power enthroned in a fixed standard of conduct.

It is obvious enough that Marlow is disturbed because Jim, a fellow English seaman, has not been true to the standards by which they all live.

> I was aggrieved against him [he says], as though he had cheated me—me! —of a splendid opportunity to keep up the illusion of my beginnings, as though he had robbed our common life of the last spark of its glamour.

But this alone is not sufficient to account for the disturbance of mind in which he is plunged. Jim has also raised doubts of the finality of the very standards themselves; he has suggested the possibility that there are hidden depths of feeling against which they are powerless. Marlow— and, as we shall see in a minute, Brierly—cannot cast Jim out as an offender and forget him, and this is not merely because he is a fellow Englishman, but because he seems to cast doubt on the values by which they could condemn him. Marlow speaks thus of the courage which Jim so signally fails to display:

> . . . an unthinking and blessed stiffness before the outward and inward terrors, before the might of nature, and the seductive corruption of men—backed by a faith invulnerable to the strength of facts, to the contagion of examples, to the solicitation of ideas. Hang ideas! They are tramps, vagabonds, knocking at the back-door of your mind, each taking a little of your substance, each carrying away some crumb of that belief in a few simple notions you must cling to if you want to live decently and would like to die easy.

Marlow would seem here to be at one with Winnie Verloc of *The Secret Agent* in her belief that life does not bear looking into very closely, and he continues with the direct implication that such courage is only possible for fools:

> This has nothing to do with Jim, directly; only he was outwardly so typical of that good, stupid kind we like to feel marching right and left of us in life, of the kind that is not disturbed by the vagaries of intelligence and the perversions of—of nerves, let us say.

He goes on to reminisce about "that good, stupid kind" and about how moved he is when a boy whom he has taken to sea for his first voyage greets him after many years, now grown into one "fit to live or die as the sea may decree," just as, in the voyage into the heart of darkness, the Marlow of that story clings for a moment to the manual of seamanship as the relief of something tangible in the midst of nightmare. The nostalgia for the normal, for the reliance on simple duties and uncomplicated virtues, is the same, and in both cases the relief can only be temporary.

The feeling of insecurity is deepened by the story of Brierly's suicide. That impeccable captain has felt the same apprehension as Marlow: ". . . the only thing that holds us together," he says, "is just the name for that kind of decency. Such an affair destroys one's confidence." We might feel the conclusion to be extreme, for in any group of men there will be some who will betray the faith reposed in them, but we know that, all the time he is enquiring into Jim's case, he is also sitting in judgment on himself and finding a verdict of "unmitigated guilt." Marlow speculates that, in his case too, it is the awakening of some idea:

> . . . the matter was no doubt of the gravest import [he says], one of those trifles that awaken ideas—start into life some thought with which a man unused to such a companionship finds it impossible to live.

We are given no hint of what the "idea" is, except that it is not a commonplace worry about drink, or money, or women, but the effect of what we are told about Brierly is to reinforce Marlow's own obliquely expressed conviction that the virtues of seamanship—all of which Brierly possesses in superabundant measure—are still vulnerable to "ideas"— that they are not enough in themselves and can easily be imperiled.

For all those issues with which Brierly's virtues can deal, the judgment on Jim is certain, but, in Marlow's words, Jim's attempt to explain his deed gives the impression that

> he was only speaking before me, in a dispute with an invisible personality, an antagonistic and inseparable partner of his existence—another possessor of his soul. These were issues beyond the competency of a court of enquiry.

The effect of muddlement which is so commonly found in *Lord Jim* comes, in short, from this—that Marlow is himself muddled. We look to him for a definite comment, explicit or implicit, on Jim's conduct and he is not able to give it. We are inevitably reminded of the bewilderment with which the Marlow of *Heart of Darkness* faces Kurtz. By appealing to "that side of us which, like the other hemisphere of the moon, exists stealthily in perpetual darkness" he confronts Marlow with "issues beyond the competency of a court of enquiry" and thus shakes the standards by which he would normally be judged.

Here, as in the short story, the experience of Marlow goes far beyond that of the man whom he cannot disown. Kurtz is only a "hollow man"; Jim himself is, by comparison with Marlow, naïve, a romantic thinking in the terms of a boy's adventure story.

But the muddlement goes farther than this. I have so far begged the question by saying "Marlow, Conrad's mouthpiece." In fact the confusion seems to extend to Conrad's conception of the story, and this reveals itself in some of the rhetoric given to Marlow. A good deal of this is imprecise and some is little more than a vague and rather pretentious playing with abstractions. It is in these terms that he speaks of the approaching catastrophe:

> *Magna est veritas et* . . . Yes, when it gets a chance. There is a law, no doubt—and likewise a law regulates your luck in the throwing of dice. It is not Justice, the servant of men, but accident, hazard, Fortune—the ally of patient Time—that holds an even and scrupulous balance. . . . Well, let's leave it to chance, whose ally is Time, that cannot be hurried, and whose enemy is Death, that will not wait.

There are many such passages, and they give the impression rather of a man who is ruminating to obscure the issue than of one thinking to clarify it. But they are not "placed"—Conrad, that is, does not so present them that we see them as deliberate, part of the portrayal of a man who is bewildered. They come rather from his own uncertainty as to the effect at which he is aiming. There is, very clearly, a conflict in his own mind; he raises the issue of the sufficiency of the "few simple notions

you must cling to if you want to live decently," but he does not, throughout the book, face it consistently.

Lord Jim is, at bottom, concerned with the same preoccupations as
Heart of Darkness and other works of this period, but Conrad has chosen
to treat them in such a way that he inevitably feels more directly concerned. As he says in the concluding words of the "Author's Note": "He
was 'one of us.' " The uncertainty which remains even at the end of the
book as to what judgment we should pass on Jim and the passages of
imprecise rhetoric are, I believe, an indication that his feelings are too
deeply and too personally involved for him to stand above the bewilderment in which he places Marlow. The fixed standards of the simple
sailor are those which, above all others, Conrad finds it difficult to treat
with detachment. He was too aware of the depths of treachery and
cowardice of which men are capable not to cherish whatever seems to
provide a defense against them, and at times we have the impression that,
just as much as Marlow, he is himself fighting to retain a faith in the
efficacy and total goodness of the "few simple notions." . . .

We have seen how, from the first, [Conrad] depicts such men of simple
courage and devotion as Captain MacWhirr, yet also raises issues with
which these attitudes and beliefs cannot deal—the "issues beyond the
competency of a court of enquiry" of *Lord Jim*. He is seen to be almost
obsessed by the "unforeseen partnership" of *Heart of Darkness,* the
"foundation of all the emotions" of "Falk."

In this pessimism and scepticism he resembles very closely that side of
Dostoevsky which is seen in the questioning of Ivan Karamazov and the
radical doubt of Kirillov and Raskolnikov. What we do not find in
Conrad is the positive side of Dostoevsky's thought which is manifested,
for instance, in the further development of *Crime and Punishment,*
where Raskolnikov finds that his logically justified decision to kill the
old woman is an unnatural violation of those parts of his personality
which his logical thought has not taken into account. Conrad's view of
human nature is, in fact, fundamentally more pessimistic, more "nihilis-
tic" than that of Dostoevsky. He has in his best novels and stories a conception of evil which is not vague and mystifying and which is not a
matter of good people and bad people. It is precise and it is conceived
profoundly in terms of the maiming power of Charles Gould's silver
mine, the "hollowness" of Mr. Kurtz and the self-deception and fear of
Mr. Verloc. But he has no conception of a goodness just as profound
(and sometimes just as hidden), rooted in a complex human nature, and
though he could echo with approval Nostromo's "God for men—religions
for women," the God is not apparent in his work; he takes no comfort
from supernatural hopes of improvement or redemption.

That this was a painful state of mind for him is clear. Though he is
pessimistic, he is never cynical; we cannot but take seriously the fate of
Mrs. Gould or Captain Whalley or Winnie Verloc. As he said, speaking

of Mr. Kurtz: "I have not treated him with the easy nonchalance of an amateur. Believe me, no man paid more for his lines than I have."

We do believe him and we can understand why, seeing no positive values to counter the force of his negative criticism, he took refuge in the unreal and unquestioned goodness of Lena and old Peyrol. For, in essence, this is Conrad's situation: he is intensely and continuously aware of the existence of a world of moral and spiritual values, yet every quality, every virtue, every position in which he might hope to rest in security, is at once undermined; the "impenetrable darkness" covers the world. He is in the position—and it is not an uncommon one for writers of the last fifty years—of feeling the reality of a moral and spiritual order sufficiently for it to condemn normal feelings and normal idealisms, but of having no beliefs that can give him hope that the forces of evil will be overcome.

His protagonists, therefore, face their problems and suffer their torments against a static background which condemns them; their struggles are futile and their fate predetermined.

Conrad's Solitaries

by Paul L. Wiley

Difficult as it is to turn without some lapse of attention from [*Heart of Darkness*] to "The End of the Tether" (1902), the realistic tale of the sea which follows [it] in the *Youth* volume, the interest of the reader quickly revives as he discovers both that the story has special merits of its own and that it restates with certain distinctive variations central themes in Conrad's first period of authorship. The hermit-like figure, representing man separated from the bonds of an established tradition, appears again in the leading character, the sixty-seven year old seaman Captain Whalley; but the shift in emphasis away from the abnormal, so that Whalley's betrayal is due rather to circumstance than to any inherent weakness of nerve or will, may seem to indicate a fundamental change in the conception of the solitary type. The causes for Whalley's disaster are, nevertheless, much the same as those which produce failure in the earlier tales. By leaving a traditional order and its safeguards and risking himself in a world ruled by the law of survival, the Captain falls victim to evils which reduce him in the end to depths without a ray of saving light. Although a man of action, Whalley resembles Jim in being fine and unfortunate; and because of his knightly and aristocratic bearing, his white beard "like a silver breast-plate over the awful secret of his heart," and his utter loss of an honorable name in the wilderness of rocky islands where his ship founders, his humiliation seems the least merited of all the blows that fall on Conrad's defeated men. Nowhere else, except in the *Patna* scene in *Lord Jim*, does Conrad appear more intent on demonstrating the sheer malevolence of a world of error than in this story of great and patriarchal strength driven to the defensive tactics of a cornered animal.

After a long and distinguished record as a commander of sailing ships in the East, Whalley severs his connection with an existence governed by a high standard of conduct when loss of his money in a banking crash forces him to sell his barque, the *Fair Maid,* and to become captain of the *Sofala,* an old coasting steamer owned by the chief engineer, Massy,

"Conrad's Solitaries" (editor's title) by Paul L. Wiley. From *Conrad's Measure of Man*. Copyright 1954 by the Regents of the University of Wisconsin. Reprinted by permission of the publisher.

a man corrupted by greed for funds to invest in lotteries. Although a presentiment warns Whalley that the bargain is a bad one, he agrees to share in the ownership of the *Sofala* partly because he believes that, despite his age, his sound health will enable him to serve competently for a few years more but mainly because he wants to provide help for his only daughter whose marriage to an invalid husband has compelled her to manage a Melbourne boardinghouse. His decision to pass from the old world of sail to the new one of steam and so to drift alone in the treacherous currents of modern life where individuals no longer count is important psychologically since it involves a radically altered view of human affairs and leaves him feeling "as if his very soul had been taken out of him forcibly." This sense of inward loss is comparable to that experienced by Willems in yielding to the temptation of Aïssa or to Jim's awareness of the cleft within his nature after the *Patna* crisis; for on removing from the *Fair Maid* Whalley comes to recognize capacities for evil in himself which were latent before. The determining motive in his sale of the ship, love for his daughter, begins through changed circumstances to encroach upon his strict principles of morality and duty, a conflict hitherto prevented by the undisturbed success of his career and the large freedoms of his past life.

In consenting to become the partner of a man whose passion for gambling has rendered him a dupe to fortune, Whalley imagines that he can establish a compromise between his high principles and the claims of a world of brute struggle and lose only a little dignity and self-respect. But when chance deprives him of his eyesight and when paternal love develops into an overmastering passion that silences the warnings of conscience, Whalley has to abandon all self-respect. He surrenders in a contest for survival which ends in the wreck of the *Sofala* through Massy's treachery and in his own death in the only ship that he has ever lost. His experience on the steamer resembles that of Jim on the *Patna* in that both men are idealists compelled to descend to the level of characters to whom honor means nothing. Massy and the mate Sterne, an ambitious schemer, are birds of prey, loyal to nothing but themselves; and Massy's absolute subservience to wilderness law is emphasized in the scene where the darkness and the odor of the tropical forest flow into his cabin below the deck:

> The ship had in that place to shave the bank so close that the gigantic wall of leaves came gliding like a shutter against the port; the darkness of the primeval forest seemed to flow into that bare cabin with the odour of rotting leaves, of sodden soil—the strong muddy smell of the living earth steaming uncovered after the passing of a deluge.

It is ironical, nevertheless, that in spite of his contempt for Massy and the difference in their moral viewpoint Whalley is partner to the engineer in guilt as much as by contract; for both are dominated by passions which lead them to place self-interest before fidelity to the ship, no matter how commendable in itself the Captain's devotion to his daughter may seem.

Still more ironical, however, by contrast to his failure under the cruelty of chance, is Whalley's strongly religious bent, his belief in Providence, combined with his faith in human goodness:

> Captain Whalley believed a disposition for good existed in every man, even if the world were not a very happy place as a whole. In the wisdom of men he had not so much confidence.
>
> The disposition had to be helped up pretty sharply sometimes, he admitted. They might be silly, wrongheaded, unhappy; but naturally evil— no. There was at bottom a complete harmlessness at least. . . .

This prominent feature of the story invites comparison again with Conrad's earlier work. A similar trust in order, backed by a more or less remote religious inspiration and a limited view of evil, found expression in Lingard and Jim; but Whalley has a positive and active faith in divine power and justice which his past experience seems to confirm. In no other tale by the early Conrad is the issue between religion and scepticism so openly debated as in the conversations between Whalley and his friend, Van Wyk, the young Dutch planter who has adopted a cynical attitude of detachment from society; and all of Whalley's defense of Providence fails to explain the insane logic of his own tragic downfall. Like Jim's belief in a world suited to the exploits of a Christian hero, the Captain's faith seems to derive from a peculiarity of temperament, his natural vigor and active disposition; and whereas this religiosity is an inherent part of the man's fine simplicity and rectitude, which the discriminating Van Wyk admires, it also stimulates unwarranted trust in himself and a consequent ignorance of evil in insidious forms.

To survive, however, Whalley needs clear sight more than faith, and the approach of blindness provides an especially bitter denial of his optimism. The descent of this wholly unforeseen affliction manifests a kind of perverse cunning behind events comparable to that exhibited in the design of the mock disaster that overwhelms Jim on the *Patna*. Neither the Captain's religion nor his ideal of duty sustains him in his reaction to this physical injury. Instead he forsakes his moral integrity and bends his mind to contriving the deception by which the eyes of his Malay steersman are made to compensate for his own loss. The mind thus becomes subservient to the organ of sight; and the story, which is replete with ocular images from the opening page description of the dazzling light blinding the eye as the *Sofala* moves toward the bar in the river, brings to fullest development the theme of vision introduced from time to time in earlier tales.

The main clue to this theme, realized in character, can be found in the portrayal of the Malay serang, upon whose sharp sight Whalley depends for the carrying out of his ruse. The eyes of the steersman are compared to the lens of a camera and his mind to a "sensitized plate" having no apparatus for speculation. Hence although, unlike the white men, he has no intellectual mistrust of his senses, which give him accurate and precise knowledge, he is incapable of comprehending the simplest motives of his superiors. This one-sidedness is, however, less morally detrimental than the deceit practiced by the officers of the *Sofala;* for by self-interest and passion they falsify both the evidence of their senses—Massy and Sterne being able to see well enough through Whalley's trick—and their interpretation of motives, whereas the Malay remains wholly loyal. Nothing distorts his exact perception, just as nothing stands between Allistoun's quick glance at Donkin's belaying pin or Singleton's at the chain cable and their capacity to act. This treatment of the division of mind and sense which marks "The End of the Tether" looks forward to the handling of the same problem in a spirit of ironic comedy in two important stories at the end of this phase in Conrad's career, *Typhoon* and "Falk."

In the brilliantly designed *Typhoon* (1902), written just after "The End of the Tether," the motif of vision occurs again in relation to Captain MacWhirr, whose extraordinary eye for fact and literal mind are reminiscent of the primitive mental equipment of Whalley's serang. But the theme appears in a subtler context than that of the preceding story; and Conrad's remark in the "Author's Note" on the "deep conviction" with which he approached the subject verifies the impression that *Typhoon,* though brief, ranks with his major work. Like *The Nigger, Lord Jim,* and *Heart of Darkness, Typhoon* reaches a high plane of allegory in its development of the familiar subject of man's limitation in a world of evil.

The hurricane, which hurls destruction upon the *Nan-Shan* with all the fury of a cannonade, is the most malevolent of all the storms in Conrad; and its full terror is kept constantly before the mind of the reader by repeated images of cataclysm. These deluge metaphors, strongly reminiscent of those employed in *An Outcast, The Nigger,* and *Lord Jim,* are supplemented by images of violent passion to make the gale a composite symbol of both natural and human evil. In its effort to drive MacWhirr's ship over the edge of the world, the typhoon attacks like a personal enemy and with the force of an explosion, a cataract, or a trampling mob:

> It was something formidable and swift, like the sudden smashing of a vial of wrath. It seemed to explode all round the ship with an overpowering concussion and a rush of great waters, as if an immense dam had been blown up to windward. In an instant the men lost touch of each other. This is the disintegrating power of a great wind: it isolates one from one's kind. An earthquake, a landslip, an avalanche, overtake a man incidentally, as it were—without passion. A furious gale attacks him like a personal

enemy, tries to grasp his limbs, fastens upon his mind, seeks to rout his very spirit out of him.

Conrad's key image of the wilderness, separating man from an ordered world, takes a new form in the circular typhoon; and MacWhirr's decision to head the *Nan-Shan* and her shipload of coolies into this heart of darkness corresponds to that initial step into the wilderness with which the action of so many of the early stories begins. But although *Typhoon* conforms thus to the general pattern of so much of the work of Conrad's first phase, it is distinguished both by its tone, which is satirical throughout, and by the skillful method employed to convey the point of the satire by indirection.

Bluntly stated, the theme of *Typhoon* is a version of Conrad's major topic of the limitation of human nature, or of the isolated individual when confronted by evil from outside his experience or beyond the protection of the community. Conrad develops the theme, however, by the dramatically successful interplay of two characters, Jukes and MacWhirr; and the clue to the story lies in an understanding not only of their relationship but also of the special function assigned to MacWhirr. Although associated as members of the seaman's craft, the two men are in everything else extreme opposites.

The mate of the *Nan-Shan,* young Jukes, a sociable person with a normal share of good sense, imagination, and sympathy, represents average humanity. He is a competent officer who is temporarily overcome by fear only when he is exposed to the fury of the typhoon which he would have avoided had the decision been his and not MacWhirr's. The analysis of his collapse during the storm corresponds generally with the longer passages on the effects of terror in *An Outcast* and *Lord Jim,* and because of the similarity in their temptation and fall Jukes appears at first sight only a more commonplace Jim. Actually, however, they differ in that Jim fails while seeking to escape the trials of his profession whereas Jukes is so much bound to the traditions of the sea that he is amazed by MacWhirr's refusal to take a simple precautionary measure to ensure the safety of the ship and the people aboard. His world is confined by the reasonable man's concept of order; and when he is forced into a situation quite unrelated to his idea of what the worst should be, he not surprisingly reaches the point where, as the French lieutenant says in *Lord Jim,* one "lets go everything."

Whereas Jukes conforms, then, to the mean of human nature, MacWhirr is so exceptional in his unerring response to fact as to border on the impossible; and one can readily accept Conrad's statement that the Captain was never seen in the flesh. With his remarkable eye for defective door locks he represents an excess of the empirical as much as earlier characters, like Almayer, illustrate an extreme in visionary habit; and his complete dependence on what he can actually see, which is the mark of his originality, is accompanied by a lack of imagination great enough to isolate him from the commonplace world of people like his wife and Jukes. Although this very deficiency accounts for his dauntless temperament, it also leaves him tinged with absurdity; for his magnificent display of courage during the storm is wasted effort from the standpoint of common sense. His determination to take the ship through the storm rather than to deviate from her course is preposterous, based as it is upon contempt for the inherited wisdom of the craft of the sea contained in the book on storms. Yet the fault is not willful indifference to tradition, since in every other respect MacWhirr is faithful to the standards of his trade. The error results from a failure of the predictive faculty which is a safeguard to Jukes with his modicum of imagination. Without MacWhirr, Jukes could not have survived the hurricane and the ordeal of initiation that he undergoes, precisely because the test is utterly beyond normal human capacities for endurance.

MacWhirr's purpose in the story is clarified, therefore, when he is seen both as a measure of the limitations of the average man, Jukes, and as a warning of what is required of the individual who expects, as Kurtz expected, to survive evils outside the communal frontier. Only on condition, in other words, that man can equal MacWhirr by a radical transformation of his very nature dare he risk an encounter with the unknown and the powers of darkness. For a moment in the typhoon Jukes and MacWhirr are bound together, but their temporary alliance only emphasizes their separation in all normal circumstances. At the height of the story Conrad again calls, therefore, upon his device of dramatic allegory to strengthen the point of what must certainly be regarded as one of the great short masterpieces of irony in English literature.

Leading out from this basic structural counterpoise of Jukes and MacWhirr, strands of irony run through *Typhoon* from beginning to end. Understandable in the light of Conrad's purpose is the use made, for example, of the type of parody on salvation and judgment developed more elaborately in *An Outcast, Lord Jim,* and *Heart of Darkness.* There is a comic element in the fact that the storm is compared to a phenomenon that might accompany the Day of Judgment and that the complacent MacWhirr manages to put this "elemental fury into its proper place." As a hero fit for a world of accident, the Captain, in one place, appears before the barometer as "a booted and misshapen pagan burning incense before the oracle of a Joss." In a crisis beyond the reach of human rational and predictive powers and on the assumption that change governs the universe, MacWhirr acquires almost superhuman stature, because his absolute reliance on immediate fact adapts him thoroughly to such an unprovidential scheme. He is, nevertheless, a creature of chance with a Damoclean sword above his head; for his survival depends ultimately upon a whim of fortune. The final shaft of Conrad's irony strikes at MacWhirr's equal distribution of the silver dollars among the coolies at the end of the voyage, an act in keeping with the Captain's rough notions of justice, formed like Lingard's, beyond the pale of custom. Although honest in its way and perhaps the most that can be expected in a lawless world, this primitive division of property is poor recompense for the grievance of the Chinese, the force of which Jukes recognizes by arming the crew with rifles.

The strongly ambivalent quality of *Typhoon* results from the adoption by Conrad of a semicomic attitude to the problem of individual divergence from a norm of conduct; and in this story, with its unwavering control of a small but perfectly chosen set of materials, he arrived at his most compact and lucid expression of the idea of man's limitation. Whereas in the earlier stories the downfall of the solitary in the wilderness had been presented as a fairly straightforward record of defeat within a surrounding frame of irony, Conrad, in *Typhoon,* completed a work ironical at the core, and in the hypothetical character of Mac-Whirr portrayed a hero who triumphs by virtue of deficiency. A similar ambivalence and sardonic humor pervades "Falk" (1903), the only other long story in the *Typhoon* volume; but this tale with its strident colors, primitive people, and almost too perceptible odor of flesh does not match its predecessor in intellectual subtlety.

Notable, however, is the fact that from his pathetic and inarticulate hero, the Scandinavian tugboat skipper Falk, Conrad stripped away all of the moral and intellectual refinements of civilized man in order to permit the one basic desire for life to exist as a single force. Feeling no tie with organized society and concerned only with preserving "the five senses of his body," Falk has survived, because he was the best man in a life-and-death struggle, the experience of cannibalism in which he shared on a derelict cargo steamer after all feelings of solidarity between the men had gone. Still burdened with this memory of ten years' standing, Falk, now an Eastern river pilot, cleanses his guilt in the tears of compassion that flow from the eyes of the woman who accepts his love, the silent and statuesque niece of Hermann, a fatherly German ship's captain whose notions of civic virtue are outraged by the knowledge of Falk's misfortune. The last view of the lovers, standing like two pagan deities in a flood of sunlight, is reminiscent of the departure of Dain and Nina in *Almayer's Folly* in that life prevails over all conventional principles of right and wrong. In "Falk," however, the Schopenhauerian implications are less pessimistic than in Conrad's first novel; and love acquires the status of a bond against the world's cruelty that it holds so frequently in his later work.

Falk is the last character in Conrad's early writing to be described explicitly as a hermit:

> The girl, with her hands raised before her pale eyes, was threading her needle. He glanced at her and his mighty trunk overshadowed the table, bringing nearer to us the breadth of his shoulders, the thickness of his neck,

and that incongruous, anchorite head, burnt in the desert, hollowed and
lean as if by excesses of vigils and fasting. His beard flowed downwards,
out of sight, between the brown hands gripping the edge of the table, and
his persistent glance made sombre by the wide dilations of the pupils,
fascinated.

Yet, his appearance to the contrary, Falk is no ascetic. The guise of a
hermit is no more appropriate to him than it is to Willems; and this
fact has more than comic significance. By suffering in the wilderness, by
the indignity of eating human flesh, Falk wears the mask of the anchorite as a token of deformity, of the wound of division between his conscience and the instincts which have caused his fall. His desperate longing for the love of Hermann's niece is evidence of his desire to rid himself of this stigma and to regain his feeling of solidarity with mankind.
Because of his simplicity he survives the division which destroys earlier
characters, and exerts his will to live.

He survives, nevertheless, through a heavy sacrifice of distinctively human attributes. His primitive valor and the physical splendor of the
girl stand out against a background of violence and cruelty in the midst
of which the image of a broken temple, the group of stony islets associated with the memory of Falk's disaster, appears to symbolize the fall
of a tradition into something resembling "the heaps of a cyclopean ruin
on a plain." In this environment, where suffering is inevitable, the only
alternatives to Falk's blind will to exist and to perpetuate life are the
Biedermeier morality of Hermann, whose floating Arcadia with its children and clotheslines is innocent of the wickedness of the sea, and
the Buddhist temple representing annihilation. Conrad seems, therefore, to concede the victory of the normal over the abnormal with a
slight toss of his hands.

As distinguished from the more civilized failures who precede them,
the heroes of *Typhoon* and "Falk" do, then, emerge battered from their
contest with the powers of darkness. Their survival depends, however,
upon conditions which are made to seem impossible for the man endowed with an average measure of imagination or reason; and in having
little or no contact with the generality of mankind, they are pitiful.
They are strange men, perhaps supermen, but in any case lopsided in
that their strength derives from acuity of the senses rather than the
mind. Since they do not break in the wilderness under the strain of internal conflict, the conclusion suggested by their experience is that only
armed with qualities, more godlike or bestial, that exceed the ordinary
human standard dares man venture to penetrate the unknown.

At the close of his first period of authorship Conrad had moved, therefore, from the depiction of men who cannot become heroes to that of
heroes who are not quite men; and this is evidence enough that he
worked not haphazardly from one story to another but under the stimu-
lus of a coherent body of intuitions and convictions that went very deep

into causes for uncertainty in his age. The peculiar ironies and tensions that develop with the progress of his writing show, however, that it is necessary to approach whatever is positive in his viewpoint by way of a screen of seemingly negative reactions. Produced at a time of crisis and transition in moral and social values, his work impresses the reader not by a statement of faith or of a few elementary moral precepts but rather by a half scornful acceptance of the results of a sweeping away of beliefs. This attitude explains in great part the emphasis upon deterioration, the reversal of traditional symbols, the ironical basis in so many of his stories. It also accounts for the lack of confidence in man outwardly manifested in his general treatment of character. Only a few of the men in his early work seem capable of enduring the trials of existence without having sacrificed some essential feature of their humanity; and these characters, the captain and mates of the *Narcissus* or the officers of the *Judea* in "Youth," are members of a craft with an inherited standard of conduct which is disappearing with their generation. Yet a code of behavior no longer valid for people of a different age may serve as a contrast to an inferior ethic which supplants it, and the non-existent ideal of man complete and assured of his place within an ordered society may be held as a norm by which deviations from it can be judged. Such an ideal, it appears, was native to Conrad's thought, even though as an artist concerned with contemporary subject matter he drew men who were incomplete and withdrawn from the communal orbit. His humanistic spirit finds utterance in his comment on Willems and Aïssa in their utter solitude and despair at the end of *An Outcast:* "They both long to have a significance in the order of nature or of society."

Conrad had no high opinion of man's significance apart from a background of order which conferred human status upon him; but since the early stories emphasize the absence of order in nature and its possible breakdown in society, the problem of how man is to remain human or whether, after all, he needs to, becomes crucial. For Conrad, man is severely limited, prone to evil rather than good; and the whole point of much of the irony in the work of this period is that in attempting to transcend his humble state the individual is thrust back into full awareness of his limitations or down to a level below the human. In another reference to *An Outcast* Conrad pointed out that "Willems fails in his effort to throw off the trammels of earth and heaven," and the same remark could be applied to Kurtz in *Heart of Darkness.* As a rebuke to pride the image of the Fall reappears steadily in Conrad's tales, usually accompanied by that of the wilderness which is symbolic not only of the loss of Eden but also of the outer and inner terrors disclosed to the man who does not share in the burden of toil. But it is noteworthy that these images are not completed according to Biblical pattern, for there is no promise of ultimate relief or divine consolation to man in his fallen state. In this partial myth Providence seems to have no role, and humiliation lies in store for men who try to assume that part themselves. The wilderness is not merely a desert to be made fruitful. It is chaos: the realm of chance, irrationality, and brute survival which accords with the grimmer interpretations of a materialistic world picture. Alone in this waste man has, literally, no chance insofar as he is merely human. Both his mind and his senses can become servants of the irrational when he is overcome by the "Dark Powers." This dilemma, in which man falls into evils worse than those decreed for Adam and inexplicable without a Providence to blame, is not far removed from the thought of Hardy in his blacker moods. It also lies at the base of Conrad's ironies as well as of his tolerance for the man who in his failure bears witness to fundamental injustice in the design of the universe.

This conception of the wilderness helps to account for Conrad's attitude to the hermit figure, the most original feature of his imagery in this phase. Adapting a familiar symbol in the French literature that he knew, Conrad gave the hermit a key function in the development of his own theme of limitation. From Flaubert's device of representing Anthony's temptations as concrete personages in an allegorical drama, Conrad seems to have obtained the hint for the objective treatment of psychological and moral conflict, of the division between mind and passion, which he used in climactic scenes in his earlier work and never afterwards abandoned completely. But the hermit figure is much more than an instrument in his method. With the French the character had come to stand, either in a serious or a semicomic light, for a pose of contempt towards bourgeois life which expressed a peculiarity of modern temperament. Conrad likewise stressed at times the temperamental peculiarities of the type. Many of his hermits—Almayer, Willems, Wait, Jim, Kurtz—are men whose mental or spiritual aberrations cause them to deviate from a norm of conduct. But for Conrad, with the possible exception of Hervey in "The Return," the anchorite is not an agent of antibourgeois satire but a figure who, in his retreat, offers a challenge to a ruling principle of order. By a system of contrasts—setting Willems against Lingard, Wait against Allistoun, Jim against the fraternity of seamen—Conrad gave dramatic expression to moral and social tensions in his age which, because unresolved, allowed for a play of reciprocal irony. But in this balance of forces the weight of the irony lies heaviest upon the hermit as a departure from the implied norm of limited man in an ordered society. In his withdrawal the anchorite becomes a victim of extremes, of the division which ensues when man tries to cast off the trammels of his middle state. He envisions paradise at the moment when he sinks deepest into the toils of the wilderness. Once again, therefore, Conrad engages in an ironical reversal of an image from a Christian background with the apparent intention of a gibe at Providence for the disorderly state of creation. Retirement to a wilderness for ascetic or contemplative purposes can be justified only on the premise that God dwells in solitary places. When, instead, the wilderness is left abandoned to the strife of savage instincts, the ascetic ideal becomes absurd and the hermit himself a prey to the evils which he seeks to reject.

Closely bound in with this view of the anchorite and his perils are the main elements of Conrad's psychological equipment which, in keeping with its time, centers in the question of will and its failure. As a result of the disturbance to his humanity involved in the division between mind and instinct, the solitary finds himself incapable of acting when that is necessary to survival. A Schopenhauerian tendency to negation enters into the detachment of Flaubert's hermit; and in the light of Conrad's dark picture of the wilderness his occasional mistrust of the will to live, with its burden of human frustration, is not surprising. Despite notes of cynicism in tales like *Almayer's Folly,* "The End of the Tether," and "Falk" it is difficult, however, to regard Conrad as an advocate of detachment. His stories imply the necessity for action even when they demonstrate its impossibility in adverse circumstances or in certain types of character. But, characteristically, he seldom portrays the norm of successful act but rather deviations from it in extremes of passivity, like that of Almayer, or of automatic response, as in Singleton. The problem of will forms a part of the larger issue of the survival of man as a human being, and the theme of action and negation continued to attract Conrad until he came to full grips with the subject in *Victory.*

It is in great part due to his discovery in the first stage of his literary career of his principal themes and of his characteristic methods, including that of allegory, that Conrad's early work must always seem vital to his reputation. The vision of life to which he gave form at this time was to remain, scarcely modified, as the source of his later writing; and it is doubtful whether he afterwards expressed it with greater force or economy of means. Yet it would be unjust to praise the achievement of this period at the expense of the technical mastery of his later books wherein he extended his range as a creator of character and scene. From a strictly literary viewpoint he succeeded best in his early work with the short novel and story. Tales like "Youth," *Heart of Darkness, Typhoon,* and "Amy Foster" are rarely surpassed by later products of the same genre. He was not yet, however, an expert craftsman in the full-scale novel. Structurally, *An Outcast* and *Lord Jim,* though provocative in content, are imperfectly massed. His improvement in the long novel is, however, a notable feature of his second stage of authorship where he turned at the same time from his contemplation of the predicament of man as an individual to that of society in which man should fulfill his limited task.

Legate of the Ideal

by Daniel Curley

The role of Leggatt in "The Secret Sharer" is commonly agreed to be that of double or second self to the captain. With this there seems little possibility of disagreement. Not so readily acceptable, however, is the almost equally widespread opinion that the self represented must be the captain's lower, darker, more evil self—that Leggatt is, in Guerard's words, "criminally impulsive."

It is quite true, as Guerard goes on to say, that ". . . every great work of art operates on multiple levels of meaning and suasion . . . and . . . may have something particular to say to every new reader." [1] But it is also true that a work of art cannot be made to say everything. In "The Secret Sharer" three sorts of evidence seem specifically to exclude the interpretation of Leggatt as "criminally impulsive." First is Conrad's own statement; second is the pattern of changes Conrad made in adapting his material from the actual voyage of the *Cutty Sark;* third is the evidence of the story itself.

In a letter to John Galsworthy, written in 1913, Conrad says: "Dearest Jack . . . I can't tell you what pleasure you have given me by what you say of the 'Secret Sharer,'—and especially the swimmer. I haven't seen many notices,—three or four in all; but in one of them he is called a murderous ruffian,—or something of the sort. Who are those fellows who write in the Press? Where do they come from? I was simply knocked over,—for indeed I meant him to be what you have at once seen he was. And as you have seen, I feel altogether comforted and rewarded for the trouble he has given me in the doing of him, for it wasn't an easy task. It was extremely difficult to keep him true to type, first as modified to some extent by the sea life and further as affected by the situation." [2]

In order to understand this completely, we would need to have the Galsworthy letter Conrad is agreeing with, but even without the letter

[1] Albert J. Guerard, Introduction to the Signet edition of *Heart of Darkness and The Secret Sharer* (New York, 1950), pp. 8-9.

[2] G. Jean-Aubry, *Joseph Conrad: Life and Letters* (New York, 1927), I, 143.

we can be sure that Conrad intended above all else that Leggatt should not be a murderous ruffian. Beyond that it seems safe to accept the evidence of the story itself for an indication of the type to which Conrad intended Leggatt to be true; that is, he is presented as the son of a parson with all that implies. In addition, he is a graduate of the training ship *Conway*. A gentleman, son of a gentleman, educated and trained to the best traditions of the sea, he is as far as possible from being a murderous ruffian, although he is involved in a violent death. Even the captain of the *Sephora,* who may be considered a hostile witness, says, "He looked very smart, very gentlemanly, and all that."

It is true that authors are not always to be trusted in their comments on their own work. In this case Conrad might have felt that the story would sooner or later speak for itself and that solidarity in friendship was more important than correcting a misinterpretation of the text. Therefore, if there were no more solid evidence than the letter, Conrad's own attitude might be discounted—although the letter does seem to go far beyond the needs of friendship and to be indeed the bitter cry of a baffled author.

The same objection of inconclusiveness can also be raised to Conrad's reference to the story in the "Preface" to *The Shorter Tales* some ten years later. "The second story deals with what may be called the '*esprit de corps*,' the deep fellowship of two young seamen meeting for the first time." [3] But here again the author, although not indicating the exact nature of the fellowship, seems specifically to exclude the possibility that it is a fellowship of violence or evil.

The second sort of evidence can also be interpreted in different ways. This evidence relates to the changes Conrad made in converting the historical material of the *Cutty Sark* into the fictional material of "The Secret Sharer." The most likely objection to a study of these changes is that Conrad was simply rearranging things to make a better story. However, it can be demonstated that Conrad in shaping his material made changes of a consistent pattern intended to produce not just any better story but a very specific better story—a story, furthermore, that can properly be understood only in terms of the answer to a very specific question: Why does the hellion mate of the *Cutty Sark* become the gentleman of the *Sephora,* a man who is by birth, education, and his own acts to be known as "one of us"?

Concerning the actual mate of the *Cutty Sark* we know little, and even that little is contradictory. The evidence at his trial lays stress on his "good character" and "humane disposition";[4] whereas, Basil Lubbock's account, drawn from the log of the *Cutty Sark* itself, presents him as a regular bucko mate in the best Yankee tradition.[5] Human nature and the

[3] Joseph Conrad, Preface to *The Shorter Tales of Joseph Conrad* (New York, 1924), p. xi.
[4] *Times,* August 4, 1882, p. 4, col. f.
[5] Basil Lubbock, *The Log of the "Cutty Sark"* (Glasgow, 1960), p. 153 *et passim*.

courts being what they are, perhaps we should give less weight to the character testimony of defense witnesses than to the account of a journalist who might at worst tend to heighten the dramatic elements of his material. In neither case, however, is there the least suggestion that the mate is a gentleman or in the least bit educated beyond the requirements of his position. He is certainly a violent and hard-bitten man in both versions. He is, in fact, exactly the man to be referred to as a "murderous ruffian" and "criminally impulsive," but he is not Leggatt.

In shaping this material to the end he desired, Conrad was faced with two really difficult problems. He had to find a way of separating his protagonist's legal and moral responsibilities, and he had to invent for Leggatt an action that would be a crime in form but not a crime in fact.

The simplest way to adapt the story of the *Cutty Sark* would have been to transfer the entire action to the new captain's ship. As a new captain he was totally unfamiliar with his officers. The mate with the terrible whiskers could easily have been the bucko mate. Events would then take their course. A man would be killed, and the captain would have to act in a morally responsible manner. But what would be the captain's responsibility in this case?

Taking into consideration Conrad's rigid concept of sea morality, there can be little doubt that he would have felt the captain to be under the same kind of obligation as Captain Vere in *Billy Budd* to honor the conditions under which he held command of his ship and to let the law take its course. This is, in fact, the very pattern followed by the captain of the *Sephora,* and he is held in contempt by the narrator and depicted as a man afraid to act. On the other hand, the actual captain of the *Cutty Sark* did act: he helped the mate escape but with fatal consequences to himself.

If, then, these two captains can be taken to represent the possibilities of the situation, there is no way in which Conrad could guide his young man safely through a trial to a new destiny. On the one hand, he would have to refuse responsibility like the captain of the *Sephora* and live on "densely distressed," or, on the other hand, he would have to accept responsibility like the captain of the *Cutty Sark* and forfeit his career and his very life. The problem is actually insoluble. The captain must slight his legal responsibility to the ship or his moral responsbiility to his subordinate. This may be a decision that an established man—Captain Vere—can make, but it is not the kind of decision to be demanded of a young man in an initiation ritual story.

Clearly, therefore, it would not do to give the young captain command of a ship like the *Cutty Sark;* but the story of the *Cutty Sark* itself suggests another possibility, and that is to have the mate of the *Cutty Sark* escape to the young captain's ship. Now the captain is freed from any legal responsibility for the death and can apply himself solely to the moral aspects of the affair.

Even as the story is finally constituted, the young captain's problem is not an easy one. It takes its most obvious form in regard to his handling the ship. He must bring the ship close enough to shore to allow Leggatt to escape safely, and he must stay far enough away from shore to keep from wrecking the ship. He could stay so far from shore that the ship was absolutely safe and leave Leggatt to drown—an obvious betrayal of Leggatt and of himself because Leggatt is, of course, himself—or he could give Leggatt absolute safety and wreck the ship—a betrayal of the crew, the owners, and himself because as he himself says, ". . . all my future, the only future for which I was fit, would perhaps go irretrievably to pieces in any mishap to my first command." But in the end he proves himself able to judge nicely in balancing against each other the dual risks of responsibility to self and responsibility to society, and he has good luck. Leggatt was as good a judge, but his luck was bad.

For both Leggatt and the captain, this concept of luck enters at the crucial moment and plays a decisive role. In one case the luck is bad and in the other it is good. The wave and the hat are the marks of the luck. They are verses from "the chapter of accidents which counts for so much in the book of success." There is a clear implication that the captain's good luck is the indirect result of his own spontaneous sympathy for Leggatt in giving him the hat, but there is no suggestion that good luck of necessity follows right action. In fact, Leggatt's case clearly shows the contrary; so it is proper only to say that right action may result in a happy outcome. However, more important than the outcome is the knowledge of one's own right action and the strength such knowledge gives for facing the outcome, whatever it may be. Ultimately it can be said that the captain and Leggatt do not represent two possibilities of character but two possibilities of outcome, both of which are met with pride and confidence.

This, then, is the meaning of the changes in the mate's character. Each change is made to increase the identification between him and the captain and to establish unmistakably the nature of that "deep fellowship" and that " 'esprit de corps' " of which Conrad speaks in the "Preface" already quoted. No such changes would have been necessary, however, if Conrad had intended the fellowship to be based on a secret bond of criminal impulsiveness. The bucko mate of the *Cutty Sark,* just as he was, would have served admirably for this purpose; but instead of using the mate as he was, Conrad carefully removed from his character all the elements that could have supported the interpretation Guerard and others have forced on the story. The result of the changes is precisely that it is not the mate of the *Cutty Sark* but Leggatt that the captain recognizes as an extension of himself, and it is not merely a possible extension but an actual extension. The very closeness of the identification indicates that Conrad was after something other than a recognition of possibility, because he proceeds quite differently when he is presenting a character who is being led to penetrate the darkness of his own heart. A case in point is that of Captain Brierly in *Lord Jim,* who apparently has nothing whatever in common with the disastrous Jim but who, because of an insight into possibility, is driven to commit suicide in a manner strikingly reminiscent of the suicide of the captain of the *Cutty Sark.*

In defining the situation within which his young captain must act, Conrad has eliminated the possibility of any automatically imposed correct solution. The captain must create out of the tradition of his life and profession an individual moral solution to meet the totally unexpected situation, and he must do it in the face of the counter moral pressure of his own crew and of the captain of the *Sephora.* It would be easy for him to act in a way that would win him social approval, to make a choice that would be universally acknowledged moral, but it requires a fully developed moral being to make a choice that he alone knows to be moral and that everyone else believes to be criminal or mad.

These observations apply equally to Leggatt. His steadiness throughout the story is the result of the moral strength he has already won by the choice he has already made, and the circumstances of Leggatt's choice involve the second major change in the *Cutty Sark* material. The change that has made the mate into Leggatt has also made the original form of death impossible to his new character. The story demands, however, that there still be something which looks like a murder; that Leggatt be made to appear to do something his character will not allow.

It must not be supposed that the choice Leggatt makes is the choice of violence; for his choice, like the captain's, is a choice of responsibility. Further, it is a choice made under trying circumstances when the natural source of responsibility, in the captain of the *Sephora,* has totally failed. Leggatt is in effect in command of the ship, thereby underlining Conrad's parallel of two morally responsible individuals. The death is merely a by-product of the choice and affects neither its correctness nor its effectiveness: "It was all very simple. The same strung-up force which had given twenty-four men a chance, at least, for their lives, had, in a sort of recoil, crushed an unworthy mutinous existence." Within the story itself Leggatt twice renounces violence as a way out. He refuses to attempt to break out of his cabin on the *Sephora:* ". . . I did not mean to get into a confounded scrimmage. Somebody else might have got killed—for I would not have broken out only to get chucked back, and I did not want any more of that work." Later he says, "Do you see me being hauled back, stark naked, off one of these little islands by the scruff of the neck and fighting like a wild beast? Somebody would have got killed for certain, and I did not want any of that."

If there is anybody in the story who recognizes violence as a possibility in himself it is Leggatt, not the captain; but Leggatt specifically renounces violence when only his personal freedom or his life is at stake. He labels it "fighting like a wild beast," and in the second instance the omission of *more* seems to indicate that he makes a clear distinction between what

happened when he saved the ship and what might happen in a struggle
to save himself. He has clearly stated his choice: "I meant to swim until I
sank." He has clearly justified the captain's repeated comment, "He was
sane."

Leggatt's resolutions are not those of a "criminally impulsive" man, nor
do they fit with the one action that is charged against him. Again it is
desirable to look at the *Cutty Sark* material to see the original action out
of which Leggatt's action grew. In both the version in the *Times* and the
version in Lubbock, the sailor is brained with a capstan bar, a device
rather more potent than a baseball bat. It really makes little difference
whether the sailor got first cracks or not, the mate's blow was not the act
of a humane and gentle man, and the mate did not have the excuse of
being under undue strain, for the maneuver was a simple change of tack
in a "nice wholesail breeze." [6]

In "The Secret Sharer" the death takes place under quite different circumstances, and the scene purely from a dramatic point of view is a
great improvement with its terrific weather, its sailor half crazed with
funk, and its awful sea. But the total effect of the scene is to commit
Leggatt to an action that he cannot control and that the reader cannot
easily evaluate. Some of the difficulties of evaluation are suggested by
the conduct of the judge who tried the much more clear-cut case of the
mate of the *Cutty Sark*. In the first place, the judge allowed the reduction
of the charge from murder to manslaughter. He also gave full weight to
testimony of good character and to the fact that the mate had an important maneuver to perform and needed to assert his authority.[7] He accepted
all these points in arriving at a sentence, for indeed there can be no
standard by which they are not relevant.

If we consider, then, the infinitely greater complexity of Leggatt's case
and the fact that Leggatt's skill and courage had just succeeded in setting
the sail that saved the ship, it is small wonder that the young captain
concluded that "it was all very simple." But in a sense Conrad has made
it even simpler than that, because Leggatt in asserting his authority had
no intention of harming the man. He just wanted him out of the way,
so he felled him like an ox. Certainly under the circumstances the action
was not only not wrong but actually the correct thing to do and of no
more significance than throwing a glass of water in the face of a screaming
child. However, when the sailor came at him again, Leggatt was forced to
adopt stronger measures and began to throttle him into submission. When
the wave broke over the ship, Leggatt's reflex led him to hold fast to anything. Unfortunately he happened to have hold of a man's throat. Here,
then, is the murder in form that is not a murder in fact. Leggatt's own
remark, "It's clear I meant business," is not at all an expression of guilt,

[6] Lubbock, p. 152.
[7] *Times*.

because the business that he meant was far from the business that resulted.

By this adaptation of the *Cutty Sark* material Conrad has removed the death from the area of the young captain's legal responsibility, and he has made Leggatt the victim of circumstances. He has so contrived things that the captain's decision must be made in purely moral terms, and he has so changed the character of the mate that Leggatt cannot be considered a "murderous ruffian" but must on the contrary be held to be what the story itself clearly suggests him to be: the ideal conception of himself that the captain has set up for himself secretly.

This signpost in the story represents the third kind of evidence about Leggatt and points the way to an interpretation that bars any conception of Leggatt as lower nature. Indeed, so clear is the sign that one would feel officious in calling attention to it if it had not been so persistently ignored by commentators on the story.

The basic error, however, is not in equating Leggatt with the captain's instinctive self but in equating *instinctive* with *evil*. Conrad himself explicitly includes instinctive action among the necessary virtues of the ideal seaman: "There are to a seaman certain words, gestures, that should in given conditions come as naturally, as instinctively as the winking of a menaced eye. A certain order should spring on to his lips without thinking; a certain sign should get itself made, so to speak, without reflection." The captain's newness in command has resulted in a self-consciousness that cripples his power of instinctive action. Leggatt is a manifestation of this instinctive nature, isolated and useless in the cabin, and it is only when Leggatt slips back into the sea that the instinctive nature of the captain slips into its proper place as part of an integrated personality. At that point the captain has, like Leggatt, passed his test and gained a right to the confidence Leggatt has displayed throughout the story.

The story is clearly an initiation ritual story. The new captain, "untried as yet by a position of the fullest responsibility," is "at the starting point of a long journey," which is to be the "appointed task" of his existence. The story must undertake to provide him with a test of his fitness to enter upon this existence, and it must also provide him with a standard by which he can measure his success in coping with his test. That he passes his test is unequivocally indicated at the end of the story, but the standard by which he is to be judged is entirely unstated if Leggatt is assumed to represent anything other than an ideal conception.

The nature of the test has already been considered in detail. It is a unique test that cannot be passed by any except a fully aware moral being. Further, the test is so devised as to take place before no witnesses or, to be more exact, "with only the sky and sea for spectators and for judges." Material help—the tug—disappears back into the land, and spiritual help —the pagoda—is left behind. The only standard by which the captain can now be judged is an entirely personal one, his own, and it is his own

as made manifest in Leggatt. His success in meeting the challenge is represented in its most obvious form when he is told that he has understood
"from first to last."

What the captain has understood is, of course, Leggatt's position, but
he has done a good deal more than understand in a passive way. He has
demonstrated his understanding by a pattern of conduct which in its
quick action and stubborn self-control closely parallels Leggatt's own conduct and which can only spring, as is said of Leggatt, from "that something unyielding in his character which was carrying him through so
finely." Specifically, the captain is carried through by that ideal conception
of himself made manifest in Leggatt, who is "one of us" by birth and training and by his own acts. Leggatt's qualification for this role, in addition to
his background, is precisely his confidence as a man who knows he has
already passed his test. From the moment he appears, it is this confidence
that most impresses the young captain. This is how he hopes he can act
when his own time comes, and it is against this that we can measure his
success and the validity of his claim to be considered a free man and a
proud swimmer.

Nostromo: Politics, Fiction, and the Uneasy Expatriate

by Jocelyn Baines

In the "Author's Note" to *Nostromo*, Conrad mentioned that "after finishing the last story of the *Typhoon* volume it seemed somehow that there was nothing more in the world to write about." All his substantial work had hitherto been based on his own experience or on hearsay within a context which he knew well and he presumably felt that he had now exhausted this source. He therefore began to search further afield and, during the period of his greatest achievement, his novels were to range over areas of which he had had virtually no personal experience.

In the same "Author's Note" he continued: "This so strangely negative but disturbing mood lasted some little time; and then, as with many of my longer stories, the first hint for *Nostromo* came to me in the shape of a vagrant anecdote completely destitute of valuable details"; this was the story of a man having stolen single-handed a lighter full of silver on the Tierra Firma seaboard during a revolution. Conrad says that he had first heard the story in 1875 or '76 when he was in the Gulf of Mexico and that he had later discovered an account of the exploit in the memoirs of a seaman which he had picked up outside a second-hand bookshop. The book to which Conrad was evidently alluding has recently been tracked down; it is *On Many Seas: the Life and Exploits of a Yankee Sailor,* by Frederick Benton Williams, edited by his friend William Stone Booth.[1] Frederick Benton Williams is the pseudonym of Herbert Elliot Hamblen and *On Many Seas* is an account of his youthful adventures as a seaman from 1864 to 1878. In Chapter XXXII Hamblen describes his association with a "swarthy, piratical looking fellow" named Nicolo who told him one night how he had been entrusted with a lighter full of silver during a

"*Nostromo:* Politics, Fiction, and the Uneasy Expatriate" (editor's title) by Jocelyn Baines. From *Joseph Conrad: A Critical Biography* (New York: McGraw-Hill, 1960). Copyright © 1960 by Jocelyn Baines. Reprinted by permission of Jocelyn Baines and of George Weidenfeld and Nicolson Ltd.
    [1] London and New York, 1897. This discovery was made by Mr. John Halverson and Professor Ian Watt of the University of California. An article by them on the subject is due to appear in *The Review of English Studies* and I am greatly indebted to the authors for their generosity in allowing me to quote from their typescript.

revolution; Nicolo had killed the two other members of the crew, then
scuttled the lighter near the shore and had since been growing rich
slowly.[2] Conrad used a few details from this story, but transformed the
character of Nicolo which was that of an "unmitigated rascal" into that
of Nostromo. It appears most likely that Nicolo's exploit had never occurred but, somewhere along the line, had been invented; in view of this
and of Conrad's tendency to disguise his indebtedness to books, his claim
to have heard the anecdote himself in the Gulf of Mexico must be treated
with circumspection.

In the "Author's Note" he goes on facetiously to say that his principal
authority for the history of Costaguana is Don José Avellanos's fictitious
History of Fifty Years of Misrule. And, until recently, it had been generally assumed that, apart from a few details picked up here and there,[3] the
whole South American background to the novel was the product of Conrad's imagination. The remarks of two of his closest friends are typical.
Galsworthy wrote that *Nostromo* was Conrad's "most sheer piece of creation. For by his own confession, very much of his work was based intimately on his own adventures and experiences; and *Nostromo* creates a
continent which he had only glimpsed." While Richard Curle has said:
"His [Conrad's] power of visualisation was immense. For example, he
built up the whole atmosphere of *Nostromo*, which breathes the very
spirit of South America, from a few days upon the coast." Conrad had
told Curle:

> As to *Nostromo*. If I ever mentioned twelve hours it must relate to
> Puerto Cabello where I was ashore about that time. In La Guayra, as I
> went up the hill and had a distant view of Caracas, I must have been two
> and a half to three days. It's such a long time ago! And there were a few
> hours in a few other places on that dreary coast of Venezuela. [22 July
> 1923]

When he was grappling with the novel, Conrad complained to Cunninghame Graham: "I am dying over that cursed *Nostromo* thing. All my memories of Central America seem to slip away. I just had a glimpse twenty-five
years ago—a short glance. That is not enough pour bâtir un roman
dessus. And yet one must live." Perhaps Cunninghame Graham then advised that Conrad should turn to books to supplement his memories and
suggested some titles or perhaps Conrad had already decided to fill in the
gaps and stimulate his imagination with some reading about South
America. At all events it is clear that at some point he carefully studied
George Frederick Masterman's *Seven Eventful Years in Paraguay*, Edward

[2] "I must git reesh slow, don' you see?" *On Many Seas*, 289. Cf. *Nostromo*, viii and 503.
[3] Conrad confessed to Cunninghame Graham that he had stolen the dentist anecdote from him and was "compunctious" about the use he had made of Ex. Sr. Don Perez
Triana's personality (presumably in the character of Don José Avellanos). Letters to
Cunninghame Graham of 7 and 31 October 1904.

B. Eastwick's *Venezuela,* probably one or more of Sir Clements Markham's books on South America, and possibly some others. From Masterman, Conrad took most of the names of his characters, including Gould, Decoud, Corbelàn, Mitchell (Mitchell in Masterman), Fidanza (Nostromo's surname), Barrios and Monygham. Masterman was a doctor and Conrad based his account of Dr. Monygham's torture and confession on that of Masterman himself; the character and career of the tyrannical dictator, Francisco Solano Lopez, supplied Conrad with material on which to draw for the Montero brothers and for the ruthless Guzman Bento.[4] There are also a number of other small details. From Eastwick, Conrad took some more names; there are names of geographical features like Mt. Higuerota and of people, like Sotillo, General Guzman Blanco, whom Conrad turned into Guzman Bento, while the reigning beauty of Valencia is Antonia Ribiera. Her surname is used for that of the benevolent President of Costaguana and although Conrad said that Antonia Avellanos was modelled on his first love there is a very close correspondence between her character and appearance and that of Antonia Ribiera. Eastwick's Antonia was, like Conrad's, emancipated and Europeanized; her opening remark to Eastwick was "Caballero, are you married?" to which he, taken aback but hopeful, replied: "Sometimes." "The other young ladies of Sulaco stood in awe of" the "character and accomplishments" of Antonia Avellanos. "She was reputed to be terribly learned and serious." Eastwick found that Antonia Ribiera "talked like a bookworm, like a politician, like a diplomatist, like a savant." In appearance Antonia Avellanos was a "tall, grave girl, with a self-possessed manner, a wide, white forehead, a wealth of rich brown hair, and blue eyes," while Eastwick said of the other Antonia: "her eyes were dark blue, her hair a rich brown, her nose Grecian, her eyebrows arched."

Eastwick describes Puerto Cabello in some detail and Conrad evidently used this to revive his own memories in order to base the topography of the port of Sulaco on that of Puerto Cabello. The latter is situated in the Golfo Triste, which became the Golfo Placido in *Nostromo* and is protected by a spit of land, like the peninsula of Azuera, on which was situated an unused lighthouse. Opposite the spit are the reefs of Punta Brava, which became the cape of Punta Mala. It is "protected from all winds, on the east, north, and south" by the land and from the west by a group of islands as well as the mainland. "In short, there is perhaps no harbour in the world where the sea is at all times so calm as at Puerto Cabello." The customs houses at Sulaco and Puerto Cabello are similarly situated, and for some of the topography of the town of Sulaco Conrad draws on East-

---

[4] It may be thought that these claims are inadequately based but curious little details, such as the fact that both Lopez and Guzman Bento had lost their lower teeth, add up to substantial evidence.

The fate of Guzman Bento's body after his death seems to be based on the history of another tyrant, Dr. Francia.

wick's description of the inland town of Valencia. It is fascinating how even the most insignificant detail would be picked up and used by Conrad. At one point, at a reception, when Eastwick was presented with a yellow flower there was much delight at his exclamation of "Viva la Amarilla" because yellow was, unknown to him, the colour of the political party in power; in *Nostromo* the most exclusive club of Sulaco is called the Amarilla.

Through the reading of these books, written at first hand by intelligent, observant men, Conrad was able to immerse himself in the authentic atmosphere of the South America of the middle of the nineteenth century. The points of view of the authors, particularly that of Eastwick, would have been sympathetic to Conrad. For instance:

> Those who think that the overthrow of a bad government implies the inauguration of a better will do well to ponder over these remarks, and the more they reflect upon them and study the history of the events to which they refer, the less will be their sympathy with the revolutionary principles which are spreading so rapidly in Europe.

But although this knowledge of Conrad's sources invalidates the assumption that he created Costaguana out of his head it in no way detracts from the far more important aspects of his achievement. There is no question of plagiarism because these books only supplied the raw material with which he built the edifice. A comparison between the sources and what Conrad made of them serves above all to underline the transmuting power of his imagination. For instance, there are mundane allusions in Eastwick to the uncompleted railroad from Puerto Cabello to San Felipe; from this hint Conrad creates the scene of the inauguration of that "progressive and patriotic undertaking," the National Central Railway, with all its philosophical overtones, the description of the trains passing old Viola's house, and Nostromo's magnificent dash to the construction camp on an engine. Equally interesting are the modifications which Conrad added to Eastwick's topographical description; Douglas Hewitt has stressed the significance of Conrad's emphasis on the isolation, the inaccessibility of Sulaco and there is no parallel to this in Eastwick or Masterman. In fact all the important elements of *Nostromo* are to be found either not at all in Conrad's sources (although the possibility of an undiscovered source cannot be ruled out) or else in the merest embryo.

Nostromo is Conrad's most ambitious feat of imagination and is worthy of comparison with the most ambitious of all great novels, *War and Peace*. Hitherto Conrad had written primarily about men in communion with themselves, and in relation to one another or within the restricted society of a ship's crew, although it is true that *Heart of Darkness* contains an implied criticism of colonialism and commercial exploitation of backward peoples and wider issues are broached in the Patusan section of *Lord Jim*. In *Nostromo* he maintained his concern with the individual and with personal relations but extended his range to include public as well as private life. He chose a far larger canvas than he had used before or was to use again; it is as large as that of any great novel except *War and Peace*. On it he placed not only the lives and fates of an array of characters but the physical and political composition of a whole country, creating it with the most meticulous though selective detail. The account of Mrs. Gould's travels through the Occidental Province is an example of the care with which he built up the visual background to the events:

> She saw them on the road carrying loads, lonely figures upon the plain, toiling under great straw hats, with their white clothing flapping about their limbs in the wind; she remembered the villages by some group of Indian women at the fountain impressed upon her memory, by the face of some young Indian girl with a melancholy and sensual profile, raising an earthenware vessel of cool water at the door of a dark hut with a wooden porch cumbered with great brown jars. The solid wooden wheels of an ox-cart, halted with its shafts in the dust, showed the strokes of the axe; and a party of charcoal carriers, with each man's load resting above his head on the top of the low mud wall, slept stretched in a row within the strip of shade.

The frequent allusions to light show the extent to which Conrad must have projected himself visually into Costaguana, while the topographical description of the surroundings of Sulaco, shut off from the sea by the vast Golfo Placido and dominated by the Cordillera, where "the white head of Higuerota rises majestically upon the blue," has such precision that it remains imprinted photographically upon the mind throughout the book.[5]

Conrad allows himself an assortment of devices to develop his subject. There is no narrator as there was in his previous long novel, *Lord Jim*. Instead most of the book is written anonymously and directly in the third person, although the anonymity is occasionally broken by phrases like "those of us whom business or curiosity took to Sulaco . . . can remember" or ". . . as I am told." Then on one important occasion Conrad uses the garrulous and portentous Captain Mitchell to relate the events and on another Decoud describes them in a long letter to his sister.

Without a narrator to perform the task of analysis and comment Conrad uses the characters to comment on each other and to reflect events. The sardonic Dr. Monygham and the skeptical Decoud are particularly exploited in this way, and Captain Mitchell is used to impart unconsciously an ironic tone. Although they can often be taken as reflecting the author's view Dr. Monygham and Decoud are characters in their own right; they reveal themselves as well as others by their comments and it is always necessary to take the commentator's own character into account when assessing the comment. Conrad does not, however, rely on this

[5] Edward Crankshaw, *Joseph Conrad; some Aspects of the Art of the Novel* (1936), pp. 178-90, has pointed out the economy with which the details are chosen to set the scene and atmosphere in chapters I-II.

method alone, but frequently intervenes with impersonal judgments and reflections.

It is perhaps the lack of a narrator which exposes the weakness of Conrad's characterization, because far more is demanded of the characters than when Marlow is there as Master of Ceremonies. It is evident that most of the characters, in particular the leading ones, exist for what they represent rather than for what they are. Although they play important roles in the development of the themes and are in that respect vivid and real, their psychology is on the whole crude, blurred, or even unconvincing. It is with the minor, picturesque characters such as Sotillo, General Montero, and Mitchell that Conrad succeeds best.

For instance, magnificent figure though Nostromo is, his psychology is rudimentary. He is summed up in a few words and the comments upon him of the other characters, as well as those of the author, tend to be repetitive. So do his own actions and words. Conrad himself does not seem to have been satisfied with him. He agreed with Cunninghame Graham's criticism, although it must be admitted that he would not have been likely to dispute the point in this context:

> I don't defend Nostromo himself. Fact is he does not take my fancy either. As to his conduct generally and with women in particular, I only wish to say that he is not a Spaniard or S. American. I tried to differentiate him even to the point of mounting him upon a mare, which I believe is not or *was not* the proper thing to do in Argentine: though in Chile there was never much of that nonsense. But truly N. is nothing at all,—a fiction, embodied vanity of the sailor kind,—a romantic mouthpiece of the "people" which (I mean "the people") frequently experience the very feelings to which he gives utterance. I do not defend him as a creation. [31 October 1904]

Nostromo might be looked on as an exception, but Gould too, on whom depends so much of the effect of the book, is far from clear. His thoughts, feelings, and actions as well as the opinions of other characters on him accumulate into a pile of separate entities but never coalesce into a vital organism.

Apart from this weakness of characterization and from the melodrama of the last two chapters presented in appropriately magazinish language the book is almost without blemish. The writing is otherwise on a consistently high level and perhaps Conrad's greatest sustained achievement; it has none of the purple passages or philosophical effusions that sometimes mar his work. He shows a wonderful versatility of style and mood ranging from deep seriousness and irony to scenes of superb comedy such as those between Sotillo and Mitchell.

The complexity of intention expressed through such a diversity of character and incident demanded an exceptionally intricate structure if the peaks of significance were not to be submerged by the flood of detail. Aside from the epilogue, the events take place in a period of a little over eighteen months, although there are numerous references to the past, particularly to the tyranny of Guzman Bento, in the biographical flash-backs of the important characters. Conrad deliberately flouts chrono-logical narration in *Nostromo* and it is here that the "unconventional grouping and perspective . . . wherein," he claimed, "almost all my 'art' consists" is most in evidence. He uses the device of the time shift to gain an effect of irony. Thus, in Part I, the day of President Ribiera's subse-quent flight across the mountains is described before the festivities in Sulaco at which he inaugurates a new era for Costaguana "emerging after this last struggle, he hoped, into a period of peace and material pros-perity." The irony is pointed at the end of the ceremony:

> As the mail-boat headed through the pass, the badly timed reports an-nounced the end of Don Vincente Ribiera's first official visit to Sulaco, and for Captain Mitchell the end of another "historic occasion." Next time when the "Hope of honest men" was to come that way, a year and a half later, it was unofficially, over the mountain tracks, fleeing after a defeat on a lame mule, to be only just saved by Nostromo from an ignominious death at the hands of a mob. It was a very different event . . .

Part II is again concerned with events leading up to Ribiera's flight and it is not for almost another hundred pages that we are abreast of the day of his escape. Thenceforth the time shifts are largely mechanical and dic-tated by the need to follow the various threads of the plot until we come to the most important of all chronological breaks: just when the book seems to be building up to an exciting climax Conrad jumps to a time some years later and makes Captain Mitchell, in the role of unofficial guide to the sights of Sulaco, tell the story of the dramatic events which led to the defeat of the Monteros and the establishment of the Occidental Republic. Then the thread is picked up again.

Apart from showing that Conrad had no intention of writing an ex-citing tale of action, the effect of these time shifts is almost to abolish time in *Nostromo*. In fact it seems to have been Conrad's aim to approach the simultaneity of visual experience which a painting offers. The elimina-tion of progression from one event to another also has the effect of imply-ing that nothing is ever achieved. By the end of the book we are virtually back where we started; it looks as if the future of Costaguana will be very similar to her past.

Unlike some great works, *Nostromo* is not a book whose subject can be summed up in a sentence. Conrad wrote in Curle's copy that it had been his "ambition to render the spirit of an epoch in the history of South Amer-ica." And in this he succeeded, creating a world compounded of tragedy and farce, brutality, pathos, idealism, and venality. But his claim was too modest because the life described in Costaguana transcends a particular epoch or continent and contains an element of the universal. It is thus not too much to claim that *Nostromo* is an investigation of the motives of human behaviour, in which idealism is set against skepticism, illusion against disillusion, and responsibility against irresponsibility. Every category of human activity which Conrad considered important, except the arts,—it is significant that religion is only dealt with in its temporal aspect —is portrayed and analyzed.

Because of the title as well as the prominent part that Nostromo plays, it would be natural to assume that the book is concerned primarily with the fate of Nostromo. But although Nostromo is constantly alluded to—it is in this indirect manner that Conrad first builds up his reputation as he did that of Kurtz in *Heart of Darkness*—he is barely concerned with the most important issues of the book and Conrad has specifically stated that he was not intended to be the hero.

In a letter to Ernst Bendz, a Swedish professor who had written a study of Conrad's work, he said:

> I will take the liberty to point out that Nostromo has never been intended for the hero of the Tale of the Seaboard. Silver is the pivot of the moral and material events, affecting the lives of everybody in the tale. [7 March 1923]

Even this statement needs modifying because although the silver is the thread which binds the book together it has only a superficial or formal connection with some of the most important moral events. In its crudest aspect, the desire for gain, the silver only influences the lives of Nostromo and of one other character, Major Sotillo, who is killed during his frantic search for the sunken lighter. But even in the case of Nostromo the theft of the silver is more the effect than the cause of his downfall. The theme of the corruptive power of riches is broached in the first chapter, in the story of the two gringos hunting the forbidden treasure on Azuera ("The poor, associating by an obscure instinct of consolation the ideas of evil and wealth . . ."), and that story is frequently alluded to throughout the book, serving the same purpose as the recurring phrases in *Lord Jim*. This theme is worked out in the fate of Nostromo.

From the start Nostromo is presented as dependable and resourceful. Whenever there is a job to be done it is Nostromo who is sent for; Captain Mitchell, the pompous and stupid representative of the O.S.N., has developed a mania for "lending" his illustrious Capataz de Cargadores. But above all Nostromo is "incorruptible"; this is insisted on again and again. He has built up his reputation for resourcefulness and incorruptibility until, as Decoud says, he is "the next great man of Sulaco after Don Carlos Gould." And it is his reputation alone about which he seems to care. In Decoud's words: "The only thing he seems to care for . . . is to be well spoken of. . . . He does not seem to make any difference between speaking and thinking." And again: "He is more naive than shrewd, more masterful than crafty, more generous with his personality than the people who make use of him are with their money. . . . It is curious to have met

a man for whom the value of life seems to consist in personal prestige."
Nostromo does indeed possess these qualities but they are, as Decoud
says, the expression only of "his enormous vanity, that first form of egoism
which can take on the aspect of every virtue." Dr. Monygham also pene-
trates to the springs of Nostromo's conduct: "I believe him capable of
anything—even of the most absurd fidelity." [6] Nostromo has been impelled by vanity to win his reputation and if this is endangered his re-
liability, fidelity, and incorruptibility are also endangered. It is only those
such as Don Pepe, a sort of South American Singleton, mounting guard
over the mine, General Barrios in his raddled way and, one should add,
Captain Mitchell, whose incorruptibility and fidelity can be relied on
because in their case these qualities derive from a belief, from their concept of service, and are not merely an expression of their egoism.

Nostromo resents being entrusted with the removal of the silver from
Sulaco because he realises that his reputation is at stake and is afraid that
he may fail. Similarly, he cannot tolerate being taken for granted by the
"hombres finos" because it belittles his reputation. That is why he pro-
claims that he is determined to make the removal of the silver "the most
famous and desperate affair of my life."

Thus when he has partially failed in his mission he begins to disinte-
grate and "the confused and intimate impressions of universal dissolution
which beset a subjective nature at any strong check to its ruling passion
had a bitterness approaching that of death itself. . . . The facts of his
situation he could appreciate like a man with a distinct experience of
the country . . . He was as if sobered after a long bout of intoxication.
His fidelity had been taken advantage of." He imagines the world on
which his reputation depends collapsing and himself a hunted man. "He
had been betrayed!"

Returning to the Great Isabel, where he has left Decoud with the hidden silver, "He descended the ridge and found himself in the open solitude, between the harbour and the town. Its spaciousness, extended in-
definitely by an effect of obscurity, rendered more sensible his profound
isolation. His pace became slower. No one waited for him; no one thought
of him; no one expected or wished his return. 'Betrayed! Betrayed!' he
muttered to himself. No one cared."

Although Nostromo's imagination has run away with him and his
world, though threatened, has not collapsed, the spell has been broken
and he persists in the feeling that he has been exploited and must hence-
forth look after his own interests. He can no longer rely on his reputation.
It is at this point, after his created world has begun to crumble, that the
silver takes hold of him:

[6] There is a discrepancy between Dr. Monygham's attitude expressed in this conversation with the chief engineer and later when he is made to appear unperceptive and
rather simple-minded.

"There is something in a treasure that fastens upon a man's mind. He will pray and blaspheme and still persevere, and will curse the day he ever heard of it, and will let his last hour come upon him unawares, still believing that he missed it only by a foot. He will see it every time he closes his eyes. He will never forget it till he is dead—and even then—Doctor, did you ever hear of the miserable gringos on Azuera, that cannot die? Ha! Ha! Sailors like myself. There is no getting away from a treasure that once fastens upon your mind."

Thus, although he goes on to transcend even his own past achievement and saves the Occidental Province in his great ride to Cayta, his thoughts remain with the silver. And when he realises that, with the death of Decoud, he is the only person who knows that the silver has not been sunk in the lighter, he decides not to disclose its whereabouts but to use it to enrich himself. And at this moment the San Tomé mine "appeared to him hateful and immense, lording it by its vast wealth over the valour, the toil, the fidelity of the poor, over war and peace, over the labours of the town, the sea, and the Campo." Thenceforth Nostromo is corrupted:

> A transgression, a crime, entering a man's existence, eats it up like a malignant growth, consumes it like a fever. Nostromo had lost his peace; the genuineness of all his qualities was destroyed. He felt it himself, and often cursed the silver of San Tomé. His courage, his magnificence, his leisure, his work, everything was as before, only everything was a sham. But the treasure was real. He clung to it with a more tenacious, mental grip. But he hated the feel of the ingots. Sometimes, after putting away a couple of them in his cabin—the fruit of a secret night expedition to the Great Isabel —he would look fixedly at his fingers, as if surprised they had left no stain on his skin.

Retribution comes in the end. When Nostromo is dying, shot in error by his devoted admirer, Old Viola, he tells Mrs. Gould with literal and symbolical truth, "The silver has killed me."

Silver is both the symbol and the embodiment of those "material interests" which are transforming Sulaco, capital of the isolated Occidental Province and once "an inviolable sanctuary from the temptations of a trading world" protected by "the prevailing calms of its vast gulf."

The power of the San Tomé mine or, in effect, of Charles Gould who controls it, dominates the Occidental Province of Costaguana and even extends to the rest of the country, because Gould has used the wealth of the mine to finance a revolution which brought to power Don Vincente Ribiera, "a man of culture and of unblemished character, invested with a mandate of reform by the best elements of the State."

Gould has not achieved this dominant position through the desire for enrichment or for power. Although the San Tomé mine has brought nothing but misfortune to his family, on the death of his father Gould is determined to accept its challenge: "The mine had been the cause of an absurd moral disaster; its working must be made a serious and moral success." But "after all his [Gould's father's] misery I simply could not have touched it for money alone" and throughout the book there is no mention of Gould becoming rich or being interested in that aspect of the situation. As for power, Gould has always shunned it. He was no "political intriguer" and had supported Ribiera primarily in order to assure the unhampered working of the mine. "He had persuaded himself that, apart from higher considerations, the backing up of Don José's hopes of reform was good business." Thus when the Ribiera regime is in danger and General Barrios's counterstroke is planned, he holds himself aloof:

> Charles Gould was not present at the anxious and patriotic send-off. It was not his part to see the soldiers embark. It was neither his part, nor his inclination, nor his policy. His part, his inclination, and his policy were united in one endeavour to keep unchecked the flow of treasure he had started singlehanded from the re-opened scar in the flank of the mountain.

The successful working of the mine is sufficient justification in itself and his satisfaction is gained through the essentially Conradian formula of the idealization of action:

> It hurt Charles Gould to feel that never more, by no effort of will, would he be able to think of his father in the same way he used to think of him when the poor man was alive. His breathing image was no longer in his power. This consideration, closely affecting his own identity, filled his breast with a mournful and angry desire for action. In this his instinct was unerring. Action is consolatory. It is the enemy of thought and the friend of flattering illusions. Only in the conduct of our action can we find the sense of mastery over the Fates.

As the chief engineer says later, "Upon my word, doctor, things seem to be worth nothing by what they are in themselves. I begin to believe that the only solid thing about them is the spiritual value which everyone discovers in his own form of activity."

Gould finds a philosophy to express this belief:

> What is wanted here is law, good faith, order, security. Any one can declaim about these things, but I pin my faith to material interests. Only let the material interests once get a firm footing, and they are bound to impose the conditions on which alone they can continue to exist. That's how your money-making is justified here in the face of lawlessness and disorder. It is justified because the security which it demands must be shared with an oppressed people. A better justice will come afterwards.

But Gould's belief in the value of action does not save him, as it did Marlow in *Heart of Darkness*; it ends by enslaving him.

Mrs. Gould, on the other hand, distrusts material interests and progress from the start. In her conversation with the chairman of the railway board she looks back wistfully to the past. The chairman is speaking:

".. . What an out-of-the-way place Sulaco is!—and for a harbour, too!
Astonishing!"

"Ah, but we are very proud of it. It used to be historically important. The
highest ecclesiastical court, for two viceroyalties, sat here in the olden time,"
she instructed him with animation . . .

and the chairman replies:

"We can't give you your ecclesiastical court back again; but you shall
have more steamers, a railway, a telegraph-cable—a future in the great world
which is worth infinitely more than any amount of ecclesiastical past. You
shall be brought in touch with something greater than two viceroyalties . . ."

But she nonetheless follows her husband in attaching a spiritual value
to the mine. Her original impulse of enthusiasm is personal and derives
from her devotion to Gould and her desire for adventure. But she soon
idealises the meaning of the mine:

. . . She had laid her unmercenary hands, with an eagerness that made them
tremble, upon the first silver ingot turned out still warm from the mould;
and by her imaginative estimate of its power she endowed that lump of
metal with a justificative conception, as though it were not a mere fact,
but something far-reaching and impalpable, like the true expression of an
emotion or the emergence of a principle.

Thus, in different ways, for both the Goulds "each passing of the escort
under the balconies of the Casa Gould was like another victory gained in
the conquest of peace for Sulaco."

The Goulds, then, are idealists, although at opposite ends of the scale;
he has become the victim of his ideal to the point of obsession whereas
she has sunk her personality in the ideal of service. Around the Goulds
there revolve the conflicting forces of idealism, skepticism, and brazen self-
interest. Among the idealists there is Holroyd, the great power in San
Francisco who is financing the mine. He has "the temperament of a Puritan and an insatiable imagination of conquest." He "attached a strangely
idealistic meaning to concrete facts" and combines a "lavish patronage of
'the purer forms of Christianity' " with ruthless exploitation of material
interests. There is Mrs. Gould's protégé, Giorgio Viola, the old Gari-
baldino, with his 'worship and service of liberty.'

The spirit of self-forgetfulness, the simple devotion to a vast humanitarian idea which inspired the thought and stress of that revolutionary
time, had left its mark upon Giorgio in a sort of austere contempt for all
personal advantage.

There are Don José Avellanos and his daughter Antonia with their profound love of their country. Don José sees in Gould's power the means
whereby his ideals may be realised. He "was ruined in every way, but a
man possessed of passion is not a bankrupt in life. Don José Avellanos
desired passionately for his country: peace, prosperity, and . . . 'an

honourable place in the comity of civilised nations.' " Then, standing apart in his fanaticism, there is Antonia's uncle, Father Corbelàn, with his demands for the restitution of the confiscated church lands.

Self-interest is embodied in the crude lust for power of the Monteros, the squalid demagoguery of Gamacho and Fuentes, the equally crude desire for wealth on the part of Sotillo, and of the unfortunate Señor Hirsch, and, in disguised form, in Nostromo's conduct.

Dr. Monygham and Decoud, on the other hand, are both self-proclaimed skeptics. Dr. Monygham's skepticism, or cynicism, has been forced on him, having its roots in a physical defeat when he had succumbed to atrocious torture during the tyranny of Guzman Bento; he had therefore lost faith in himself and others. This event placed him in the same situation as Jim and Razumov. He feels cut off from social communion with others and because of his uncouth behaviour is distrusted by them. He is sustained only by his devotion to Mrs. Gould, which is "like a store of unlawful wealth." Decoud's skepticism, on the other hand, is a mental attitude; he "recognised no other virtue than intelligence" and "had pushed the habit of universal raillery to a point where it blinded him to the genuine impulses of his own nature." He feels bound to explain away such impulses, or relate them to self-interest. Later he is able, like Dr. Monygham, to attribute all his actions to one passion, his love for Antonia. "I have no patriotic illusions," he says; "I have only the supreme illusion of a lover." He is confronted with Antonia's "belief in the cause" and with her accusation that he never sees "the aim."

To Mrs. Gould, Decoud ruthlessly analyses Gould's character:

> "Don't you see, he's such an idealist. . . . It's a wonderful thing to say with the sight of the San Tomé mine, the greatest fact in the whole of South America, perhaps, before our very eyes. But look even at that, he has idealised this fact to a point—— . . . Are you aware to what point he has idealised the existence, the worth, the meaning of the San Tomé mine? Are you aware of it?" . . .
>
> "What do you know?" she asked in a feeble voice.
>
> "Nothing," answered Decoud, firmly. "But, then, don't you see, he's an Englishman?"
>
> "Well, what of that?" asked Mrs. Gould.
>
> "Simply that he cannot act or exist without idealising every simple feeling, desire, or achievement. He could not believe his own motives if he did not make them first a part of some fairy tale. The earth is not quite good enough for him, I fear. Do you excuse my frankness? Besides, whether you excuse it or not, it is part of the truth of things which hurts the—what do you call them?—the Anglo-Saxon susceptibilities, and at the present moment I don't feel as if I could treat seriously either his conception of things or—if you allow me to say so—or yet yours."

In Decoud's mind there is only one step from idealism to sentimentalism. He claims that both Gould and Holroyd are sentimentalists. He tells Mrs. Gould that her husband is a "sentimentalist, after the amazing manner of your people" and expounding his scheme for the Occidental Republic he says: "I think he [Gould] can be drawn into it, like all idealists, when he once sees a sentimental basis for his action."

It is Decoud who sees that Gould's idealisation of the mine has become an obsession. He speaks of "this 'Imperium in Imperio,' this wealth-producing thing, to which his [Gould's] sentimentalism attaches a strange idea of justice. Unless I am much mistaken in the man, it must remain inviolate or perish by an act of his will alone. A passion has crept into his cold and idealistic life."

Gould has eventually reversed the order of values. Instead of the mine being justified by its service to "law, good faith, order, security," these ideals have become subordinated to the importance of the mine. He has become a monomaniac who can only think of the mine as identified with himself and plans to blow it up rather than let it fall into the hands of another. Decoud realises that the mine represents a tragedy in the personal relations of the Goulds, for Mrs. Gould "has discovered that he [Gould] lives for the mine rather than for her." It is Mrs. Gould's "mission to save him from the effects of that cold and overmastering passion which she dreads more than if it were an infatuation for another woman." She has found that her husband is becoming gradually estranged from her:

> Mrs. Gould continued along the corridor away from her husband's room. The fate of the San Tomé mine was lying heavy upon her heart. It was a long time now since she had begun to fear it. It had been an idea. She had watched it with misgivings turning into a fetish, and now the fetish had grown into a monstrous and crushing weight. It was as if the inspiration of their early years had left her heart to turn into a wall of silver-bricks, erected by the silent work of evil spirits, between her and her husband. He seemed to dwell alone within a circumvallation of precious metal, leaving her outside with her school, her hospital, the sick mothers and the feeble old men, mere insignificant vestiges of the initial inspiration.

She sees that "the mine had got hold of Charles Gould with a grip as deadly as ever it had laid upon his father," or, it might be added, as deadly as that which bound the ghosts of the two gringos to the treasure on Azuera. "She saw clearly the San Tomé mine possessing, consuming, burning up the life of the last of the Costaguana Goulds." She only once tries to break down the wall and regain the intimacy of their early days together. Otherwise she accepts her isolation fatalistically, but confesses at Nostromo's deathbed: "I, too, have hated the idea of that silver from the bottom of my heart." Even she herself has been tainted by the silver because, persuaded by Decoud, "for the first and last time of her life she had concealed the truth from her husband about that very silver. She had been corrupted by her fears at that time, and had never forgiven herself."

The silver, or the mine, happens to have been the cause of the tragedy, but the real cause is in Gould's obsessive character. He could have dedicated himself to something unconnected with wealth, with the same tragic consequences because:

> A man haunted by a fixed idea is insane. He is dangerous even if that idea is an idea of justice; for may he not bring the heaven down pitilessly upon a loved head?

To Decoud it seemed that "every conviction, as soon as it became effective, turned into that form of dementia the gods send upon those they wish to destroy." But his skepticism leads him to a fate even more tragic than that of the Goulds. For when he is put to the ultimate test he fails. Alone on the Great Isabel his sense of his own personality disintegrates, as does that of Nostromo in similar circumstances. "He had recognised no other virtue than intelligence, and had erected passions into duties. Both his intelligence and his passion were swallowed up easily in this great unbroken solitude of waiting without faith." Finally he can stand it no longer and shoots himself:

> He died from solitude, the enemy known but to few on this earth, and whom only the simplest of us are fit to withstand. The brilliant Costaguanero of the boulevards had died from solitude and want of faith in himself and others.

Thus idealism and skepticism, faith and want of faith, both seem to lead to disaster. *Nostromo* is an intensely pessimistic book; it is perhaps the most impressive monument to futility ever created. Apart from Captain Mitchell with his comfortable old age secured by his seventeen shares in the San Tomé mine, no one achieves satisfaction; and Mitchell is certainly among those, like MacWhirr and Hermann, who have been "disdained by destiny or by the sea."

The fate of the individuals with whom *Nostromo* has been particularly concerned and of Costaguana as a whole are equally hopeless. Antonia Avellanos and Linda Viola both have the men they love taken away by death. Mrs. Gould virtually loses her husband to the mine and is in the end disillusioned: "She resembled a good fairy, weary with a long career of well-doing, touched by the withering suspicion of the uselessness of her labours, the powerlessness of her magic." She is engulfed by "an immense desolation, the dread of her own continued life." Don José Avellanos dies "vanquished in a lifelong struggle with the powers of moral darkness, whose stagnant depths breed monstrous crimes and monstrous illusions." Decoud dies "a victim of the disillusioned weariness which is the retribution meted out to intellectual audacity" just as Nostromo is the "victim of the disenchanted vanity which is the reward of audacious action." This is the most deeply pessimistic judgment of all, because their "audacity" has produced the two most constructive actions in the book. It is due to Decoud that the Occidental Republic is proclaimed and to Nostromo's ride to Cayta that it is established.

The country as a whole comes off no better. In an article on Anatole France written just after finishing *Nostromo* Conrad said: "Political institutions, whether contrived by the wisdom of the few or the ignorance of the many, are incapable of securing the happiness of mankind." It is not surprising therefore that no section of the community seems to offer any hope for a permanently better future. The Democrats naturally get short shrift from Conrad, who goes out of his way to make their leaders, Gamacho and Fuentes, thoroughly disreputable and unscrupulous. Don Juste Lopez, the conservative champion of parliamentary institutions, is made to appear pathetic and craven in his readiness to propitiate the villainous Pedrito Montero "in order to save the form at least of parliamentary institutions"; Conrad cannot even resist making him ridiculous by having half his beard blown off. Similarly, Ribiera, the "hope of honest men," flees ignominiously from the Monteros; and it is significant that he is a particularly poor physical specimen, "obese to the point of infirmity," "almost a cripple." And at the end the fanatical Father Corbelàn is threatening the overthrow of the material interests which have made the Occidental Republic secure, justifying Dr. Monygham's verdict of "incorrigible" on the Costaguaneros.

Then although at the end of the book justice and order have temporarily triumphed and Sulaco is "growing rich swiftly," material interests, which dominate the Occidental Republic, have their own form of tyranny. This has been foreshadowed from the start and is expressed in one of those sentences whose full significance only becomes apparent later:

> The sparse row of telegraph poles strode obliquely clear of the town, bearing a single, almost invisible wire far into the great campo—like a slender, vibrating feeler of that progress waiting outside for a moment of peace to enter and twine itself about the weary heart of the land.

Thus when Mrs. Gould asks: "Will there never be any peace?" Dr. Monygham prophesies:

> There is no peace and no rest in the development of material interests. They have their law, and their justice. But it is founded on expediency, and is inhuman; it is without rectitude, without the continuity and the force that can be found only in a moral principle. Mrs. Gould, the time approaches when all that the Gould Concession stands for shall weigh as heavily upon the people as the barbarism, cruelty, and misrule of a few years back.

Mrs. Gould cannot deny this, and her vision of the future is as black as Dr. Monygham's because, although in the development of the San Tomé mine her husband had achieved a "colossal and lasting success," "there was something inherent in the necessities of successful action which carried with it the moral degradation of the idea. She saw the San Tomé mountain hanging over the Campo, over the whole land, feared, hated, wealthy; more soulless than any tyrant, more pitiless and autocratic than the worst Government; ready to crush innumerable lives in the expansion of its greatness." So much for Gould's hope of the mine becoming "that little rift in the darkness" which his father had despaired of seeing.

The future of Costaguana is as ominous as its past has been gory. Dr. Monygham does "not believe in the reform of Costaguana," and this seems to be the conclusion implicit in the novel. To seek out a hopeful interpretation Robert Penn Warren, who has written perhaps the most perceptive essay on *Nostromo* and incidentally on Conrad, is forced to search beyond the limits of the book. But perhaps the most apt implied comment on the world of *Nostromo* is contained in "Autocracy and War," an essay which Conrad wrote a few months after finishing the novel. After saying that, in a world dominated by industrialism and commercialism, there can only be an uneasy peace based on fear, he continues: "The true peace of the world . . . will be built on less perishable foundations than those of material interests. But it must be confessed that the architectural aspect of the universal city remains as yet inconceivable—that the very ground for its erection has not been cleared of the jungle." A few paragraphs later he probes deeper:

> The intellectual stage of mankind being as yet in its infancy, and States, like most individuals, having but a feeble and imperfect consciousness of the worth and force of the inner life, the need of making their existence manifest to themselves is determined in the direction of physical activity. The idea of ceasing to grow in territory, in strength, in wealth, in influence—in anything but wisdom and self-knowledge is odious to them as the omen of the end. Action, in which is to be found the illusion of a mastered destiny, can alone satisfy our uneasy vanity and lay to rest the haunting fear of the future—a sentiment concealed, indeed, but proving its existence by the force it has, when invoked, to stir the passions of a nation. It will be long before we have learned that in the great darkness before us there is nothing that we need fear.

In *Nostromo* Conrad portrayed the world as he saw it, not as he hoped it might become; nor does he allow any trace of a hope to appear without exposing the illusion on which it is based. It is clear that he regarded the dominance of material interests and the "feeble and imperfect consciousness of the worth and force of the inner life" as a condition of humanity and not peculiar to Costaguana.

Costaguana is, however, primarily a prototype of a politically inexperienced nation and it is tempting to see an analogy between it and Poland. It is likely that Conrad was able to express some of his feelings about Poland consciously or unconsciously using the disguise of Costaguana. He might well have been thinking of Russian-dominated Poland when he referred to the "political immaturity of the people . . . the indolence of the upper classes and the mental darkness of the lower," or when Gould complains: "The words one knows so well have a nightmarish

meaning in this country. Liberty, democracy, patriotism, government—
all of them have a flavour of folly and murder," or when "The cruel futility of things stood unveiled in the levity and sufferings of that incorrigible people; the cruel futility of lives and of deaths thrown away in the
vain endeavour to attain an enduring solution of the problem." So, too,
when Decoud says: " 'We are a wonderful people, but it has always been
our fate to be'—he did not say 'robbed,' but added, after a pause—'exploited!' " And his analysis of the predicament of Costaguana fits closely
to that of Poland:

> There is a curse of futility upon our character: Don Quixote and Sancho
> Panza, chivalry and materialism, high-sounding sentiments and a supine
> morality, violent efforts for an idea and a sullen acquiescence in every
> form of corruption. We convulsed a continent for our independence only
> to become the passive prey of a democratic parody, the helpless victims of
> scoundrels and cut-throats. . . .

There is little doubt that Conrad had strongly ambivalent feelings towards
Polish aspirations which were closely bound up with his attitude towards
his father. He had seen at first hand one of the tragic consequences of
the political agitation which culminated in the 1863 rising; the exile and
disillusionment of his father and the premature death of his mother. In
fact the situation between Mr. and Mrs. Gould is analogous to that between Conrad's parents if political action is substituted for material interests; it is particularly emphasized when Conrad says that Gould is
haunted by a fixed idea, and "a man haunted by a fixed idea is insane.
He is dangerous even if that idea is an idea of justice; for may he not
bring the heaven down pitilessly upon a loved head?" or when Decoud,
speaking of Mrs. Gould, points to "some subtle wrong . . . that sentimental unfaithfulness which surrenders her happiness, her life, to the
seduction of an idea."

As a result of his experiences, and above all because he had left Poland,
Conrad, while retaining a deep attachment to the country, refused to take
her political aspirations seriously; for if he admitted that there was a
genuine chance that Poland might regain her freedom he would have felt
bound to remain and participate in the struggle. In the "Author's Note"
to *Nostromo* he says that Antonia Avellanos is modelled on his "first love"
and adds: "I was not the only one in love with her; but it was I who had
to hear oftenest her scathing criticism of my levities—very much like poor
Decoud—or stand the brunt of her austere, unanswerable invective." Although this must be treated circumspectly in view of Eastwick's Antonia
Ribiera it is not too far-fetched to see Conrad's own dilemma reflected in
Decoud's attitude. Decoud at first, like Mrs. Gould, finds it hard to take
the affairs of Costaguana seriously; they smack of *opéra bouffe*. But he
cannot withhold his sympathy for long: "He was moved in spite of himself by that note of passion and sorrow unknown on the more refined

stage of European politics," and: "To contemplate revolutions from the distance of the Parisian boulevards was quite another matter. Here on the spot it was not possible to dismiss their tragic comedy with the expression, 'Quelle Farce!' . . . 'I suppose I am more of a Costaguanero than I would have believed possible,' he thought to himself." In several of his utterances, and even of his actions, he shows signs of a passionate concern for his country's fate akin to that of Don José and Antonia Avellanos.

When Conrad condemns Decoud's attitude to life, or at least his pose of skepticism, he is perhaps recalling his own situation in Marseilles:

> He imagined himself Parisian to the tips of his fingers. But far from being that he was in danger of remaining a sort of nondescript dilettante all his life. He had pushed the habit of universal raillery to a point where it blinded him to the genuine impulses of his own nature.

When Decoud says: "What is a conviction? a particular view of our personal advantage either practical or emotional," he is the witty, cynical boulevardier but when "it seemed to him that every conviction, as soon as it became effective, turned into that form of dementia the gods send upon those they wish to destroy," he is expressing the view of the mature Conrad. The statement that Decoud "had no faith in anything except the truth of his own sensations" expresses in negative form what was the cornerstone of Conrad's own outlook, and when Father Corbelàn calls Decoud "neither the son of his own country nor of any other," he designates Conrad's own predicament.

The Secret Agent Reconsidered

by E. M. W. Tillyard

I

Responses to Conrad's *Secret Agent* have ranged from total capitulation to coolish approval; and it is not at all yet clear what position in the future hierarchy of his works it is destined to occupy. A reconsideration needs no apology.

First, we can accept the virtue of the writing throughout and of the different scenes considered in themselves as scenes. Any blemishes here are incidental. We may tire of hearing Comrade Ossipon called "robust" and we may find a speech or two of the Assistant Commissioner to the Home Secretary (in spite of the latter's appeal for brevity) clotted and obscure. And of course there are mistakes in the English. But all these are small matters; and the only serious mistake of detail is in the psychology of Ossipon. Granted his previous presentation, is it likely that he would have been haunted permanently by the thought of Mrs. Verloc's death and permanently put off his amorous adventures? I can find nothing in his previous states of mind to justify such fidelity to an impression. I suspect that Conrad here unconsciously sacrificed psychological probability to certain demands of plot, to which I shall refer later. But in its context of the last chapter this blemish does not count for much; it affects our pleasure in reading very little, for it coexists with so much else to think about.

Next, I can only concur in most of the praise that writers have bestowed on Conrad's ironic method, on his success in keeping his dreadful story within the bounds of comedy. His prevailing ironic method is to make very large the distance between the way things appear to the persons in the story and the way they are made to appear to the reader. The theme of Verloc's hat provides typical instances. Verloc's hat and heavy overcoat, constantly worn indoors, are powerful agents in building up Verloc's character; they are symbols of his physical and mental frowstiness. Then, rather more than halfway through the book, Conrad gives us the reasons

"The Secret Agent Reconsidered" by E. M. W. Tillyard. From *Essays in Criticism*, XI, No. 3 (July 1961), 309-318. Copyright © 1961 by the editors of *Essays in Criticism*. Reprinted by permission of the editors of *Essays in Criticism*.

for Verloc's habit of retaining his clothing: "It was not devotion to an out-
door life, but the frequentation of foreign cafés which was responsible for
that habit, investing with a character of unceremonious impermanency
Mr. Verloc's steady fidelity to his own fireside." And of course Verloc has
no notion of this discrepancy between appearance and reality. The culminating chapter containing the murder ends thus:

> Then all became still. Mrs. Verloc on reaching the door had stopped. A
> round hat disclosed in the middle of the floor by the moving of the table
> rocked slightly on its crown in the wind of her flight.

These words are perfect in deflating the murder—that is, as it concerns the
victim. The grotesque rocking of the inverted bowler resembles and mocks
Verloc's precarious state of mind in the last weeks, just as its dethrone-
ment from the eminence of his head duplicates and minimises his own
downfall. The hat figures for the last time when Ossipon, now convinced
that he is the victim of a plot to murder him, returns with Winnie Verloc
to the house in Brett Street. He is standing in the shop looking through
the glass of the door into the parlour, where Verloc lies, apparently
asleep; Ossipon is still under the illusion that he had been blown to
pieces in Greenwich Park:

> But the true sense of the scene he was beholding came to Ossipon through
> the contemplation of the hat. It seemed an extraordinary thing, an omi-
> nous object, a sign. Black and rim upward, it lay on the floor before the
> couch as if prepared to receive the contributions of pence from people
> who would come presently to behold Mr. Verloc in the fullness of his do-
> mestic ease reposing on a sofa.

There is, of course, more than one kind of irony here. For instance, there
is the contrast between the appearance of domestic ease and the reality of
its opposite. But the main irony consists in the fantastic distance between
what Conrad instructs the reader to think of, the likeness of the hat to a
beggar's inviting coins, and Ossipon's vision of it as a symbol of chaos
come again. And by achieving that distance Conrad makes the reader very
happy indeed.

Further, Conrad is tactful in his use of this ironic tool. Winnie Verloc
is pathetic and even noble. It would be a piece of very bad taste to submit
her to the kind and the degree of ridicule that is apt for her husband.
Nevertheless, she cannot be allowed to engage our sympathies too seriously, or the whole tone of the book will be ruined. So in the murder
scene, where her sufferings are great, Conrad avoids irony as far as she is
concerned and concentrates on reducing the scale of the potentially tragic
action. Before the scene he had kept on insisting that her view into things
did not go deep, as when he tells us that "Mrs. Verloc wasted no portion
of this transient life in seeking for fundamental information." And this
insistence is continued into the scene itself with such remarks as "The
visions of Mrs. Verloc lacked nobility and magnificence." She is indeed

a woman with small range of mind, incapable of holding more than one important thing in it at the same time. Hatred of Verloc as the murderer of Stevie at first quite usurps it, to be expelled by her use of the carving knife. Then the vision of the gallows takes complete possession. In her extremity she is too ignorant to know how to escape abroad. By such means Conrad succeeds in rendering innocuous the powerful sympathies the reader might have had with her obsessive devotion to her helpless brother. And that devotion too had come in for its share of criticism before the catastrophe, for it is a short-sighted devotion, quite preventing Winnie from seeing why her mother had left Brett Street for the almshouse. Thus Conrad contrives to deflate Mrs. Verloc, but without the impropriety of an ironic deflation. He does something similar before her suicide, which in its turn must not be allowed to cross the borderline into tragedy. The scene that follows Mrs. Verloc's flight from her house and her accidental encounter with Ossipon is both macabre and richly comic. And the comedy is that of cross purposes and mutual misunderstanding. Thinking that it is Verloc who was blown up and ignorant of the murder, Ossipon at first believes that Winnie is a genuine pick-up, a windfall, and prepares to make use of his good luck. But he soon sees he is wrong and flies to the opposite error of diagnosing her as a homicidal maniac, from whom at all costs he must escape. Conrad is able, and without impropriety, to include Winnie in the comic context and in so doing to spotlight her stupidity. The climax comes when, waiting for the Southampton train to leave, she misinterprets Ossipon's words about Stevie (Comrade Ossipon, it will be remembered, was a devoted student of Cesare Lombroso and his theory of the "criminal type"):

> "He was an extraordinary lad, that brother of yours. Most interesting to study. A perfect type in a way. Perfect."
>
> He spoke scientifically in his secret fear. And Mrs. Verloc, hearing these words of commendation vouchsafed to her beloved dead, swayed forward with a flicker of light in her sombre eyes, like a ray of sunshine heralding a tempest of rain.
>
> "He was that indeed," she whispered, softly, with quivering lips. "You took a lot of notice of him, Tom. I loved you for it."

After Mrs. Verloc has reached that degree of stupidity, of total grossness of misapprehension, we cannot think of her suicide as a tragic event.

But *The Secret Agent* is pervaded by another kind of irony, and one which, like the first kind, helps towards making the book a unity. It is the irony of great plans having trivial results and of the weightiest results being effected by trivial means. It is the kind of irony that encourages men to keep their eyes open and not to expect too much logic and tidiness from life; and Shakespeare gave it its classic embodiment in *Much Ado About Nothing*. There Claudio and Hero are the chief figures in the main plot, although they are less fitted to be so than Benedick and Beatrice. Through a freak of fate their story nearly ends in disaster, but not quite.

They arouse unnecessary passions in other people, and all the pains that these folk take to clear up the trouble are futile because the fantastic incompetence of Dogberry and his fellows anticipates the carefully directed efforts of their betters: "What your wisdoms could not discover, these shallow fools have brought to light." Beatrice, the potentially tragic figure, and with a brilliant intellect, not only wastes her efforts in setting Benedick against Claudio, but has her love awakened by a trick that a much less brilliant person might have evaded; and the trick itself may have been superfluous since Benedick and Beatrice are in fact deeply attracted to each other. Conrad writes in the mode of *Much Ado;* since this seems to be a new contention, I had better go into the details.

The first hint of expectations being falsified occurs in the opening scene at the (German or Austrian?) Embassy. There, Privy Councillor Wurmt questions the vigilance of the English police, but the vigilance turns out to be embarrassingly greater than he had ever expected. Later, in the same scene, Vladimir announces that England must be brought into line with the Continent in the way she deals with revolutionaries: in the end his action only helps to perpetuate the difference of methods. Chief Inspector Heat hopes to use the explosion of the bomb to justify the imprisonment of Michaelis, whom he dislikes seeing at large; but this dislike awakens the suspicions of his superior and leads to a rebuff. The domestic set-up of the Verlocs is a humble and small scale affair, yet it makes itself felt in embassies and offices of state; while in turn the feelings thus aroused there are destined to lead nowhere. The mother of Mrs. Verloc, thinking that her presence in the Brett Street house may ultimately annoy Mr. Verloc and finally lead to his turning against her mentally deficient son, heroically contrives to retire to an almshouse. Her act is rich in unforeseen consequences. It leads first to Mr. Verloc's taking more notice of Stevie and finally to his using him to deposit the bomb that blows Stevie up, and second to Winnie's sewing the address of the house under Stevie's coat collar, an act which identifies him as the blown-up man. Mrs. Verloc did another thing to help Stevie. She joined with her daughter in impressing on him the measureless "goodness" of Mr. Verloc. Thus impressed they thought he would be more docile in Mr. Verloc's presence and hence more acceptable. It was through Stevie's blindly loyal belief in this "goodness" that he let himself be persuaded to carry the bomb and so meet his death. The Assistant Commissioner of Police hoped that the Greenwich explosion might become a *cause célèbre* and show up the iniquities of foreign embassies; and immediately, with Verloc's death, it lapsed into impenetrable obscurity. Most obvious of all, Verloc's efforts to pacify Winnie over Stevie's death serve instead to enrage her into committing murder. And lastly there is Ossipon, whose exposure to the same process is the *coda* of the novel. Ossipon, as well as affecting to be a revolutionary, was the *gigolo* of a steady succession of mature women not without means. He expected Winnie Verloc, widow of a man obviously possessed of means, to take her place in the succession. Finding her a murderess and haunted by the horror of her end, he is put off women altogether and takes to drink instead. I have questioned the motivation of this part of the novel, but in ironic idea it is strictly in accord with the rest. Thus, the theme of ends miscarrying goes right through and can hardly not have been intended by its author to be a means towards unity of impression.

Conrad used yet another means towards that end: he constantly makes an earlier passage or episode presage a later. I can be brief here, for the critics are well aware of this. The following examples will serve to illustrate the point. When Stevie was tried in an office job, the other office boys worked on his feelings and induced him to let off fireworks on the stairs. Their persuasiveness presages Verloc's influence on Stevie, as the fireworks presage the enlarged explosive that caused his death. The effect of the fireworks in the building was sensational: "silk hats and elderly business men could be seen rolling independently down the stairs." And it presages the sensation in other places where silk hats are worn—embassies and government departments—after the bomb went off in Greenwich Park. The conversation between the Verlocs at the end of the third chapter prepares us for the conversation that leads up to the murder. While Adolf is obsessed by the orders of Mr. Vladimir, Winnie is obsessed by her anxiety over Stevie. Neither will listen to the other; both are wholly self-absorbed. Near the end Winnie says she has had to take the carving knife from Stevie in his excitement; it is the knife she used later to stick into Adolf. All Winnie can achieve in the way of curiosity over her husband's troubles is the sleepy remark at the end, "Comfortable, dear? shall I put the light out now?"

II

I might have remarked at the end of the last paragraph that the cross references are rarer in the parts concerning the police, as I could have remarked earlier that in those parts there occurs a conspicuous exception to Conrad's usual ironic method. Both remarks could have served to introduce the rest of this essay, which questions whether Conrad achieved the unity he intended. I will not support my first assertion, for this would involve the intolerable boredom of giving a list of certain or possible examples; but I shall have to explain in a degree of detail that Conrad suspends his ironic method in dealing with the Assistant Commissioner and perhaps also with the Home Secretary.

As first presented, the Assistant Commissioner might well be within the scope of Conrad's ironic method:

> At headquarters the Chief Inspector was admitted at once to the Assistant Commissioner's private room. He found him, pen in hand, bent over a great table bestrewn with papers, as if worshipping an enormous double

inkstand of bronze and crystal. Speaking tubes resembling snakes were tied
by the heads to the back of the Assistant Commissioner's wooden armchair,
and their gaping mouths seemed ready to bite his elbow.

Here we might easily think of the Commissioner as an unconscious
Laocoön caught in the coils of officialdom. But very soon we learn that
he is as well aware of the coils as we are and as averse to them as Conrad
would like his readers to be. The ironic distance between character and
reader has been closed. Far from welcoming the sedentary imprisonment
of administration, the Assistant Commissioner had an adventurous nature
and would have preferred an active post in the tropics, such as he once
had. He is denied his wish because, in a moment of blindness alien to his
usual discriminating nature, he has married the wrong woman. Here is a
perfect opportunity for the ironic method; but Conrad passes it by, allowing the Commissioner to have his own ironic situation quite under
control:

> Chained to a desk in the thick of four millions of men, he considered him-
> self the victim of an ironic fate—the same, no doubt, which had brought
> about his marriage with a woman exceptionally sensitive in the matter of
> colonial climate, besides other limitations testifying to the delicacy of her
> nature.

In fact, far from distancing him, Conrad creates in the Assistant Commissioner a man pretty close to himself. With the Home Secretary the case
is slightly different. His physique and his clothes receive ironic treatment,
presenting themselves to us and to himself differently, as when we learn
that "the eyes, with puffy lower lids, stared with a haughty droop on
each side of a hooked, aggressive nose, nobly salient in the vast pale cir-
cumference of the face." But there is nothing especially ironic in the way
Conrad tells us how he coped with the problem presented to him by the
Assistant Commissioner.

Another point. Not only does the Assistant Commissioner remain outside the area of Conrad's irony; he is the one person whose plans do not
miscarry. True, he had hoped, as I have noted, that the Greenwich Park
bomb would be the occasion of a *cause célèbre,* and his hopes were disappointed. But he scores substantial successes. He brings his subordinate to
heel, as his two predecessors had failed to do; he had at last (in spite of
his wife) been caught up in a job with a spice of adventure in it; and he
managed to flatten Mr. Vladimir, whose methods of dealing with revolutionaries he abhorred. Conrad dismisses him with, "he had had a full
evening." He might with equal truth have added, "and a very successful
day."

These matters, little touched on by the critics, have their bearing on
the better known dispute as to whether or not the police scenes are integrated with the rest, which is almost identical with the dispute about
unity. Of course Conrad had every right to bring in the police. Anar-

chists are among the characters; a bomb was exploded: the police are doubly entitled to be present. The questions remain: do the police and their activities harmonise with the rest of the novel? are they to scale? Chief Inspector Heat is in keeping with the dominant ironic trend. He is duly distanced, and his plans turned out not as he expected. But we have seen that it is far otherwise with his superior: the Assistant Commissioner is not in keeping with the whole. Set against his subordinate he is admirable for the time being, within the detached sense; but that excellence does not extend to the whole book. It looks as if Conrad's short term interest in him prevailed over his regard for the whole. Then there is the question of scale. The affairs of the police are largely concentrated into a long section of three consecutive chapters (V, VI, VII). They are brilliantly presented and they engage our attention and sympathy deeply. In fact, they whet our appetite for more. And we do get more in chapters IX and X. And yet somehow this addition does not satisfy; it does not suffice the appetite set up. The two chief characters have been elaborated too successfully; they have reached statures that demand scope in some major action and then perforce they have to dwindle into subordination to the affairs of the Verlocs. The disappointment is felt acutely when their direct interference in the action ends:

> The Assistant Commissioner himself did not turn into the noble building. It was the Explorers' Club. The thought passed through his mind that Mr. Vladimir, honorary member, would not be seen very often there in the future. He looked at his watch. It was only half-past ten. He had had a very full evening.

This is a feeble dismissal, as if Conrad had no faith in it. "Yes," we feel like saying, "it is only half-past ten and you led us to believe that you would prolong these fascinating men's doings to midnight at least, if not into the small hours. You have let us down." Troubled by such thoughts and by the incongruity of the treatment given to the Assistant Commissioner, we cannot but conclude that the theme of the police is not perfectly integrated with that of the Verlocs.

The majestic scale of the scenes between the two police officers prompts a last doubt as to the perfection of *The Secret Agent*. Is not the scale of the separate scene-units perhaps too big for the general scale? Conrad called his novel "a simple tale," and it is nothing of the kind. He may have meant it to be, but when it came to the execution he wove a complex plot and gave us some highly developed characters. More important, he worked through a series of massive, long-drawn-out scenes. It would be wrong to complain of the length of the culminating scene ending with the murder; but should it have been matched by scenes equally massive? Think of the long opening scene in the embassy, of the intricate sparring between Heat and his superior, of the cab drive from Brett Street to the almshouses. I believe that Conrad, intending a simple ironic tale, could not resist the urge to employ the technique of the long novel and so allowed the supporting incidents to acquire an excessive consequence.

The parts of the novel are so good that in the act of reading them we are not likely to be bothered with their disproportionate scale, or with their relation to the whole. In the reading it would be a sacrilege to find fault with the glorious abundance of Conrad's account of the cab drive. Further, he makes his story so interesting that we are carried along with our critical exactions mollified. Then there *are* the various features making for unity that I mentioned in the first section of this essay; and these help powerfully to distract us from the novel's failings. It is only when we have ceased reading and look back and reflect on the whole that our doubts arise and we reach this conclusion: that with all its merits *The Secret Agent* hovers a little uneasily between a novel in the grand manner and the long short-story.

Introduction to *Under Western Eyes*

by Morton Dauwen Zabel

I

Late in 1907 Conrad, now fifty and in his thirteenth year as a published author, began the writing of a new novel—the book that was not to appear until four years later as *Under Western Eyes*. He was at this time crossing the decade of his severest tests in authorship, and of problems that mark the years between 1902 and 1912 as a crucial phase in his career. Such tests had never been lacking in his writing life, but once the impulse of what he called his "first" or "Malayan phase" was spent, and once he had completed the series of tales and novels, culminating in "Typhoon" and "Falk," that had derived from his life at sea, they took on a new and formidable appearance.

His early stages in his art, however persistent in labor and accomplishment, had been anything but easy. It took him five years, between the ages of thirty-two and thirty-seven, to complete *Almayer's Folly* before it was published in 1895. *The Rescue,* begun in 1896, proved so baffling that he abandoned it after more than three years of struggle and did not return to it, as to an unsettled account in his conscience, until seventeen years later. His doubts in conceiving and finishing *Lord Jim* run through the letters he wrote during the year of its writing, and even after its appearance in 1900. His work in the shorter forms of fiction veered between the almost spontaneous exhilaration that produced his masterpieces in these forms and the profound uncertainty that yielded his mistaken efforts. Critical recognition had come to him early but practical success lagged to the point of bringing him to desperate crises in his financial prospects. When he arrived at a virtual point of rupture in his relations with William Blackwood of Edinburgh, the publisher who had done most to advance his literary fortunes in the early years, he felt that his struggle at "labouring against an anxious tomorrow, under the stress of an uncertain future," had brought him to a crisis more forbidding than any he had yet faced.

"Introduction to *Under Western Eyes*" by Morton Dauwen Zabel. From *Under Western Eyes* by Joseph Conrad, Anchor Books, Doubleday & Co. Copyright © 1963 by Morton Dauwen Zabel. Reprinted by permission of the Estate of Morton Dauwen Zabel.

Yet against these hazards he had carried to completion a remarkable body of work in a short space of years—four novels, two book length collaborations, four long tales, eight short stories—which testifies to the sustained energy, the sometimes astonishing intensity of excitement and labor, that had impelled him. "Youth" had been written in three weeks; *Heart of Darkness* in about three months; *The Nigger of the "Narcissus"* in less than six; *Lord Jim,* once its tentative beginnings were past, in about twelve. The long-stored, long-meditated years of his youth and sailing life; the restraints he had put on his imagination until the hour of his first effort at writing a novel struck in 1889; his three decades of dramatic encounters in Poland, in Russia, in France, in the East, and on the high seas—all these had combined to produce a succession of tales that make Conrad's first decade as a published author one of the most productive in modern literature. He had kept his mind and nerves steadily on the stretch. He had reaped a swift harvest from his past. Neither his personal responsibilities nor his creative need had allowed him to rest. The cumulative strain and tension of his work were bound to arrive at a point of snapping—of a radical climacteric in his imaginative life; and by Conrad's own account that point came in 1902.

"I don't mean," he wrote fifteen years later, "to say that I became then conscious of any impending change in my mentality and in my attitude towards the tasks of my writing life. And perhaps there was never any change, except in that mysterious, extraneous thing which has nothing to do with theories of art; a subtle change in the nature of the inspiration; a phenomenon for which I cannot in any way be held responsible. What, however, did cause me some concern was that after finishing the last story of the *Typhoon* volume it seemed somehow that there was nothing more in the world to write about." [1] Few writers have escaped such moments of spent energy or impasse, and Conrad was still to meet more than one of them before his life ended. But several circumstances combined to make the crisis of 1902 particularly significant in his career.

The East and the sea had already given him the most powerful tales he was to write on these subjects. For the moment their force had been exhausted. Blackwood, having published four of the best of these works, had found them too unprofitable to make it possible for him to agree to a financial scheme Conrad had proposed to him as a means of future support. ("He was very kind but told me plainly that I was a loss to the Firm. That's hard enough to hear at any time.") The sting of this refusal, the momentary sense of failure it brought to Conrad ("I admit that after leaving you I remained for some time under the impression of my 'worthlessness' "), caused him to write the most serious defense of his work and aims that he had yet attempted—crucial even beyond the

---

[1] "Author's Note" to *Nostromo,* dated 1917, in *Conrad's Prefaces to His Works* (London: J. M. Dent & Sons, 1937), p. 85.

credo he had written in 1897 as his preface to *The Nigger of the
"Narcissus,"* because this time it came in the face of a direct challenge
to his personal fortunes and future. It was more than a defense. It was a
stubborn affirmation of his vocation and of his pride as an artist and a
moral dramatist.

> I am conscious of having pursued with pain and labour a calm conception
> of a definite ideal in a perfect soberness of spirit . . . I have nothing but a
> faith—a little against the world—in my reasoned conviction . . . Now my
> character is formed: it has been tried by experience. I have looked upon
> the worst life can do—and I am sure of myself, even against the demoralising
> effect of straitened circumstances. I know exactly what I am doing . . . I
> want to make good my contention that I am not writing "in the air." It is
> not the haphazard business of a mere temperament . . . Therefore I am
> emboldened to say that ultimate and irretrievable failure is *not* to be my
> lot. . . . My work shall not be an utter failure because it has the solid basis
> of a definite intention . . .[2]

It was in this conflict of self-doubt and enforced resolution that Conrad lived out the year 1902, and its acuteness, already evident in so
many of the past phases of his life, was to persist in a renewed form in
the years that lay ahead. He pressed on with the completion of "The
End of the Tether," the last tale he wrote for Blackwood, even after
most of the manuscript of its first draft had burned one night when the
lamp on his writing table exploded. He saw the publication of the *Youth*
volume and told Edward Garnett he was "overcome" by the appearance
of the "three-headed monster in the green cover. I hate the sight of the
thing." He assembled the four stories of the *Typhoon* volume for Heine-
mann and said he was "ashamed of them all; I don't believe either in
their popularity or in their merit. . . . My mind is becoming base, my
hand heavy, my tongue thick—as though I had drunk some subtle
poison, some slow poison that will make me die, die as it were without
an echo." Such were his private comments on some of the finest tales he
had yet written or was ever to write.[3]

But another ferment was working in his mind. Blackwood's rebuff,
the prolonged strain of the past five years, recurring ill health and
domestic worries that prolonged themselves into 1903, apparently joined
with the sense that he had run out of his material to compel Conrad to-

[2] Conrad to William Blackwood, May 31, 1902, in *Joseph Conrad: Letters to William
Blackwood and David S. Meldrum,* edited by William Blackburn (Durham, N.C.: Duke
University Press, 1958), pp. 152-56. Conrad's situation in 1902, also traced in the letters
included in *Joseph Conrad: Life and Letters,* edited by G. Jean-Aubry (Garden City,
N.Y.: Doubleday, Page & Co., 1927), and in *Letters from Conrad, 1895-1924,* to and
edited with introduction and notes by Edward Garnett (Indianapolis, Ind.: The Bobbs-
Merrill Co., 1928), and other records, is most closely documented in the letters to Blackwood and Meldrum.

[3] Letters to Edward Garnett of November 27, 1902, and June 10, 1902, in *Letters from
Conrad, 1895-1924,* pp. 186-87, 183-84.

ward a different subject matter, a new direction in his work, an attack on themes more closely actual and contemporary than those of his exotic or maritime tales. The drama of modern life, modern politics, the social crisis and the future of nations, was in the air. Novelists like his friend Wells and various popular entertainers were making a success of it. Newspapers were full of the unease of the world that lay behind the outward shows and successes of imperialism or *ententes*. The Russian novelists were seizing the public attention in Constance Garnett's translations, and though Conrad expressed himself as "think[ing] but little" of these books, they must have struck his old memories of his Polish youth and its tragedy with the impact of a profound hereditary recognition. A part of his personal life and inheritance that was older and more deep-seated in his mind than anything he had experienced at sea or in the East was stirred to action in him. Whatever attempts he had made to come to grips with the problems of modern history in "An Outpost of Progress," *Heart of Darkness,* and the abandoned *Rescue* were now feeling the claim of a more pressing actuality.

Imperialism, autocracy, nationalism, and revolution had been living presences to Conrad in more than the news of the day. They were conditions of his intimate history and personal knowledge. He now sensed himself to be at the edge of a new and bolder undertaking in his art. His "so strangely negative but disturbing mood" having "lasted some little time," there strayed into his mind the "first hint" of a new book "in the shape of a vagrant anecdote completely destitute of valuable details"— a memory of having heard "in 1875 or '6, when very young, in the West Indies, or rather in the Gulf of Mexico," the "story of some man who was supposed to have stolen single-handed a whole lighter-full of silver, somewhere on the Tierra Firme seaboard during the troubles of a revolution." Now, "twenty-six or seven years afterwards," he "came upon the very thing in a shabby volume picked up outside a second-hand bookshop." The germ of a new book was in his hands; and though he could scarcely have anticipated it at the moment, its writing was to involve him in almost two years of unremitting labor that resulted in the "most anxiously meditated" of his novels, and in "an intense creative effort on what I suppose will always remain my largest canvas." [4]

Early in 1903, on an undated Thursday, he wrote in a letter to John Galsworthy that "with my head full of a story, I have not been able to write a single word—except the title, which shall be, I think: *Nostromo* . . .". Twenty months later, on September 1, 1904, he announced, again to Galsworthy, "Finished! finished! on the 30th in Hope's house in Stanford in Essex"; and two days later, in letters to Garnett and William Rothenstein, that the completion of the book was "a fact upon which

[4] "Author's Note" to *Nostromo* in *Prefaces;* and to *The Secret Agent,* 1920, *Prefaces.* For a further note on Conrad's derivations in *Nostromo,* see supplementary note 4 at the end of this volume.

my friends may congratulate me as upon a recovery from a dangerous illness," and that "What the book is like, I don't know. . . . Personally I
am not satisfied. It is something,—but not *the* thing I tried for. There
is no exultation, none of that temporary sense of achievement which is
so soothing. Even the mere feeling of relief at having done with it is
wanting. The strain has been too great, has lasted too long. But I am
ready for more. I don't feel empty, exhausted. I am simply joyless,—
like most men of little faith." [5]

"I don't know whether I really felt that I wanted a change, change in
my imagination, in my vision, and in my mental attitude," he recalled
in 1920; "I rather think that a change in the fundamental mood had already stolen over me unawares." The change, though not radically dis-
continuous with the mood and impetus of certain of his earlier works,
was to remain with him for almost a decade. Though interrupted by re-
currences to his more familiar maritime or Eastern subjects, it was to
sustain him through the writing of three of his most ambitious and searching books between 1903 and 1910, and to produce, in *Nostromo, The
Secret Agent,* and *Under Western Eyes,* the works that give him his
major rank among the political novelists of the twentieth century.

II

"Books have their fate," Conrad said in one of his early essays, "and
it is very much like the destiny of man. They share with us the great
incertitude of ignominy or glory—of severe justice and senseless persecution—of calumny and misunderstanding—the shame of undeserved success." Nor can they rely on "the formulas of art" for assurance against
these hazards of chance or fortune, for such formulas too "are dependent
on things variable, unstable, and untrustworthy; on human sympathies,
on prejudices, on likes and dislikes, on the sense of virtue and the sense
of propriety, on beliefs and theories that, indestructible in themselves,
always change their form—often in the lifetime of one fleeting generation." [6]

The fate of Conrad's own books supports his contention. From early
neglect to later success; from public admiration for the romantic glamour
and atmosphere of his exotic or maritime tales to a lingering public indifference to the serious values that were masked by these; from the impatience of careless readers to the respect of his fellow artists and to a
gradually insistent critical esteem, the fortunes of his art during the past
seven decades describe the destiny of his resolutely individual talent and

[5] The letters to Galsworthy are in Jean-Aubry's *Life and Letters,* Vol. I, pp. 308,
332-35; those to Garnett and Rothenstein, pp. 335-36. Conrad's following remark is in
his "Author's Note" to *The Secret Agent* in *Prefaces,* p. 105.
[6] "Books" in *Notes on Life and Letters* (Garden City, N.Y.: Doubleday, Page & Co.,
1921), pp. 3-10. The essay was first published in *The Speaker,* July 15, 1905.

of the risks to which it was fated. Some of his tales were admitted to the rank of modern classics as early as half a century ago, but certain others —among them some of his most serious achievements—have had to wait much longer for the turn of taste or of events that had to appear before they won their hearing and a measure of justice.

The tales of Conrad that have remained most widely read during the past sixty years happen to be those he wrote early or late in his career. *Almayer's Folly, The Nigger of the "Narcissus," Lord Jim,* "Youth," *Heart of Darkness,* and *Typhoon* were all completed by 1902, in his first eight years as a professional writer. *Chance, Victory, The Shadow Line, The Arrow of Gold, The Rescue,* and *The Rover,* the novels that won him public success in the last decade of his life, came after 1913. But between these two groups of tales he wrote the series of novels that may be called the works of his middle period—books that deviated from the maritime, exotic, or romantic scenes of his more popular fiction by addressing themselves to the drama of modern society and politics. These novels show not only some of his most serious subjects but some of his most ambitious art; and if their value was largely neglected at the time of their appearance, it has been made unmistakable by the events and crises that have followed them in the twentieth century. *Under Western Eyes* was a failure when it was first published in 1911 and must still be one of his least read novels. But it profits by the irony of circumstance more than any of the others, and it is without question one of the books that must be read by anyone concerned to know Conrad's art in its full dimensions and resonance. Today, even after so many novels have been written on its subject, and when the developments of Russian and international history have made its drama more familiar to Western readers than ever before, it shares with its two immediate predecessors in Conrad's canon the stature of a classic drama of modern history and one of the few English books of the century that calls for a rank among its Russian and European companions.

Nostromo, appearing in 1904, and variously rated by critics as his most difficult or perplexing book and as "one of the great novels of the language," gave Conrad, in its complex drama of civil war, revolution, and rival moralities in the South American state of Costaguana, his first full test as a dramatist of politics and statecraft. *The Secret Agent* of 1907 is now readily recognizable as a pioneer in its genre—the tale of political intrigue, espionage, and moral anarchism in modern Europe which has become a typical mode of fiction in our age of *Machtpolitik,* scientific violence, and "international evil." *Chance,* the book that turned the tide of Conrad's fortunes when it ran serially in the *New York Herald* in 1912, though not a political novel, combined its maritime theme with a drama of modern finance, ethical confusion, and social persecution in which Marlow, the narrator Conrad had created to tell the tales of "Youth," *Heart of Darkness,* and *Lord Jim,* reappeared to manipulate, in the history of Flora de Barral, one of his most intricate tales of moral duplicity and alienation. All three of these novels are radically and recognizably Conradian in their subjects and craftsmanship. All of them develop themes and motives that were essential to his work from its beginnings. But *Under Western Eyes,* as Conrad himself admitted, has a personal relevance that gives it a special interest among his books. Its subject—Russian character, despotism, and revolution—is one with which, as a Pole whose nation and family had suffered under the heel of Russian imperialist occupation, he was sooner or later bound to come to terms in his art. And beyond this it forms, along with *The Secret Agent,* his most serious effort to describe the forces at work in the body politic of modern Europe. It also serves as his closest link with the Dostoevskian tradition in Russian fiction—a tradition which, though he persistently repudiated it and professed himself both baffled and repelled by it, opens a radical question of temperamental affinity and influence in his work. And lastly the book presents a theme which, however remote from the public interests of fifty years ago, has become of absorbing concern to the West during the past four decades, and never more so than at the present moment.

The novel fell almost completely flat in England and America, but in Europe and Russia it won serious attention. It was translated into Russian (by E. Pimenova, for the house of Polza) as early as 1912, and numerous editions were printed before 1917; and while it has not been possible to trace its recent fate there—the recent editions of the *Great Soviet Encyclopedia* do not mention either *The Secret Agent* or *Under Western Eyes* in describing Conrad as a "bourgeois decadent" who abandoned true social subjects in favor of the exotic and the subjective —it must still be the book by which Conrad is best known to such Russian readers as have access to his work. The present time of crisis between Russia and the West has given it the force of a prophecy; and an age that has been bred on such classics as *Virgin Soil, Crime and Punishment,* and *The Possessed,* and that has found images of its ordeal in books like Kafka's *The Trial,* Koestler's *Darkness at Noon,* Orwell's *1984,* as well as in the tales of Sartre, Camus, Graham Greene, Aldanov, Victor Serge, Schwarz-Bart, and a host of other recent novelists of ideological conflict and political terror, must encounter *The Secret Agent* and *Under Western Eyes* with the shock of recognizing novels which, written well in advance of the wars and crises of the twentieth century, have become appallingly corroborated by the events of contemporary history.

The present writer has found himself returning to *Under Western Eyes* during the past thirty years as often as to any of Conrad's books, and discovering in it a force and achievement that only two of his other novels and three or four of the tales rival. This may be a matter of personal taste, but it has been supported by several of Conrad's distinguished readers. Ford Madox Ford once said that for himself the book was "in a long way the greatest—as it is the latest—of all Conrad's great novels"; and André Gide, who on first making its acquaintance in 1917, admired its "prophetic reflections about the Russian soul," continued to read and ponder it, saying of the theme it shares with *Lord Jim* that "there is no more pathetic subject for a novel," and finding in it a reflection of his own persistent concern with "that *irresponsible act* of the hero, to redeem which his whole life is subsequently engaged." The English critic V. S. Pritchett has said that the novel has become "more and more suggestive to the contemporary reader," and another, F. R. Leavis, has rated it one of Conrad's best—"a most distinguished work," which "must be counted among those upon which Conrad's status as one of the great English novelists securely rests." [7] More recent studies have given it increasing attention and a major place in his achievement. And Conrad himself had a special feeling for his effort "to capture the very soul of things Russian," and one of the last projects of his life was to make a play out of the novel under the title he originally gave it, *Razumov*.[8]

To these opinions there has been a certain amount of critical dissent, and it is possible that at a first reading or casual glance the reader will find that the book, especially in its second and third parts, shows Conrad at his densest and most discouraging. Yet there can be little in modern fiction more acutely conceived and written than its first and final parts; and while it must be allowed that between these there are stretches of dramatic indirection, calculated delay, and psychic or moral dissection

[7] Ford Madox Ford in *Return to Yesterday* (London: Victor Gollancz, 1932) , p. 193; André Gide in *Journal* (Paris, 1941), December 13, 1917, p. 641, and February 23, 1930, p. 971 (as here translated by Justin O'Brien in *Journals* [New York, 1948, 1949], Vol. II, p. 219; Vol. III, pp. 94-95); V. S. Pritchett in *The New Statesman and Nation* (London), July 15, 1950, pp. 72-73; F. R. Leavis in *The Great Tradition* (1948), pp. 219-22. [Gide adds to his comment of February 23, 1930: "Much interested by the relationship I discover between *Under Western Eyes* and *Lord Jim*. (I regret not having spoken of this with Conrad.) . . . For the thing that leads to the heaviest responsibility is just the *irresponsibilities* in a life. How can one efface that act? There is no more pathetic subject for a novel, nor one that has been more stifled in our literature by belief in Boileau's rule: that the hero must remain, from one end to the other of a drama or a novel, 'such as he was first seen to be.' "]

Since the present essay on *Under Western Eyes* was first published in 1951 a number of studies of the novel have been made: among them Douglas Hewitt's in *Conrad: A Reassessment* (1952), pp. 80-88; Robert F. Haugh's in *Joseph Conrad: Discovery in Design* (1957), pp. 119-35; Albert J. Guerard's in *Conrad the Novelist* (1958), pp. 218-53; and Eloise K. Hay's in an as yet unpublished doctoral thesis on *The Political Novels of Joseph Conrad*, Radcliffe College, 1961. Other comment has appeared in more incidental form in other recent criticism. The present study appears in a revised and expanded version from that which appeared as an introduction to the novel in 1951 (New York: New Directions) and as an essay in the author's *Craft and Character* (New York: The Viking Press, 1957).

[8] The play, sketched and apparently partly written, was never finished. For a further note on it and Conrad's other plays, see supplementary note 8, where a French film version of *Under Western Eyes* is also described.

that are likely to put any reader's patience to a test, the narrative repeatedly rises to points of extraordinary intensity and in the end achieves a depth of penetration, of cumulative effect and resonance, that brings it into the company of the most memorable books of its period and certainly of Conrad's own finest powers. Even its attenuations put less of a strain on credulity or attention than many distinguished modern books do; and one can only advise the reader to stay with the book, to keep his patience alert, and to see what becomes of the novel's long-drawn tensions. He is likely to find himself rewarded with a remarkable experience in fiction, and to discover a reason in Conrad's method which, though it may not be as compelling as in some of his shorter tales, will have much to say about the kind of art Conrad here practised at its maturity and about the difficult theme of conscience and retribution with which the novel deals. If *Nostromo* shows a larger vision and a more comprehensive conspectus of history, and *The Secret Agent* a more sustained focus of tragic action and irony, it may be argued that *Under Western Eyes* combines these elements in the proportions that make it finally more penetrating, more akin to a classic tradition in European fiction, than either of its companion books. And if the ominous test of Dostoevsky's novels looms behind it, it is for the Western reader to decide what *Under Western Eyes* does to bring an acuteness of moral concentration and insight to bear upon its Dostoevskian subject and even, perhaps, to refine upon and rival it.

III

The writing of the book, as so often with Conrad, gave him severe difficulties. The prolonged ordeal of *Nostromo* in 1903-4, though it did not baffle him as *The Rescue* had done or involve him in an unexpected elaboration of his subject as in the case of *Lord Jim,* had drained him of strength, and it was almost eighteen more months before he ventured on a new novel. Meanwhile he wrote a number of essays, among them his first and most important treatise on politics, "Autocracy and War," in 1905. He turned to the writing of his sketches of sea life, largely at Ford Madox Hueffer's prodding, and by 1906 had accumulated enough of them to publish *The Mirror of the Sea.* He wrote "Gaspar Ruiz" as a pendant to *Nostromo* in 1905, and later in the same year he significantly tackled the themes of modern political intrigue and anarchism that resulted in the two slight but premonitory tales of "An Anarchist" and "The Informer."

By these steps he brought his political subject out of its Eastern and South American settings and closer to contemporary Europe and England. The compelling need of dealing with the forces of contemporary history which had counted in the shaping of *Nostromo* was obviously becoming more insistent in his thought. Early in 1906 his chronic sense of feeling "powerless in an exhaustion of thought and will" was alleviated by a vacation in southern France at Montpellier—a change that not only proved more successful than a trip to Capri in the previous year but that also gave him hints that were to contribute, years later, to *Victory* and the French historical dramas of his final years. He was soon able to begin a new book. "A few words uttered by a friend in casual conversation about anarchists or rather anarchist activities" combined with his memory of the "blood-stained inanity" of the "already old story of the attempt to blow up the Greenwich Observatory" in 1894 and with some other "not very recondite" sources to shape a drama of London espionage in his mind. In "a matter of about three days" its plot was decided; and in an unusual stride of steady application the novel of *The Secret Agent* was completed by early November.

   The Secret Agent, which derived in large part from London itself— "the vision of an enormous town . . . a monstrous town more populous than some continents"—is one of the most concentrated of Conrad's books and his most sustained feat of "ironic method." It undoubtedly acted as a resolving test of his political insight. Less nebulous or remote than the Eastern dramas of *The Rescue* and *Lord Jim,* less riddled by complex plotting and dramatic diffusion than *Nostromo,* more convinced in its action and language than "An Anarchist" and "The Informer," it concentrated his political imagination more effectively than anything he had yet written. Though it carries some effects of the *tour de force,* it shows what was for Conrad an unusual excitement and movement of inspiration. "All of a sudden I found myself stimulated. . . . It was at first for me a mental change, disturbing a quieted-down imagination, in which strange forms, sharp in outline but imperfectly apprehended, appeared and claimed attention as crystals will do by their bizarre and unexpected shapes." It gives the impression that Conrad was now more forcibly propelled toward the drama of Europe than ever before, and toward the more intimate treatment of it that was soon to come.

   Having completed the novel he found himself again spent, "horribly seedy and depressed." Another vacation in Montpellier was undertaken in December 1906. He wrote "Il Conde," worked on "The Duel," and cast about in the lore of Napoleonic history. He also began to struggle with a longer project, the novel *Chance,* whose germinal idea had first come to him as early as 1898. But *Chance* at this point was spurred by no such impetus as had produced *The Secret Agent,* and proving intractable throughout 1907, it was finally put aside, to remain unfinished for another five years. During the Montpellier visit an alarming illness of the Conrads' son Borys took the family to a hydropathic cure at an old scene, Champel, near Geneva, which Conrad had visited in the nineties. At this distracted juncture he remembered "something told [him] by a man in Geneva many years ago," when he had gone to Switzerland on an earlier search for health and inspiration. Now, revisiting Geneva, he seized on the earlier memory and by January 1908 was at work on the novel that became *Under Western Eyes*. At that point he called it *Razumov* and his conception of it differed radically from the book he completed, after another series of delays and interruptions, two years later (on January 22, 1910, according to the date he wrote on the manuscript) and published on October 5, 1911, with its dedication to his American friend Agnes Tobin of San Francisco, "who brought to our door her genius for friendship from the uttermost shore of the West." [9]

The strands of suggestion and memory that combined in Conrad's shaping of his tale were thus both immediate and remote, and they included some of the most profound and deeply rooted emotions of his life. There was first the suggestion of Geneva itself, "the respectable and passionless abode of democratic liberty, the serious-minded town of dreary hotels, tendering the same indifferent hospitality to tourists of all nations and to international conspirators of every shade": Voltaire's

> ville froide et fade, où tout est entamè,
> Où l'on calcule toujours, et ne sent jamais—

the city of Calvinist rectitude and Swiss sobriety which from the time of Herzen, Bakunin, and Kropotkin to that of Lenin and Trotsky had offered its impervious sanctuary to the exiles of Tsarist autocracy. There, perhaps in the quarter which, "on account of many Russians residing there, is called La Petite Russie," Conrad heard from his unknown acquaintance the hints of the story which served as his germ. (He was as avid as Henry James was for those chance suggestions that illustrate what James called "that odd law which somehow always makes the minimum of valid suggestion serve the man of imagination better than the maximum," although, as Graham Greene has pointed out, there is a striking difference between the germs Conrad seized upon, "remarkable as a rule for their anarchy" or "their ambiguity," and "those neat little dinner-table stories which set James off constructing his more intricate and deeper fictions, holding up his hand in deprecation to prevent the whole story coming out.")[10]

What Conrad remembered of the stranger's tale he heard in Geneva in 1895 must have fallen in with the mood that still possessed him after the writing of *The Secret Agent* and its two short companion pieces.

[9] The manuscript of *Under Western Eyes* is in the Keating Collection in the Yale University Library. It shows many revisions and some lengthy deletions of details and episodes before the novel reached its published form; there were other revisions between the serial and book form. The novel was first serialized in *The English Review* (London) and in *The North American Review* in America, December 1910-October 1911, before being published by Methuen in London and Harper & Brothers in New York in 1911.

[10] Henry James, preface to *The Aspern Papers, etc.*, in the New York Edition of 1907-09, and in *The Art of the Novel* (1934), pp. 161-62. Graham Greene in *The Lost Childhood and Other Essays* (1951), p. 99.

That novel of intrigue, anarchism, and treachery in the London of the
1890's, with its plot of terrorists, bomb makers, and *agents provocateurs*
manipulated by an unnamed foreign power in the interests of inciting
the western European nations to suppress the alien revolutionary groups
to whom they gave asylum, was his first full portrayal of two of the
evils he feared most profoundly in his life and age—the "plague spots"
of radical socialism and anarchism that undermined the solidarity of
European society, and the "ferocity and imbecility of an autocratic rule"
that bred them. The shadow of the Tsarist tyranny and violence was
already falling heavily across Europe. Nineteen hundred five was the
year of the aborted Russian revolution that foreshadowed 1917. Nihilism,
anarchism, and revolutionary terrorism had spread westward through the
past five or six decades. The First International at The Hague in 1872
had brought to a head the conflict between the scientific socialism of
Marx and the anarchist policy of Bakunin, resulting in the expulsion of
the anarchists. The *Communist Manifesto* of 1848 and *Das Kapital* had
descended and proliferated into a widespread lineage of tracts, texts,
theses, programs of action, systems of organized protest, and crises of
crime and persecution, extending across Europe and to both Asia and
America. And from the time of Turgenev's *Smoke, Rudin,* and *Virgin
Soil* or the novels of Dostoevsky, the modern novel had become increasingly concerned with themes of despotism, protest, and revolt.
Conrad's friends Constance and Edward Garnett were busy in England
translating and writing propaganda for the Russian classics, or mixing
in the circles of refugees like Kropotkin, Stepniak, and other exiles from
Russia. His collaborator Ford Madox Hueffer was involved in the socialist
activities of the younger Rossettis and other sympathizers with Continental radicalism.

Twenty-five years before Conrad wrote his novel Henry James had
dealt with the subject of revolutionary anarchism in *The Princess Casamassima*. That book, the first notable work of fiction in English on its
theme and the most impressive novel of its kind to appear in England or
America before 1900, was inspired by the radical activity of the 1880's;
and Lionel Trilling[11] and others have shown in their studies of the
book how closely its material tallies with such events as the Lyons riots
of 1882, with a series of attempts to assassinate the rulers of Germany,
Spain, Italy, and Russia, with the Phoenix Park murders in Ireland and
the Haymarket Riots in Chicago, with dynamite conspiracies in England
and Germany, and with the activities of such anti-scientific rivals of Marx
as Bakunin and Johann Most. In Russia the "Socialist Revolutionary"
Party and its terrorist Battle Organization were augmented by the student
revolutionary groups that sprang up in the eighties and nineties. And
against them stood the organized forces of Tsarist officialdom and the

[11] In his introduction to the novel (New York: Macmillan Co., 1948), included in *The
Liberal Imagination* by Lionel Trilling (1950), pp. 58-92.

political secret police, the *Okhrana*. All these served to provide Conrad—as they were to provide many other novelists—with his situation and background. From their activities he fastened upon the episode of recent history with which his novel opens: "an event characteristic of modern Russia in the actual fact"—the "successful attempt on the life of Mr. de P——, the President of the notorious Repressive Commission of some years ago, the Minister of State invested with extraordinary powers."

The novel—of which Conrad was later to say that "I was induced to write" it "by the rubbishy character of stories about Russian revolutionists published in magazines"—thus hinges on an occurrence which had only recently shaken Europe and figured in the world's news. "De P——" was the celebrated Viatscheslav Konstantinovitch Plehve, whose assassination took place in July 1904. Born in 1846 of Lithuanian stock, educated in Warsaw and at the University of St. Petersburg, he had ascended by carefully calculated stages from assistant Solicitor-General to become the director of the Russian state police, Secretary of State, member of the Council of the Empire, and eventually in 1902 Minister of the Interior. He had attracted the favor of Alexander III for his work in investigating the assassination of Alexander II; had earned the hatred of Poland, Lithuania, and Finland for his ruthless "Russification" of those subject provinces; had manipulated pogroms against the Jews and persecutions of Armenians in the Caucasus; was credited with being accessory to the Kishinev massacres; opposed Witte's policy of commercial development in Russia along European lines because it tended to further both a dangerous proletariat and a prosperous middle class; and in time became the fanatical archetype of the autocratic principle and an archvillain in revolutionary history. Long-plotted by the Battle Organization, his murder was finally brought off by a bombing as he was driving to the Petershof to make his regular report to the Tsar, and it made an enormous impression on all strata of Russian society and throughout Europe. The assassin indicted and executed for the murder, Sasonov, enacted a role comparable to that of Victor Haldin in Conrad's story.

Plehve's assassination involved another person who became notorious in Russian revolutionary history. This was Azeff, one of the most notorious of the police spies and double agents of the time who, double-dealing as revolutionary conspirators and as tools of the Tsarist police, became a familiar product of the politics of despotism. From the time of Vidocq and Balzac's Vautrin they had figured in modern European intrigue, but Azeff achieved a special celebrity. Born of poor parents in 1869, he absconded from Russia with some stolen money at the age of twenty-three; went to Karlsruhe in Germany (like Stuttgart, Baden, and Geneva, one of the centers of Russian conspiracy abroad); joined there a group of Russian student revolutionists among whom he appeared as a student of engineering; and at the same time offered his services as a spy to the Russian state police. Thus while, as a member of the Socialist Revolutionary Party and head of its terrorist section, he was instrumental in plotting the assassination not only of Plehve in 1904 but of the Grand Duke Sergei in 1905 and of Dubasov, Governor-General of Moscow, in 1906, he simultaneously remained the best paid and most valued secret agent of the *Okhrana*.

His double life was symptomatic of the fantastic world he lived in. The drawn battle between the Tsarist state and the revolutionary anarchists was little less deadly than the rivalries within each of these bodies. State officials were willing to see their rivals assassinated and their policies discredited by terrorist outrages. Frequent atrocities increased the importance of the *Okhrana*. A police spy against whom suspicion might be directed by one set of officials could find patronage in another set. Official intrigue, time-serving, and opportunism taxed the wits of vested authority quite as much as its declared enemies did. And against these tangled lines of a corrupt officialdom stood the equally tangled loyalties and intrigues within the revolutionary circles themselves, riddled by sectarian careerism and rivalries through which a conspirator like Azeff might pick his way if he possessed a sufficient genius for duplicity. The situation was as typical of the deadly world of Tsarist politics as it was later to become of Soviet and Praesidium machinations; and it took the stubborn persistence of V. L. Burtzeff, editor of the revolutionary historical review *Byloye (The Past)*, to track Azeff's treachery down by extracting the truth about it from a disappointed ex-director of the Police Department, Lopuhin, and exposing the sordid case in the pages of his journal. Whereupon Azeff, his dual standing as terrorist and spy shattered, had to flee Russia and go into hiding in Germany, where he lived incognito on a false passport as an apparently respectable citizen and member of the Berlin Stock Exchange in the company of his mistress Madame N—— (known also as "La Bella Heddy de Hero"), until, to his horror, he was arrested in 1914 by the German authorities as "a dangerous revolutionary, anarchist, and terrorist, who, according to the international police conventions, was to be handed over to the Russian authorities at the end of the War." He was thrown into the Moabit Prison, but was released on the outbreak of the Bolshevik Revolution in 1917, was given a minor post in the German Ministry of Foreign Affairs, and died in Berlin in 1918. His onetime notoriety was to become obscured after his death by a proliferation of men of his type among the spies, double agents, and *intrigueurs* of our time, but during his life his name became a legend and Azeff himself a classic model of political duplicity.

It is not to be assumed that Conrad took the career of Azeff as a model for his story of Razumov. The two characters are quite different. But there is a strong possibility that Conrad followed Burtzeff's exposure of Azeff while he was writing his novel. It took place in 1908 while *Under Western Eyes* was in its first stages; it became headlined in the news of the day; it had a direct connection with the Plehve murder of 1904 which Conrad explicitly incorporated into his story; and before the novel was finished it had already become the subject of learned scholarship in France and Germany. And Conrad had already fixed upon the police spy and *agent provocateur* as a radical symptom of the whole sinister machinery of European corruption and Russian duplicity. The hero of *The Secret Agent,* Mr. Verloc, was precisely such a character in the squalid circles of London anarchist life and activity, simultaneously employed by a foreign embassy (unspecified but obviously Russian) to foment public outrages among his confederates, and accepted as a fellow conspirator by the gang he harbored in the back room of his shop in Soho. A similar type appears in the police agent Servin of the story "The Informer," whose exposure brings confusion to all his confederates in the house they have used as their headquarters in Hermione Street, London. There is also the different but related figure of the anarchist victim in Paul, the modest workingman engineer in the story called "An Anarchist," who becomes ruined as much by his exploiting radical friends as by the police machinery of Paris. As Henry James, in *The Princess Casamassima,* shows his hero Hyacinth Robinson becoming fatally involved in the anarchist machinations of Paul Muniment, of the ambiguous dilettante-radical Princess, and of the great mastermind Hoffendahl, so Conrad shows both his squalid Verloc and his high-minded Razumov trapped by the treacheries and furtive guilt into which the dupe or the willing self-deceiver falls when he trafficks with the evil genius of despotism or anarchy.

IV

But Conrad, in treating this subject, unquestionably felt the force of it more intimately and personally than James could have felt it. The subject was part of his life and memory; it had conditioned his experience from his childhood; and no distance he put between himself and the country of his birth or the empire that occupied it could possibly have effaced his memory of them. Politics, nationalism. the forces of imperialism and rebellion, were the first and deepest part of his inheritance; and few novelists in English—perhaps none—could have brought a more tenacious sense of those forces to their work and art.

He was a Pole, born in the Russian-occupied Poland of 1857 as the son of one of the most spirited participants in the Polish National Committee, and with a profound fear of Russian autocratic power in his blood. Three of his uncles had been killed or exiled during the Polish rising against Russia in the 1860's, and his father, Apollo Naleçz Korzeniowski, poet, translator, patriot, and member of the "Red" or extremist wing of the Polish cause, had been arrested by the Russian authorities in 1861 for his part in the illegal National Committee and in framing its seditious mandate against the occupying powers. With his wife Ewelina Bobrowska, named in the penal document as his fellow exile, he was sentenced to deportation in a remote province of Russia, the Government Vologda. Their five year old son accompanied them into this exile in May 1862. Both of Conrad's parents later died as a result of their hardships soon after their return to Poland—the mother in 1865, the father in 1869—leaving Conrad an orphan at the age of eleven, bereft of his immediate family by the repressive hostility of the Tsarist autocracy. The stamp of that tragedy was never effaced from his mind or emotion.

Thus Conrad brought into his early manhood two strains of his native inheritance—the patriotic and nationalistic ardor of his father's nature and the more conservative "land-tilling gentry" temper of his mother's people, the Bobrowskis. And while he was to become confirmed in the conservative leanings of his mother's family, now represented by his uncle Tadeusz Bobrowski who soon took over the guardianship of the young Conrad, he carried into his mature life a divided allegiance. One side of his nature was ardent, excitable, strenuous, adventurous, self-willed, and haunted by the memory of his father's and his country's dedication—it was the side that led to his first youthful ventures of bravado, Carlist enthusiasm, amateur seamanship, and reckless living in France and Spain between 1874 and 1878. The other side of his character was incurably committed to caution and doubt, a somber pessimism, fearing violence, fanaticism, anarchy, and Slavic instability, all of them symptoms of the autocratic or revolutionary extremism which both Russia and the Polish nationalist enthusiasm came to represent in his mind, and which eventually led him to seek his future in western Europe and finally in the "sanity and method" of England and her Merchant Service. "The obligation of absolute fairness" which he claimed for the writing of *Under Western Eyes* was, as he said in his "Author's Note" to the novel, "imposed on me historically and hereditarily, by the peculiar experience of race and family. . . . I had never been called before to a greater effort of detachment: detachment from all passions, prejudices, and even from personal memories." Those passions and prejudices were personally present in his formative years in the characters of his father and uncle. Apollo Korzeniowski and Tadeusz Bobrowski conditioned in him a moral character whose divided temper and conflicts of emotion were to remain with him for life.

When Razumov, in *Under Western Eyes*, finds himself caught in the trap of Haldin's act of violence and of his own betrayal of the man who came to him for help, he writes certain lines on a sheet of paper and impales them on his bedroom wall with his penknife. They describe the antagonism of forces which Conrad knew in his own history and define the reaction to which his deep-seated historical pessimism finally compelled him:

> History not Theory.
> Patriotism not Internationalism.
> Evolution not Revolution.
> Direction not Destruction.
> Unity not Disruption.

When he spoke of the novel in 1920 Conrad confessed that his "greatest anxiety" in writing it had been "to strike and sustain the note of scrupulous impartiality," and to obey his "primary conviction that truth alone is the justification of any fiction which makes the least claim to the quality of art or may hope to take its place in the culture of men and women of its time." He had claimed that justification for his work from its beginnings: the argument is expressed in the first two statements he wrote on his craft, his prefaces to *Almayer's Folly* in 1895 and to *The Nigger of the "Narcissus"* in 1897. But whatever the tests he had met, whatever the strains he had suffered, in writing his other books, they could hardly have equaled in emotional and intimate immediacy the challenge he faced when he wrote *Under Western Eyes*. The fear or suspicion of Russia he expressed in his letters; the fear of revolutionary zealotry he felt in his blood; the distrust with which he regarded political extremism or racial mysticism, whether Russian or Polish; his cautious view of all such excesses in thought or action—these were now subjected to the test of an aesthetic or moral justice more demanding than any he had yet confronted. He must have felt himself under the scrutiny of a judicious criticism in every line he wrote. In 1920 his final judgment on the novel and on the modern Russian history to which it refers—he is now writing three years after the Bolshevik revolution of 1917—was emphatic:

> The ferocity and imbecility of an autocratic rule rejecting all legality and in fact basing itself upon complete moral anarchism provokes the no less imbecile and atrocious answer of a purely Utopian revolutionism encompassing destruction by the first means to hand, in the strange conviction that a fundamental change of hearts must follow the downfall of any given human institutions. These people are unable to see that all they can effect is merely a change of names. The oppressors and the oppressed are all Russians together; and the world is brought once more face to face with the truth of the saying that the tiger cannot change his stripes nor the leopard his spots.

This is the Conrad who speaks in his own person, and in the simplified language of argument. When he wrote as a novelist he had another kind of truth to contend with, and his artist's doctrine of "the highest kind of justice to the visible universe" fell under the demands of a severer conscience, a more complex intelligence. It is these that give *Under Western Eyes* its moral and dramatic quality, its Conradian dimension. If there remain for some readers of the novel evidences of a prejudice that mars the ultimate or abstract justice of the tale, there can be no question that his consciousness of that prejudice is as intense in its pages as his struggle to redress it. One of Conrad's recent critics, Miss M. C. Bradbrook, writing in 1941, said that "No wonder the book was unpopular in 1911. It might have been equally unpopular in 1931, but at the moment its premises are familiar." [12] The remark has become even more to the point in the decades that have followed. And as for the charge that Conrad harbored an unbalanced "Russophobia," a comment E. M. Forster once made on him is also relevant:

> Conrad's passions are intelligible and frank: having lived thus, thus he feels, and it is as idle to regret his account of Russians as it would be to regret Dostoevsky's account of Poles in *The Brothers Karamazov*. A philosopher would moderate his transports, or attempt to correlate them. Conrad isn't that type: he claims the right to be unreasonable when he or those whom he respects have suffered.[13]

The effort to moderate or correlate exists in the book; Conrad himself boasted of it. But he was, in the end, writing a novel, not a treatise in scientific or historical impersonality. Had his moderation fully succeeded, he would not have achieved the book he wrote.

What he called a "senseless desperation provoked by senseless tyranny" epitomized for Conrad the Russian danger and its effects on the Polish cause that had led him to leave Poland in 1874 and to identify his personal fate with the West. Yet his divided allegiance between East and West, between the Slavic world and the European or English, remains basic to his tale and it was referred to explicitly when he decided on what he called its "awkward title." It became his special purpose to hold in double focus two views of the Russian fate—that of the Russians themselves (and the respect the book first won in Russia perhaps testifies sufficiently to his success on this score) and that of their alien observers who represent the standards of Western life. This alone, quite apart from its difficult moral theme, gives the work its characteristic Conradian complexity. It also gives it what no Russian novelist—except possibly a Turgenev or Tolstoy in the nineteenth century or a Pasternak in the twentieth—would be likely to give it: a quality of intense personal commitment combined with a severe discipline in moral and humanistic objectivity. A distinguished critic to whom I once gave the book remarked, after expressing some impatience with its method and construction, that its handling of Russians ("about whom," he allowed, Conrad "says many things that seem to me true and penetrating") has "a little the second-hand quality of most sketching of national types by

---

[12] M. C. Bradbrook, *Joseph Conrad: Poland's English Genius* (1941), p. 9.
[13] E. M. Forster, "Joseph Conrad: A Note," in *Abinger Harvest* (1936), p. 136. This "note" is a review of Conrad's *Notes on Life and Letters* (1921), but it has a wider relevance to his work, and it includes some essential statements on Conrad and his art.

foreigners." "Isn't it," he asked, "much more satisfactory to read *The Possessed* or *Crime and Punishment?*" Possibly in the interests of a final authority it is. Conrad, as Thomas Mann once said, "is far from being the size of Dostoevsky"; and it is both impossible and unnecessary to read *Under Western Eyes* in the expectation of finding another Dostoevsky novel in it, whatever its links with the Dostoevskian art and subject matter. But Mann added that though Conrad's "objectivity may seem cool," it is informed by "a passion—a passion for freedom," the "refusal of a very much engaged intelligence to hang miserably in the air between contraries." [14] The expression of such a passion is never possible in a wholly engaged participant or an undivided nationalist. And a foreigner may have a contribution of importance to make in writing about another nationality. His outsider's point of vantage, if sufficiently informed by knowledge and sympathy, makes it possible for him to add something of importance, in critical insight and judgment, to a native tradition. Stendhal made such a contribution in writing about Italians, James in writing about the English and the French, Forster in writing about India, Lawrence in writing about Mexico or Australia, Orwell and Koestler in writing about the Burmese and the Russians. Conrad, divided between a reasonable fear of tyranny or fanaticism and the demands of the justice to which his art committed him, achieved in *Under Western Eyes* what is possibly the most searching portrayal of Russian character and history that has yet been arrived at in a non-Russian novel. Perhaps only one other in the past fifty years—*Darkness at Noon*—can be said to rival it. Its justice is more than a matter of the detachment or impartiality he claimed for it. It is a matter of the charity and compassion that have their origins in sympathy and suffering.

V

But the book he wrote is, of course, more than a document on Russian character or history; more than an exemplum of his conviction that "the old despotism and the new Utopianism are complementary forms of moral anarchy." It is a novel whose subject and artistry are continuous with his other work; and the reader of *Lord Jim, Nostromo, Heart of Darkness,* "The Secret Sharer," and *Victory* will soon realize that *Under Western Eyes* offers yet another version of the hero and moral drama that Conrad made his own. In fact, the novel shows his theme and method in essence, as well as the ordeal of doubt and creative intensity that had, by the time he wrote it, become habitual with him.

---

[14] Thomas Mann, "Vorwort zu Joseph Conrads Roman *Der Geheimagent*," a preface he wrote for the German translation of *The Secret Agent*, included in *Die Forderung des Tages* (1930), pp. 325-40; translated by H. T. Lowe-Porter in *Past Masters and Other Papers* by Thomas Mann (1933), pp. 231-47, here 238, 246-47.

On January 6, 1908, he wrote a letter to his friend Galsworthy in which he described his first steps in the writing of his manuscript:

> *"Et le misérable écrivait toujours."*
> He is writing now a story the title of which is *Razumov*. Isn't it expressive? I think that I am trying to capture the very soul of things Russian,— *Cosas de Russia*. It is not an easy work but it may be rather good when it's done. . . .
> Listen to the theme. The Student Razumov (a natural son of a Prince K.) gives up secretly to the police his fellow student, Haldin, who seeks refuge in his rooms after committing a political crime (supposed to be the murder of de Plehve). First movement in St. Petersburg. (Haldin is hanged, of course.)
> 2d in Genève. The Student Razumov meeting abroad the mother and sister of Haldin falls in love with that last, marries her, and, after a time, confesses to her the part he played in the arrest of her brother.
> The psychological developments leading to Razumov's betrayal of Haldin, to the confession of the fact to his wife and to the death of these people (brought about mainly by the resemblance of their child to the late Haldin), form the real subject of the story.
> And perhaps no magazine will touch it. . . . Ah! my dear, you don't know what an inspiration-killing anxiety it is to think: "Is it saleable?" There's nothing more cruel than to be caught between one's impulse, one's act, and that question, which for me simply is a question of life and death. There are moments when the mere fear sweeps my head clean of every thought. It is agonizing,—no less. And,—you know,—that pressure grows from day to day instead of getting less.
> But I had to write it. I had to get away from *Chance,* with which I was making no serious progress.[15]

Two years later, on December 23, 1909, we find him still laboring at the book and writing to Norman Douglas:

> The novel hangs on the last 12,000 words, but there's neither inspiration nor hope in my work. It's mere hard labour for life—with this difference, that the life convict is at any rate out of harm's way—and may consider the account with his conscience closed; and this is not the case with me. I envy the serene fate and the comparative honesty of the gentlemen in gray who live in Dartmoor. I do really, I am not half as decent or half as useful. . . . All the same, don't give me up in your thoughts entirely. In the light of a "tormented spirit" I am not to be altogether despised.

It was another month before the manuscript was finished and almost two years before the novel reached book form, not under the title Conrad gave to Galsworthy but as *Under Western Eyes*—a change which, in indicating a shift of the post of observation from the hero to a disinterested spectator (the old English teacher of languages in Geneva who tells the

<hr>

[15] As given in *Joseph Conrad: Life and Letters,* by G. Jean-Aubry (1927), Vol. II, pp. 64-65. The letter following, to Norman Douglas, is in Vol. II, p. 105.

story, partly from his own witness of it but largely from evidence gained from other characters or from Razumov's secret diary) and to a critical attitude alien and largely incomprehensible to the Russian, tells much about the narrative method Conrad had by this time made his own and outside of which he seldom trusted himself to work. It was, of course, more than a method. It was a temperamental necessity and compulsion. When Henry James described Conrad as "a votary of the way to do a thing that shall make it undergo most doing," and his method as "a prolonged hovering flight of the subjective over the outstretched ground of the case exposed," [16] he put his finger on the radical factors that operate throughout Conrad's art at its best—its exhaustively empirical workmanship, the subjective commitment of its imagination, its intensity of scrutiny and analysis, and the origins of these in personal conditions of temperament and sympathetic intimacy that stamp it from beginning to end. If these factors sometimes betrayed him into an excessive identification of his emotion with his material in his weaker work, and if they produced at times an exaggerated solicitation of effect in his language and argument, their necessity to him is clear and their part in his originality is unquestionable. They, even more than his dramatic subjects, are the essential *donnée* of his work. Without them it would lack both its occasional weakness of control and its radical power.

Conrad's letter to Galsworthy shows that he first conceived the story in strongly active terms, embodied in physical encounters and external conflict of an almost melodramatic tendency. But what had already happened in the writing of *An Outcast of the Islands, Lord Jim,* and *Nostromo,* and what was to happen again in *The Rescue* and *The Rover,* happened in this case. The title was not the only thing that was changed. The plot was also transformed. Razumov and Nathalie Haldin never marry. They never have a child who resembles the dead Haldin and thus "brings about" the "death of these people." And the "psychological developments" which Conrad planned as leading to the marriage and these deaths were altered to take a different direction. As in so many of his tales, the more Conrad pondered his theme, the more he came to grips with the shaping of it, the less he was able to adhere to an objective dramatization of it. What he retained was his initial episode—the assassination of Plehve by Haldin; Haldin's seeking refuge with Razumov; Razumov's betrayal of that trust to Prince K—— and General T——; Haldin's arrest and execution; and then the trap of official suspicion snapping down on Razumov when, resolving "to retire" into his solitude and win the University's prize that will rescue his life from its lonely nonentity, he finds his illusion of safety suddenly shattered by Councillor Mikulin's quiet and ominous question: "Where to?"

[16] Henry James, "The New Novel, 1914," in *Notes on Novelists* (1914), pp. 314-61, here pp. 345, 348. The novel under discussion is *Chance,* Conrad's latest book at the moment

On that question the novel pauses and hangs. By the time Razumov reappears in Part II, we see what the question means. "Isolation and conscience are the dominant motifs in the novels of Conrad": the fact has been remarked by Mr. Pritchett and every attentive reader of the books. Razumov is to enact a drama that has already been played by Lord Jim, by both Kurtz and Marlow in *Heart of Darkness,* by Decoud, Dr. Monygham, and Nostromo himself in *Nostromo,* by the young ship captain in "The Secret Sharer"; and it will be enacted again by Flora de Barral and Captain Anthony in *Chance,* by Axel Heyst in *Victory,* and by Tom Lingard in *The Rescue.* Geneva, where, unknown to the Russians among whom he is accepted as a fellow revolutionary and dedicated spirit, Razumov comes as a spy for Mikulin, becomes the stage for his test of conscience. There his ordeal of guilt, self-condemnation, and expiation will, by driving him to confession, first to Nathalie Haldin and then publicly to the revolutionists, and to the virtually suicidal disclosure of his part in Haldin's death, save him from the damnation of living his lie and his treachery.

In that drama of conscience all the exiles will play their parts.[17] Their roles in Razumov's ordeal—at times so protractedly digressive, sometimes tangential or trivial, oftener unconscious, trusting, or confident—will embody and objectify the agonized movement of his mind from passivity to action, from a benumbed fatalism to expiatory truth. The fatuous philosophical pretensions of Peter Ivanovitch, the seedy dilettantism of Madame de S——, the devoted ardor of Sophia Antonovna, the dedicated zeal of Laspara, the cowed humility of Tekla, the anthropoid brutality of Nikita—all these lenses of delusion, vanity, self-deception, cruelty, and devotion in the cause will turn and refract the light of truth or falsehood on Razumov's agony of mind and conscience. All of them will serve to objectify or "transfer" the lie his treachery toward Haldin, his deception of Nathalie, and the unrealized egotism of his secret self have trapped him

---

[17] The novel offers a gallery of types and characters familiar in the literature and history of Russian life and politics, and comparisons can be made with those in the novels of Turgenev, Dostoevsky, Tolstoy, and in the biographies of revolutionary leaders. The reader of *Under Western Eyes* will find special interest in the literature of the Russian exiles, notably the memoirs of Alexander Herzen (*My Life and Thoughts*), Prince Peter Kropotkin (*Memoirs of a Revolutionist*), Stepniak (*Underground Russia, The Russian Storm Cloud,* and *The Career of a Nihilist*), as well as accounts of Bakunin and Ogarev. Especially relevant among books in English are Edward Hallett Carr's excellent account of *The Romantic Exiles* (1933) and his *Michael Bakunin* (1937), Edmund Wilson's *To the Finland Station* (1940), and George Woodcock's and Ivan Avakumovic's biography of Kropotkin, *The Anarchist Prince* (1950); there are numerous other accounts of Russian, anarchist, and communist activity in the past hundred years. Conrad's Peter Ivanovitch (obviously derived from Bakunin, with possible suggestions of the later Tolstoy), Madame de S——, Tekla, Laspara and his daughters, Yakovlitch, Ziemianitch, Kostia, Sophia Antonovna, etc., suggest their analogies in this literature and place the novel in a large context of historical and literary characters.

into living. They will reveal to him the "everlasting black hole of his life" into which, like the hero of *Lord Jim,* his ignorance or failure in moral courage forced him to jump. They will take him, step by step, on his downward journey into the "destructive element" of moral reality which, by destroying him, may finally save him. But most of all he will be condemned and saved by Nathalie herself. Her pure and credulous spirit—one of Conrad's exceptional successes among his portrayals of women—will drive him to self-condemnation and confession, to the test of honor that at last breaks and redeems him.

Razumov is what the Conradian hero invariably is: a solitary. He is the man designed by nature or circumstance to live not by the law of his kind but by self-law. Like Willems, Kurtz, Tuan Jim, Nostromo, Decoud, and Heyst, he is Conrad's version of the man—descendant of the self-willed heroes of Balzac, Stendhal, Turgenev, Dostoevsky, and Melville, and brother to those of Mann or Gide—who chooses or is compelled to live a life of egoistic self-regard or compulsive self-assertion: the existence *pour soi* or the fate of estrangement and isolation. As we are later told of Heyst, confirmed in his father's nihilism by the treachery he has encountered in human society, that "not a single soul belonging to him lived anywhere on earth . . . he was alone on the bank of the stream. In his pride he determined not to enter it"; so we are told of Razumov that "he was as lonely in the world as a man swimming in the deep sea. . . . He had nothing. He had not even a moral refuge—the refuge of confidence." And on the heels of that statement comes another no less terrifying: "Who knows what true loneliness is—not the conventional word but the naked terror? To the lonely themselves it wears a mask. The most miserable outcast hugs some memory or some illusion. . . . No human being could bear a steady view of moral solitude without going mad."

When, in one of the novel's greatest scenes, Razumov walks the wintry night streets of St. Petersburg, furious that Haldin has suddenly erupted into his lonely life of high resolve and secret ambition with his crime and his appeal, he stamps his foot in desperation upon the snow-sheeted ground, suddenly to discover that he has stamped the earth of Russia herself, "inanimate, cold, inert, like a sullen and tragic mother hiding her face under a winding-sheet—his native soil!—his very own—without a fireside, without a hearth!" He looks upward and "as if by a miracle" he sees "above his head the clear black sky of the northern winter, decorated with the sumptuous fires of the stars." He receives "an almost physical impression of endless space and of countless millions," of "an inheritance of space and numbers." His pathetic solitude and desperate egoism find refuge in the "sacred inertia" of the Russian earth, with its "guarantee of duration, of safety, while the travail of maturing destiny went on—a work not of revolutions with their passionate levity of action and their shifting impulses—but of peace." Without warning he finds himself standing "on the point of conversion"—"fascinated by its approach, by its overpowering logic." "Don't touch it," a voice cries within him, and another says "Haldin means disruption." And "like other Russians before him, Razumov, in conflict with himself, felt the touch of grace upon his forehead." But cutting across that sudden benediction there comes one of Conrad's most acute comments: "a train of thought is never false. The falsehead lies deep in the necessities of existence, in secret fears and half-formed ambitions, in the secret confidence combined with a secret mistrust of ourselves, in the love of hope and the dread of uncertain days." And presently, in the struggle to rationalize his confused impulses of treachery and self-justification, Razumov articulates another and even deadlier truth: "All a man can betray is his conscience." He will betray Haldin too, and later he will carry his deception to Geneva and the trusting soul of Nathalie; but he will be condemned to discover that it is the greater betrayal that tracks him down.

Though he does not yet know it, his existence has become committed to that implacable test of truth—committed by what Gide has called those fatal acts or unconscious treacheries for which "a whole lifetime, afterward, is not enough to give them the lie and to efface their mark." The novel becomes a drama of their consequences. There is no escape from them. As we watch the unfolding of Razumov's fate in Geneva— watch it through the shifting focus of the Russian eyes and the Western; follow it through Razumov's encounters with all the disclosures of delusion, conceit, sincerity, or honor in the characters who surround him; trace it through the splendidly imaged scenes that shift from the Haldin apartment to the Château Borel, from the promenade of the Bastions to Rousseau's island in the lake, from Razumov's tormented colloquies with Nathalie and the other exiles to his bitter vigils in the Rue de Carouge or on the bridge beneath which the water, "violent and deep," rushes headlong in "its vertiginous rapidity, its terrible force"—we see where that fate is leading him. It is carrying him remorselessly to the moment when his confession will break through his torment in the white boxed glare of the Haldin vestibule, thence into the storm-lashed streets of Geneva where the rain will wash him clean, and thus to Laspara's house where his guilt is made public and Nikita's brutal fist deafens him forever.

The prolonged attenuation and indirection of Conrad's narrative seems as if designed to put the reader's senses on the rack as much as Razumov's. The art and method of Conrad's work had by this time arrived at this almost excruciating refinement of sensory and moral impressionism, this extreme elaboration of the *progression d'effet*. But the process is continuously relieved and condensed in superb moments of imagery and action—moments that mount toward the novel's shattering climax and thus toward its bitter conclusion, poised between pathos and irony. The humanity of Conrad's pessimism insists on both. Razumov, deafened and crippled, lies at last in Russia, tended by the faithful Tekla and broken

to the law of "unavoidable solidarity" which all of Conrad's estranged
souls must finally sense or recognize—"the solidarity in mysterious origin,
in toil, in joy, in hope, in uncertain fate, which binds men to each other
and all mankind to the visible earth." Nathalie too returns to Russia to
carry her faith into the ominous future of her country and the end that
awaits her there. The truth that wrecked his life and the hope that sustains hers both offer the coldest of comforts to those who ask "from men
faith, honour, fidelity to truth in themselves and others." But there is
no other comfort possible—perhaps no comfort at all except in that
"resignation, not mystic, not detached, but . . . open-eyed, conscious, and
informed by love," which Conrad believed to be "the only one of our
feelings for which it is impossible to become a sham." The "solidarity"
he so insistently invoked as a mode of moral salvation offered little but
this grim consolation to his skepticism; but that much it did offer, and
on that principle of trust and sincerity he staked his personal and
aesthetic faith. A more certain confidence lies with such characters as
Sophia Antonovna and Peter Ivanovitch, and it is for her stubborn faith
and his triumphant self-conceit that the novel's final touch of irony is
reserved. "There are," said Conrad in *Typhoon,* "on sea and on land
such men thus fortunate—or thus disdained by destiny or by the sea."

VI

In *Under Western Eyes* Conrad wrote a political novel which today,
half a century after its publication, still stands as pre-eminent of its kind
in English fiction and calls for a rank in European fiction as well. The
literary genre of the political novel admits a large variety of content and
method, and has perhaps never been very clearly defined; but Conrad's
book is recognizably a descendant of the type classically established by
Stendhal, Turgenev, Dostoevsky, and James, and prophetic, as much
through its acumen of historical insight as through the accident of the
contemporary events it foreshadowed, of the novels that were to come
after it from writers like Malraux, Silone, Sartre, Koestler, Camus, Orwell, and Pasternak. Its continuing and increasing relevance to the twentieth century takes on the force of a compensation for the neglect to which
it was treated on its first appearance in 1911. Its "precarious hold on life,"
for Conrad always a lurking fear in his struggles as a novelist, has been
proved mistaken by the events and conflicts of our time. It has declared its
value as a drama of that "pursuit of happiness by means lawful and unlawful, through resignation or revolt," which he once defined as "the
only theme that can be legitimately developed by the novelist who is the
chronicler of the adventures of mankind amongst the dangers of the king-
dom of the earth."

It forms a judgment on modern history and on the morality of political
actions; and on this score it constitutes, even more specifically than *No-*

stromo or *The Secret Agent,* his commitment to a position on the future of Europe and the West. What that position came to be for Conrad involves a consideration of his intelligence not only as a man of historical vision but as a Pole and an exile from Poland, whose life and thought were conditioned by one of the most complex political and nationalistic situations of his age. He was thus involved "antecedent to choice," long before he became a novelist. But it was in his novels more than in his practical conduct or expressed political convictions that he had to meet the test of what his inherited situation imposed on him as a political thinker and critic of history. *Under Western Eyes* necessarily became in his hands something more than a political argument, tract, or parable. It became a story of the soul of man under tyranny and rebellion, the drama of a character subjected to the most searching tests of challenge, moral probity, and self-knowledge to which the human spirit can be exposed. It is finally in this drama that the book achieves its essential strength as well as its continuity with Conrad's work as a whole. The book remains a novel, a work of human and moral relevance, well after its specific political reference is taken into account. But this is not to minimize the urgency of that reference to Conrad when he created the book, or to relegate to an incidental role the problem he faced when he undertook to dramatize its Russian (and by extension its European) subject—*cosas de Russia.*

That problem—granting his prejudice and inherited emotion regarding Russia—was less one of the "impartiality" to which he addressed himself than of an engagement in the Russian fate and drama: of entering that drama not as a critic or observer—a man of "Western eyes"—but as a participant and sharer in the Russian destiny. Had he failed to penetrate his subject in this way, his novel would have failed in substance as much as in art. But in spite of his use of the old English professor as his narrator, with all its attendant emphasis on incomprehension and bafflement before the riddle of Russian character and psychology, the book finds its strength in its penetration of the riddle, its distributed insight, and its identification with its characters and their fate. Conrad, like any valid novelist, had to become in some sense a Russian to write the book, and it became his paradox as the artist of his subject to convert his Polish life and inheritance into a means of that imaginative and moral authority.

We may agree with him when he said that he "had never been called before to a greater effort of detachment: detachment from all passions, prejudices and even from personal memories." The effort was doubtless acute to the point of paralyzing his mind and hand. But it is not detachment that finally counts in the strength the novel achieves. It is sympathy, compassion, participation, insight. In these the novel met its test, and Conrad himself one of the most severe personal and aesthetic tests of his career.

It would not have required Conrad's personal temper, so radically divided between a skeptical intellect and an imperative human feeling, between moral pessimism and a deep-seated racial and political emotion, to make that test a complex one. This was a conflict that existed in all his treatments of history.[18] Nor would it have required the presence in his immediate family of a collision between his father's romantic and patriotic idealism and his uncle's conservative caution to bring the divided mind of Polish nationalism home to him in an intimate form—though that collision was one of the decisive factors in the formation of his character. The conflict was an immediate personal condition of his youth, but the division was a larger fact in the mind and culture of his people. Poland, possibly more consciously and acutely than the other nations of central Europe, is a traditional ground of the conflict. East and West, Slavophilism and "Westernism," a precarious location between the rival powers of Russia and Germany, an aristocratic and Catholic tradition joined with democratic humanism and liberal impulse, a strong conviction of a mystical and religious national destiny at grips with a polity of ethnic necessity and pragmatic compromise—these factors have for three centuries formed the condition of Poland's physical and historic entity, and they continue to show themselves in the form of a major European crisis down to the present moment.

When Conrad argued the cause of Poland and "Polonism" in his essays at the time of the First World War he defined his country as "the offspring of the West," as "universal" in its "sentimental attitude towards the Western Powers," as Latin, Western, and "humanistically" European in its roots, as a "racial unity" compressed between "Prussian Germanism on one side and the Russian Slavonism on the other," toward the first of which it felt "nothing but hatred," and toward the second "not so much hatred as a complete and ineradicable incompatibility." These have been the claims of Polish nationalism at various points of its modern history, and they remain its claims among the Western councils today; but the

---

[18] The larger outlines of Conrad's view of history are discussed by the present writer in the introduction to a collection of nine *Tales of Heroes and History* by Joseph Conrad (Anchor Books, 1960), where these stories are related to Conrad's political novels as well as to his political ideas as they appear in his letters and essays. The latter include "Autocracy and War" (1905), "The Shock of War" (1915), "To Poland in Wartime" (1915), "Poland Revisited" (1916), "The Crime of Partition" (1919), and "A Note on the Polish Problem" (1916), all included in *Notes on Life and Letters* (1921).

The evolution of the political novel from Stendhal and Dostoevsky to the present has been traced by various writers in recent years—by, for one, Irving Howe in his study of *Politics and the Novel* (1957), which includes a chapter on "Conrad: Order and Anarchy." This is the most stimulating and suggestive recent study of the genre in its European and American scope. An early, but now very tentative and limited, treatment of the subject was Morris Speare's *The Political Novel: Its Development in England and America* (1924); other recent studies have been Joseph L. Blotner's *The Political Novel* (1955) and W. M. Frohock's *The Novel of Violence in America* (revised edition, 1957). There is a larger Continental literature on the subject; Albert Camus' *L'Homme révolté* is a notable example.

Polish situation has never been as simple as this. If its deprivation of independence and its partition among three imperial powers during the nineteenth century inflamed the cause of Polish nationalism to a pitch of passion and bred a *mystique* of cultural salvationism among its defenders, the opposite bent of self-criticism, ethnic necessity, and pragmatic compromise also existed. If "anti-Slavonism" and "Russophobia" had their adherents, so did the critical prudence that was induced by the need of survival among the powerful military oppressions that hedged the country in. The visionary Christian idealism—*"le messianisme polonais"* —of Mickiewicz, Malczewski, and the Polish romantics was reproved by realistic nationalists and historians: by, for one, the romantic poet Slowacki, whom Conrad's uncle Tadeusz Bobrowski once quoted to his nephew as having charged Poland with a morbid pride and persecutory bent: "a nation who consider ourselves great and misunderstood, the possessors of a greatness which others do not recognize and will never recognize." [19] Mystical dedication and realistic caution, the elation of a sacred martyrdom and the mortifications of political and military defeat—these formed the opposing elements of the Polish temper throughout its tragic ordeals of the nineteenth century; and they came to Conrad in the form of a direct challenge to his personal and political identity. He was not alone in contending with that challenge. It is one of the radical facts in the arguments of modern Polish intellectuals and cultural historians, and a primary feature of it is Poland's division between the claims of its Slavic and European elements. But to Conrad, in his exiled life and vulnerable conscience, the challenge came in a particularly disturbing and sensitive form. Reflecting a division within his own family, increasing as he matured in his own thought and sensibility, it exposed him to what the exile from a persecuted country is bound to feel—that he is open to the charge of deserting a native trust and inherited obligation.[20]

[19] The letter, of November 9, 1891 is given by Jean-Aubry in *Life and Letters,* Vol. I, pp. 147-48; the original text appears in "Listy Tadeusza Bobrowskiego do Conrada," ed. Jabłkowska, *Kwartalnik Neofilologiczny,* Vol. III, pp. 110-11. This and other Polish letters and documents by Conrad, his father, his uncle, and others are to appear in a book on *Joseph Conrad's Polish Background,* by Zdzislaw Najder, announced for publication by the Oxford University Press, London, in 1963, which will be the most complete collection of these materials and the only comprehensive one in English.

[20] The word "guilt," often used in studies of this aspect of Conrad's life and psychology, and encouraged by Joseph Morf's study of his "Polish heritage" of 1929, is a decided simplification of an elusive problem, though some element of "guilt," or at least of acute moral sensitiveness, certainly figured in Conrad's relations with Poland and his family. Several times in his career the problem impinged on him severely. It did so at the time of the First World War and can be sensed in the essays he wrote on the Polish cause at that time; they are listed here in footnote 18. An earlier episode occurred in 1899 when Vincent Lutosławski, following a visit to Conrad in England, defended his exile from Poland and his service to "the cause of Poland" abroad ("as loyally as those who stayed at home"), in an article on "The Emigration of the Talents" in the Polish journal *Kraj,* published in St. Petersburg (March 1899). This essay was answered vehemently by Eliza Orzeszkowa in the April issue, accusing Conrad and other

What this situation stimulated in Conrad—apart from any probing of his personal conscience to which he may have subjected himself or his sensitivity to the debates of his compatriots—was a profound sympathy with these divisions of mind or loyalty in other peoples: the men of his Eastern kingdoms in *An Outcast of the Islands, Lord Jim,* and *The Rescue,* the rival factions of Costaguana in *Nostromo,* even in the Russians whom he was bred to fear as Poland's traditional enemy and oppressor. When he expressed himself on Russia in his letters or essays it was invariably in terms of a convinced aversion, an open fear, or a contemptuous hostility. But it was part of his personal and Polish instinct, and most of all of his artist's intelligence, to know that Russia too was a sharer in the moral and political destiny of mankind; that its Slavic temper had a kinship with his own; and that what he and his people knew of moral and civil conflict had laid an even greater and more crushing burden on the Russian soul.

It was this burden that he had to deal with when he wrote *Under Western Eyes*—"this pitiful fate of a country held by an evil spell, suffering from an awful visitation for which the responsibility cannot be traced either to her sins or her follies." More portentously he could say of the Tsarist autocracy (again in his essay on "Autocracy and War" in 1905): "this dreaded and strange apparition, bristling with bayonets, armed with chains, hung over with holy images; that something not of this world, partaking of a ravenous ghoul, of a blind Djinn grown up from a cloud, and of the Old Man of the Sea," which "still faces us with its old stupidity, with its strange mystical arrogance,"—the "decrepit, old, hundred years old, spectre of Russia's might [that] still faces Europe from across the teeming graves of Russian people." He could, even at the point of turning his indictment to the rival "enemy" of Prussianism, quote with approval Bismarck's *"La Russie, c'est le néant"*—a *"Néant* which for so many years had remained hidden behind this phantom of invincible armies"; but, more than a *Néant* or "empty void," a "yawning chasm open between East and West: a bottomless abyss that has swallowed up every hope of mercy, every aspiration towards personal dignity, towards freedom, towards knowledge, every ennobling desire of the heart, every redeeming whisper of conscience." We know too little about Conrad's actual reading of Dostoevsky to connect his aversion to the Russian novelist with this contempt of the Russian evil, but his reaction

---

expatriates of desertion to more rewarding and lucrative fields, and supporting the protest of one of the journal's editors, Tadeusz Zuk-Skarszewski, in the March issue. This episode was dealt with by Jean-Aubry in his *Vie de Conrad* (1947; translated as *The Sea Dreamer,* 1957, pp. 237-38); by Jocelyn Baines in his book of 1960 (pp. 352-54); and at length by Józef Ujejski in his *O Konradzie Korzeniowskim* of 1936 (French translation as *Joseph Conrad,* 1939). An interesting speculation on the possible bearing of this episode on the writing of *Lord Jim* is given in an article by Eloise K. Hay, "*Lord Jim:* From Sketch to Novel," *Comparative Literature,* Vol. XII (Fall, 1960), pp. 289-309.

to *The Brothers Karamazov* when Edward Garnett sent him his wife's translation in 1912 put Dostoevsky down as an embodiment of all he despised or dreaded in the Russian mentality: "I don't know what D. stands for or reveals, but I do know that he is too Russian for me. It sounds like some fierce mouthings from prehistoric ages." [21] In Dostoevsky he evidently found in combination the elements he most feared in Russia and its history—its Panslavic messianism, its mystical illuminism, its contempt for subject peoples (Poland among them), its moral confusion and militant arrogance, its emotional excess and "convulsed terror-haunted" morbidity.[22]

But as if to restore a balance to this aversion he found in another Russian the virtue that indicts the Dostoevskian excess as emphatically as any indictment of his own. Inevitably that Russian was the one who most impressively embodied to the Western world the nobler soul and vision of his country—Turgenev. For Conrad it was Turgenev who created an art of "absolute sanity and the deepest sensibility, the clearest vision and the quickest responsiveness, penetrating insight and unfailing generosity of judgment, an exquisite perception of the visible world and an unerring instinct for the significant, for the essential in the life of men and women, the clearest mind, the warmest heart, the largest sympathy"; and whose characters were "human beings, fit to live, fit to suffer, fit to struggle, fit to win, fit to lose, in the endless and inspiring game of pursuing from day to day the ever-receding future"—"not strange beasts in a menagerie or damned souls knocking themselves to pieces in the stuffy

[21] The quotations above are from "Autocracy and War" in *Notes on Life and Letters* (1921), pp. 83-114. The letter to Garnett is given in *Life and Letters* (1927), Vol. II, p. 140, and in Garnett's *Letters from Conrad* (London, 1928), pp. 260-61 (under the date May 27, 1912). The question of Conrad's possible derivations from or relationship to Dostoevsky has been touched on by various writers during the past four decades. Richard Curle touched on it in his early study *Joseph Conrad* in 1914 and again in *The Last Twelve Years of Joseph Conrad* (1928), pp. 28-29 and elsewhere ("I have an idea that his real hatred for Dostoevsky was due to an appreciation of his power. . . . Dostoevsky represented to him the ultimate forces of confusion and insanity arrayed against all that he valued in civilization. He did not despise him as one despises a nonentity, he hated him as one might hate Lucifer and the forces of darkness."). Jocelyn Baines, in his *Joseph Conrad* (1960), has noted comparisons between *Under Western Eyes* and *Crime and Punishment,* including some verbal similarities, pp. 360-61, 370-71 ("It seems almost as if *Under Western Eyes* were a challenge to Dostoevsky on his own ground."). There are comparisons in Gustav Morf's *The Polish Heritage of Joseph Conrad,* numerous perceptive insights in Albert Guerard's *Conrad the Novelist* (1958), and other comments in the work of Polish scholars. Others appear in Eloise K. Hay's Radcliffe dissertation of 1961; and one of the earlier treatments of the problem was written by Henri Daniel-Rops in his essay on Conrad in his *Carte d'Europe* (Paris, 1928).

[22] Those concerned with Conrad's hostility to Russia may find interest in the condemnations of another vehement critic and accuser of Russia and the Russians, Karl Marx. Marx's letters on Russia at the time of the Crimean War (1853-56), written for the *New York Tribune,* have recently been collected as *Marx vs. Russia* (New York: Ungar, 1962).

darkness of mystical contradictions." The humane justice of Turgenev
stood, among Conrad's models in his craft, as an example of the novelist's art at its finest—of its power to bring "all [its] problems and characters to the test of love." But whatever Conrad's repugnance or disclaim-
ers, the "turmoil and darkness" of Dostoevsky's vision evidently had as
much to say to the Pole's experience of excess and contradiction as
Turgenev's classic balance did; and if a novel like *Under Western Eyes*
is to be referred to a Russian precedent, it is as much to that of the
"terror-haunted" Dostoevsky as to that of the "impartial lover of *all*
his countrymen." [23]

It refers inevitably to both precedents, for it combines with its sense
of human evil and corruption the necessity of sympathy—sympathy
"with common mortals, no matter where they live," with the "multitude
of the bewildered, the simple, and the voiceless"—which Conrad defined
as the basis of the moral community to which all valid art is dedicated
and of which he made a principle whenever he wrote his credo as a
novelist. But an abstract or generalized sympathy, the "malady of the
quotidian," is hardly possible for a realist or moral critic. When he came
to write his drama of Russia Conrad put himself to the test of reconcil-
ing his effort at sympathy ("impartiality") with a realistic view of what
the Russian threat to Europe involved. That view required both the
practical judgment of a political realist and the humane objectivity of
a historical intelligence. Being by nature a novelist and moral dramatist,
he could fill neither of these offices—that of the scientific politician or
that of the philosophic historian—with systematic logic or competence;
and it has been possible for some critics to see in him a case of evasion or
ambiguity in both these roles.[24] His real ground lay between them. For
the extremes of the forces at work in the Russia he depicts—Tsarist
tyranny and revolutionary brutality or fanaticism—he declares an equal
indictment. It is in the sincere and distraught "souls," the idealists,
dreamers, or characters of dedicated conscience, caught between these
evils, that he establishes his true moral bearings and the ground of his
most searching insight. And the circumstance that he brought to bear on
these his personal experience of historical and political fact is what
gives his novel its actuality, its dialectic substance, and its weight as a
document on the crisis of his age.

The factor of "contradiction" which repelled Conrad in Dostoevsky
was in truth a factor in his own sensibility and intelligence, rooted there
fully as "historically and hereditarily, by the peculiar experience of race

---

[23] Conrad's essay on Turgenev, his single formal writing on a Russian author, was
written as an introduction to Edward Garnett's *Turgenev: A Study* in 1917. It is included in *Notes on Life and Letters* (1921), pp. 45-48.

[24] One of the perceptive studies of this problem appears in two essays by G. H. Ban-
tock: "The Two 'Moralities' of Joseph Conrad," *Essays in Criticism*, April 1953, pp. 125-
42; and "Conrad and Politics," *English Literary History*, June 1958, pp. 122-36.

and family," as any "obligation of absolute fairness" he professed. To
turn to evidences of it in his letters or personal statements is to find that
he was as subject to conflicts of skepticism and partisan passion as any of
the characters he created in his political novels. To Cunninghame
Graham and his other Socialist friends in the nineties, as to his old
Polish friend Spiridion Kliszczewski earlier, he could express a pessimism
on political reforms or social programs amounting to a complete cynicism.[25] It was this temperamental disillusionment that led him to view
later creeds or programs of political or revolutionary action with revul-
sion; and the forms such action took in his lifetime—imperialism, anarchism, militant nihilism or communism, power coalitions, the tactics of
Realpolitik—gave him sufficient occasion for distaste and contempt, as
the casuistry of "balances of power" among the Western nations gave
him cause for alarm for the future of the West. But against his profes-
sions of indifference or disgust there played a tenacious sense that there
is a social and political community in the affairs of men no less than a
moral one, and that a man repudiates it at his peril.

The imperative for Conrad was specifically the Polish question, far
beyond any loyalty he professed for England—his exile's fealty to an
adopted nationality, usually conservative, conventional, and reactionary,
which could nettle or disgruntle his liberal and skeptical English friends.
When he wrote outside his fiction it was in the Polish cause that he
centered his commitment. In his fiction the case was otherwise. Only
once, in the story "Prince Roman" of 1911, did he employ the Polish
subject there, and he employed it then in its traditional heroic form.
But into his treatments of polity, honor, and political casuistry elsewhere—in South America, England, the colonial East, or Russia—he
carried a critical insight which, however bred in his own native nationalism, could exercise itself more objectively, realistically, and far more
searchingly than a situation personally prejudiced could allow. It may
be true that in practical terms Conrad's political fiction, as has more
than once been said, "finally solves nothing." It provides no prescriptions
for actionable policy, party or sectarian maneuver, tactical action, or
concerted protest. But it is doubtful if the serious political novel has
ever provided these. They are not provided by Turgenev, Stendhal,
Tolstoy, or Dostoevsky, or even by such later novelists as Malraux,

[25] E.g.: "Disestablishment, Land Reform, Universal Brotherhood are but like mile-
stones on the road to ruin." "Faith is a myth and beliefs shift like mists on the shore."
"Socialism must inevitably end in Caesarism." "You want from men faith, honour,
fidelity to truth in themselves and others . . . [this to Graham]; What makes you
dangerous is your unwarrantable belief that your desires may be realized." "I look with
the serenity of despair and the indifference of contempt upon the passing events. . . .
there is no earthly remedy for those earthly misfortunes, and from above, I fear, we
may obtain consolation, but no remedy. 'All is Vanity.' " These passages are from letters
given in *Life and Letters*, Vol. I, pp. 79-86, and 268-70, 215-16, 221-23, 229-30; the
strain appears in many of Conrad's letters at this time and later.

Camus, Hemingway, or Pasternak, who have experienced political warfare and ideology in more immediate and physical forms. The fiction
of political policy is the preserve of party journalists and propagandists.
The serious novelist has a more vital and radical subject to contend
with—not the tactics of power but the morality of power, of political
responsibility, and of social intelligence; and from that obligation there
is no shirking or evasion. It is an imperative continuous with a man's
moral existence. Perhaps the two phrases in *Under Western Eyes* that
are most likely to echo in the reader's mind as the focal epigram of the
book are those that come at the end of Part I—Razumov's declaration to
Mikulin that he intends "To retire," and Mikulin's sinister and comprehensive question "Where to?" In that defiance and reply Conrad, by
means of an oral image as resolving as his great visual images can be,
condensed not only this particular novel's radical issue but the issue of
his own experience in social and moral engagement.

To its dramatization he brought a narrative method and a sequence
of motifs that had by this time become his typical usages. There is, at
the outset, Razumov's isolation, his secret illusion of his destiny, his ignorance of his moral identity. Abruptly there enters into his solitude the
challenge, the test, that cuts across that illusion and puts it to proof—
Haldin's confidence and appeal. There follows the derangement of
Razumov's mind and purpose that invariably accompanies the collision
of the secret self with external circumstance: his perception that his life
and fate have become inescapably identified with Haldin's—the hallucination of walking across the man lying in the snow, the imprint of
Haldin's outstretched body on his bed. Having resolved to betray Haldin
to the police, he senses, even if dimly, that his youth is over, his young
manhood hurtled into the maelstrom of political and revolutionary conflict, his "shadow-line" crossed: hearing Prince K—— murmur of "a
quarter-life-size smooth-limbed bronze of an adolescent figure, running,"
in General T——'s reception room, "Spontini's. 'Flight of Youth.' Exquisite," he assents faintly. "Admirable." Then comes the interview with
Mikulin which snares him as a spy for the official police; then the be-
wildering shift to Geneva, wrenching him out of his life's purpose,
casting him into the company and confidences of the exiles, exposing
him to their challenges of delusion or fidelity, hypocrisy or truth. Thus
he goes on, another trapped conscience, to enact his lie, his deception of
Nathalie, his recognition by agonized stages of her dedicated sincerity
and his own falsehood, eventually his confession, the breaking of his
will and body, and his final return to Russia and to the living out of the
remorseless logic of his personal fate that awaits him there. The drama
recapitulates the logic of destiny that Conrad had already traced in the
lives of Almayer, Willems, Jim, Kurtz, Nostromo, Decoud; and the law
which operates in it—that "no man can escape his fate"—was to remain
the law of life that Conrad carried to the end of his career in fiction.

If that law became attenuated by sentiment or moral compromise before the end, it found, in this novel, one of the most rigorous and consistent embodiments that Conrad ever achieved; and here it arrived at a strength of social and historical reference that brought it out of its earlier remote or exotic versions into the full light and actuality of a crisis that is a radical fact and test of the twentieth century.

Under Western Eyes shows Conrad writing in the strength of his sincerity and despair, his lacerating irony and his passionate humanism. If the book lacks the stronger intimacy of *Lord Jim* and *Heart of Darkness,* the more complex reverberations of *Nostromo,* the ironic tautness of *The Secret Agent,* or the overt symbolic dimension of "The Secret Sharer" and *Victory,* it shows his power to memorable effect and ends by making its unquestionable impression of authority and justice. The justice with which it deals is painful and baffling, but his treatment of it, whatever its complexity of sympathy or insight, is not evasive, and the workings of truth and conscience are neither shirked nor disguised. Perhaps, as Mr. Pritchett has said, Conrad wrote the book "to bring a harder Western focus upon a theme of Dostoevsky." The book has, at any rate, the quality of translating the Dostoevskian vision and ethos into the terms of a moral necessity which the West, whatever its compromises or failures of principle, can never forget, and which it will forget now only at its peril. That Conrad should have been able to illuminate that necessity by means of a subject so deeply involved in his personal history, and to achieve in doing so a version of the Russian fate that calls for comparison with the art of the Russian masters themselves, testifies to the risks he was willing to take in his art and to the vision and insight that rewarded him. The novel, as strenuous in its craft as in the drama it describes, carries his reading of the human destiny to a pitch of sometimes unendurable intensity, and the judgment at which it finally arrives is as exigent and as stern in its conclusions as any we are likely to find in modern fiction. It proposes a major question to the age, and it leaves that question pending the moral decision of Europe and the West. The novel thus becomes more than an experience in the drama and craftsmanship of one of the most scrupulous and searching of modern novelists. It becomes an example and a portent for an era in history whose crisis Conrad, through his own experience of it and the severity of vision it yielded him, was able with a remarkable prophetic instinct to foresee.

Conrad's Later "Affirmation"

by Thomas Moser

[In the works of Conrad's later period, his interest in the significance of test and betrayal seems to] yield to an acceptance of chance as the force controlling human action. Our discussion of Conrad's altered view of the world will center in four novels, *Chance* (1913), *Victory* (1915), and *The Shadow Line* (1917), because they are the most respected of the later works, and *The Rescue* (1920), because it attempts to fuse the early interests with the later. Accident plays an important part in the resolution of the love affairs. In *Chance,* for example, Powell's lucky peep at de Barral is possible only because of the "precise workmanship of chance, fate, providence, call it what you will!" *Victory,* too, moves by accidents: Heyst just happens to go in to see the orchestra and is actually on the point of leaving when he notices Lena; the evil trio appear utterly unexpectedly at Schomberg's hotel; they almost fail to reach Heyst's island; "their apparition in a boat Heyst could not connect with anything plausible." Love comes by chance to Captain Lingard in *The Rescue*. The nonromantic *Shadow Line* depends also upon chance happenings: the young narrator gains his first command by a series of "miracles"; the crisis arises when he discovers, to his amazement, that the quinine he is counting on to cure the crew is not quinine at all.

To be sure, chance serving the plot, creating the crisis, is hardly a new development in Conrad. In *Lord Jim,* nothing could be less expected that serene night than that the *Patna* should strike a submerged derelict. In *Nostromo,* too, the collision of the lighter with the troopship (the only two ships moving in a huge bay) is utterly unexpected, and this absurd accident destroys Decoud and Nostromo. . . . The early Conrad is interested in these unlooked-for disasters in terms of the human response they evoke as well as the irony of fate that brings them about. Chance in the early Conrad remains subordinate to its result, the test. The crisis tests one's fidelity to the solidarity of mankind, tests one's humanity, essentially. Never to be tested is to be disdained, as Captain MacWhirr is disdained until the typhoon strikes. Even Jim recognizes this and longs

"Conrad's 'Later Affirmation' " by Thomas Moser. From *Joseph Conrad: Achievement and Decline.* Copyright © 1957 by the President and Fellows of Harvard College. Reprinted by permission of the Harvard University Press.

for a second chance, that perfect opportunity to prove his superiority to ordinary men.

Not only does the chance crisis in the early Conrad try one's physical courage; it also tries the inner man. In fact, the accidental test usually symbolizes the weaknesses of those to be tested. In *The Nigger of the "Narcissus,"* there are two tests: of the outer man in his response to the fury of a storm; of the inner man through James Wait, who personifies the terror that each member of the crew (except, perhaps, Singleton) feels about his own death. In "The Secret Sharer," chance and inner weakness are equated. Only because the young captain unaccountably violates sea tradition to take the watch himself is the ladder permitted to hang over the side and save Leggatt, the captain's other, darker self. Mr. Zabel effectively defines chance in the early Conrad:

> an . . . enemy lies in wait . . . leaping from unknown coverts, sometimes from the hiding places that fate has prepared, but more often and seriously, like James's beast in the jungle, from the unfathomed depths of our secret natures, our ignorance, our unconscious and untested selves.

For the true heroes of the early Conrad, whether simple and unthinking or complex and perceptive, chance is never an excuse for failure. Only those who are morally insensitive try to make excuses and blame fate. This is Jim's case. He feels sure that "on the square" there is nothing that he could not meet. Marlow answers:

> "It is always the unexpected that happens," I said in a propitiatory tone. My obtuseness provoked him into a contemptuous "Pshaw!" I suppose he meant that the unexpected couldn't touch him; nothing less than the inconceivable itself could get over his perfect state of preparation. He had been taken unawares. . . .

Nostromo responds to the accidental sinking of the lighter with the feeling that, somehow, he has been "betrayed." His further response, like Jim's aboard the *Patna,* is to betray in return. Marlow and the ironic narrator of *Nostromo* know that their heroes are guilty of betrayal. To the obtuse Captain Mitchell, on the other hand, disasters are unrelated to character and can all be explained under the simple heading of "fatality."

If chance remains essentially a *device* for exploring moral failure in the early novels, it has, or seems to have, more important meanings in the later Conrad. Marlow, in *Chance,* his last appearance in Conrad's works, talks a good deal about it. He points out unfailingly how vital a part it plays in the story: the reader can easily find twenty chance happenings which elicit a Marlovian comment. But Marlow does more than simply point; he asserts a serious justification: chance serves to bring about awareness of evil. The first crisis in Flora de Barral's life comes, we recall, wholly as a result of chance. It is none of her own doing. De Barral has hired the evil governess by chance; the disaster occurs through the collapse of de Barral's fortunes, an event unrelated to Flora. Marlow comments that the night before the disaster is Flora's last sleep in

> unconsciousness of the world's ways . . . her unconsciousness was to be broken into with profane violence, with desecrating circumstances like a temple violated by a mad, vengeful impiety. Yes, that very young girl, almost no more than a child—this was what was going to happen to her. And if you ask me how, wherefore, for what reason? I will answer you: Why, by chance! By the merest chance, as things do happen, lucky and unlucky, terrible or tender, important or unimportant.

Conrad thus underlines the importance of the ensuing scene with the governess. After all, it is then that Flora comes to the conclusion that she is absolutely unlovable. Her reaction to the governess' cruelty is as determining to her career as Jim's jump is to his. After Flora collapses in her arms, Mrs. Fyne says to herself something which reminds us of the early Marlow's idea about Jim: "That child is too emotional—much too emotional to be ever really sound." But the later Marlow's comment upon Mrs. Fyne's statement does not sound like the Marlow of *Lord Jim*: "even in the best armour of steel there are joints a treacherous stroke can always find if chance gives the opportunity." The early Conrad believes that the *best* men can withstand any assault of the dark powers.

The first half of *Chance* is, in some ways, a feminine version of *Lord Jim*. Flora and Jim both suffer unexpected disasters which affect their way of looking at life and partially incapacitate them for effective action. Both contemplate suicide as a way out, but both feel contempt for such an escape. Friends (the Fynes in *Chance*, Marlow in *Lord Jim*) try to find jobs for them, but because of their psychic wounds, their hypersensitivity, they prove unsatisfactory. Yet the difference between the two chance disasters gives us a key to the shift in Conrad's attitude. In *Chance*, the evil is *outside* Flora. All that is required of Flora is that she open her eyes to it. She has no responsibility during her crisis. She remains passive until the governess says that de Barral is a swindler, and then she screams. When the governess and her lover leave the house, Flora runs next door to the Fynes, the only people she knows. Jim's response to his disaster does resemble Flora's in certain respects. Like Flora, he remains passive at the beginning, and then he jumps. Yet there are many things Jim could have done, things he ought to have done as a responsible ship's officer; and Jim is aware of these responsibilities at the time, and afterwards, when talking with Marlow. " 'Ah! what a chance missed! My God! what a chance missed!' he blazed out . . ." The *Patna* disaster had been Jim's chance, his test, which he failed because of weakness *within himself*. For Flora, the inner problem is secondary to her discovery of how bad *other people* can be. Throughout the novel, Flora's conduct is impeccable. All her difficulties result from the inhumanity of her father and the timorous and chivalric behavior of Captain Anthony. Flora herself perfectly justifies Marlow's confidence in her: "How far Flora went I can't say. But I will tell you my idea: my idea is that she went as far as she was able—as far as she could bear it—as far as she had to. . . ."

The disaster that comes by chance to Lena in *Victory,* Ricardo's attack on her, brings about the same kind of moral awareness as the governess' attack on Flora. As Lena and Ricardo sit facing each other, Lena ponders the meaning of her test: "It seemed to her that the man sitting there before her was an unavoidable presence, which had attended all her life. He was the embodied evil of the world." The key phrase here is "of the world." Ricardo represents for Lena the wickedness of other people. This is very different from *Heart of Darkness.* When Kurtz is confronted with an "instinctive savagery" far more powerful than Ricardo's, Kurtz is able to pronounce judgment, not only against the world, but against himself.

These opposite responses to crises might seem simply to reflect Conrad's inability to understand women, his tendency to sentimentalize female characterizations. Let us look, therefore, at the chance disaster in the later Conrad's only masculine story, *The Shadow Line.* On the surface, the young captain's response to his crisis seems to be quite different from Flora's and Lena's. When he finds that the bottles do not contain the quinine that his crew needs so badly, he immediately acknowledges his own responsibility: "The person I could never forgive was myself. Nothing should ever be taken for granted. The seed of everlasting remorse was sown in my breast." Throughout the rest of the novel, the captain periodically accuses himself of failure; he feels oppressed by a "sense of guilt," the "weight of [his] sins," his "sense of unworthiness": "My first command. Now I understand that strange sense of insecurity in my past. I always suspected that I might be no good. And here is proof positive, I am shirking it, I am no good."

Certainly, these are explicit references to inner weakness, rather than to evil embodied in others. Yet we have found the early Conrad most seriously involved with his material and most convincing where he is most ironic, where meanings are implicit rather than explicit. Perhaps, then, we should look a little more carefully at evil in *The Shadow Line* by comparing the novel with its predecessor, "The Secret Sharer." It can be demonstrated that *The Shadow Line* is essentially a reworking of the materials of the earlier, shorter novel. But our present purpose is simply to examine some of the ideas in the two novels to see if they reflect the same or different attitudes toward moral awareness. In "The Secret Sharer," the captain lets evil board the ship in the person of Leggatt; he immediately reveals through his own *actions* that he knows that he is guilty. He calls no one to help; he talks in a whisper to Leggatt; he hides Leggatt in his cabin; and he deals with his crew in such a bizarre manner that he makes himself suspect to everyone.

Although the captain in *The Shadow Line* says that he feels guilty, his actions belie his statement. He makes no effort to conceal his "guilt" about the quinine or to put the blame on anyone else. Instead he rushes out of his cabin, tells his mate, Mr. Burns, and the faithful Ransome of his discovery. Then he makes a speech to the crew, suffering during it more than a "confessed criminal" would have. To his surprise, the men do not reproach him at all; in fact they encourage the captain in a "low assenting murmur." This is very different from the attitude of the crew of "The Secret Sharer." When they hear it said that Leggatt may be hidden aboard their ship, they immediately pass judgment against such a deception: "As if we would harbour a thing like that." Until the end of the novel, they show no confidence whatsoever in their peculiar and distraught young captain. In *The Shadow Line*, however, the crew behaves as faithfully as could be expected of men almost dead from fever. Through all their suffering, they never blame their captain: "I expected to meet reproachful glances. There were none."

Conrad tries to suggest the presence of evil in *The Shadow Line* in two ways: by references to the former captain, and by emphasis on the physical disability of Ransome, the faithful and heroic cook. By frequently calling the former captain the "old man," and the "old dodging Devil," Conrad indicates that he intends him to be symbolic. Yet he remains a very external evil. He does not make his presence felt aboard the ship; he tempts no man's soul. Rather, he lies buried at the entrance to the Gulf afflicting the ship with calms and unfavorable winds in order to bar her passage. The young captain, his mate, Ransome, and the crew, all, like Flora, act impeccably. In the case of Ransome, however, Conrad tries to symbolize the presence of an internal weakness. He pictures him "going up the companion stairs cautiously, step by step, in mortal fear of starting into sudden anger our common enemy it was his hard fate to carry consciously within his faithful breast." When we recall that the common enemy which Ransome carries is his heart trouble, a purely physical flaw, we realize that, in *The Shadow Line*, the only evil lies at the bottom of the sea.

"The Secret Sharer" contains no satanic figure like the late captain. Rather, evil is represented by a straggler from the ranks, Leggatt, the captain's double, who looks "like a patient, unmoved convict." Leggatt reveals his nature through action; he kills a man. While there are extenuating circumstances, Leggatt is responsible, and his act of violence is the result of a flaw in character. Moreover, the flaw does not exist in Leggatt alone; the captain shares it:

> "Fit of temper," I suggested confidently.
> The shadowy, dark head, like mine, seemed to nod imperceptibly above the ghostly grey of my sleeping-suit. It was, in the night, as though I had been faced by my own reflection in the depths of a sombre and immense mirror.

In short, "The Secret Sharer" belongs to Conrad's early period where the dark powers lurk within us all. The attitude toward evil that *The Shadow*

Line dramatizes places it, however, with *Chance* and *Victory*. In these, the crises that come to us by chance reveal that, while we may be surrounded by disease and evil, we are basically sound. When trouble comes to us, we are in no way responsible for it. The fault lies elsewhere, in other people.

Old garrulous Captain Giles sounds the moral at the end of *The Shadow Line* in very interesting language: "a man should stand up to his bad luck, to his mistakes, to his conscience, and all that sort of thing." We note that Conrad's *raisonneur* here equates "bad luck" and "conscience." This reminds us that in the later novels chance serves not only to reveal an evil external to the main characters but also to blur the problem of their moral responsibility, to confuse failure of luck with failure of conscience. We need only think of the quinine. Conrad nowhere establishes that the captain has a clear-cut responsibility for the contents of every bottle in the medicine chest. A "humane doctor," the captain's closest friend during the weeks of delay because of the crew's ill health, anticipates the captain's worry about the medicine chest and carefully inspects the ship's supply of drugs before it departs. "Everything was completed and in order." It is not surprising that the crew do not blame their captain for the absence of quinine. On the other hand, the "chance" of the ladder that saves Leggatt in "The Secret Sharer" is really no chance at all, but the result of the young captain's violation of sea tradition in taking over a watch himself. His own "strangeness" prompts "that unconventional arrangement," and although his first mate conceals "his astonishment," the second mate raises his voice "incredulously" at the "unheard-of caprice." In short, the captain's strange act betrays an inner weakness which his officers immediately and correctly judge as unworthy of a ship's captain.

Chance blurs responsibility in *Chance* and *Victory*, too. We have already noticed how young Powell's chance peep at de Barral and the poison saves Captain Anthony's life and gives him Flora. It also effectively prevents Anthony from having to face the real problems in his marriage. In *Victory* there is a series of perfectly plausible misunderstandings between Heyst and Lena rising out of her secret plan to trick Ricardo. Heyst finally becomes suspicious of Lena. His chance arrival with Mr. Jones at precisely the wrong moment, when Lena is bending over Ricardo, results in Heyst's natural misinterpretation of the scene. Heyst makes no effort to prevent Mr. Jones from shooting, and the bullet intended for Ricardo kills Lena. At the end Heyst blames himself for not putting his "trust in life," but surely chance, not conscience, is at fault.

We have been trying to define the quality of the later Conrad's "affirmation." We have seen how his use of chance makes this a very evasive affirmation: the point is not that man is basically good or even his potentialities for good, but rather that the world is full of evil, except in certain characters whom Conrad likes. Furthermore, when pain and suffering

come by chance to the untainted, the responsibility for the evil lies elsewhere. That is, the heroes and heroines of the later Conrad are sinned
against, themselves unsinning.

We may well wonder if there is any positive value in the later affirmation. In the early Conrad, we found that the unquestioned values were
integrity and work for its own sake. Marlow says in *Lord Jim* that the
"only reward" of life at sea is the "perfect love of the work." The value
of work is rarely referred to in the later period; instead Conrad asserts
that man can achieve goodness and fulfill himself through romantic love.
While this affirmation may be defensible, we should scrutinize it carefully
to see whether Conradian love is really positive and creative.

The most noteworthy affirmation through love in the later novels is
Lena's unequivocal (Mr. Leavis' word) victory for life. Yet an examination
of the last pages of *Victory* reveals that the terms of Lena's victory are all
against life. Mortally wounded, she feels "relieved at once of an intolerable
weight"; she is "content to surrender" to Heyst an "infinite weariness."
She looks at her own form on the bed and feels "profoundly at peace."
Lena's triumphant union with Heyst is a curiously possessive one. "I was
thanking God with all my sinful heart for . . . giving you to me in that
way—oh, my beloved—all my own at last!" She will look "for his glance
in the shades of death."

In *Chance,* however, neither lover dies until long after the reconcilia-
tion. Yet even here, where we know so little of the relationship between
hero and heroine, Conrad gives us one brief hint of the meaning of
Flora's and Anthony's triumphant embrace. Young Powell approaches the
door of the captain's cabin where the two are at last consummating their
marriage and comments: "It was very still in there; still as death."

Once again, *The Shadow Line* seems to be an exception to our generalizations about the later works. Since it has no love affair, it cannot be
guilty of asserting that the love which brings escape into eternal peace
is man's greatest good. In fact, *The Shadow Line* appears to stand against
peace and to reaffirm the early Conrad's faith in work. The young captain
tells old Captain Giles at the end of the novel that he will be off at day-
break, despite the fact that he has spent seventeen days on deck and has
had no sleep at all in the last forty hours. "There's no rest for me till
she's out in the Indian Ocean and not much of it even then." Captain
Giles approves of the young captain's vigorous attitude toward life and
adds, "Precious little rest in life for anybody. Better not think of it."
Nevertheless, even in *The Shadow Line,* Conrad cannot quite criticize the
longing for death. The novel ends with the reader's attention directed,
sympathetically, upon Ransome "in a blue funk" about his heart, moving
cautiously, headed for the "quiet" to which he has a "right." We cannot
fail to contrast this with our last view of the secret sharer, "a free man,
a proud swimmer striking out for a new destiny."

Our analysis of the meaning of chance and love in the later novels has revealed that a new moral attitude now obtains. Conrad no longer sees his characters as part of the world community of suffering and damned humanity; rather he sees them as figures of purity afflicted by an external evil. Their greatest good is to lose themselves in a love that will blot out all awareness of the world and bring the semblance of death.

Conrad's new attitude clearly separates him from his early convictions. Those of his early characters who are in love with death he consistently views ironically and judges adversely, even though, at the same time, he is sympathetically aware that longing for peace is a universal human failing. We think of the terrified Jukes, "corrupted by the storm that breeds a craving for peace." We think, especially, of Jim. Conrad treats ironically his longing to be lord, to be perfect, to be dead, from the very first page, with its account of Jim "appareled in immaculate white," and with "Ability in the abstract," to the end of the novel when Jim embraces death. The true Conradian hero of the early period stands firmly against death, and for life.

Although the early Conrad associates love with death, as *An Outcast of the Islands* makes abundantly clear, he nevertheless views that association with horror. It is difficult to point precisely to the time when his attitude shifts from horror to passive acceptance, but this seems to have taken place shortly after the completion of *Chance*. We have already seen the theme in *Victory*, which Conrad says, in a prefatory note, that he finished May 29, 1914, after, according to M. Jean-Aubry, nineteen months of work. This would put the beginning of *Victory* in the fall of 1912, some six months after the completion of *Chance*. Conrad abandoned *Victory* only once, toward the end of 1913, to write "The Planter of Malata." Though the story has, on occasion, been taken seriously, Conrad's own doubts about it seem well founded. It is interesting, however, as a "break" from *Victory* and important as an aid to dating the beginning of Conrad's willing acceptance of the association between love and death.

"The Planter of Malata" closely resembles its exact contemporary, *Victory*, both in characters and story. The hero, Renouard, is another Heyst, sensitive, romantic, withdrawn from society. Like Heyst, Renouard has retired to an island after gaining a dubious reputation from explorations that cost several of his associates their lives. Renouard, too, falls in love and takes his beloved with him to his private island. When she discovers that he has lied to lure her there, she rejects him and leaves. Renouard's only friend, a newspaper man, visits the island to see what has happened and finds evidence that Renouard has committed suicide by drowning.

By the end of 1913, Conrad's surrender to the association between love and death is fairly complete. Renouard equates his love for Felicia Moorsom with a return to unconsciousness, even before he has lost her and decided to commit suicide. In fact, immediately after Felicia gives the first hint that she may be attracted to Renouard, he slips off his yacht into the water: "He swam away, noiseless like a fish, and then struck boldly for the land, sustained, embraced, by the tepid water. The gentle, voluptuous heave of its breast swung him up and down slightly. . . ." As he swims back to the ship, toward his "desire," he feels a "mournful fatigue."

> It was as if his love had sapped the invisible supports of his strength. There came a moment when it seemed to him that he must have swum beyond the confines of life. He had a sensation of eternity close at hand, demanding no effort—offering its peace. It was easy to swim like this beyond the confines of life looking at a star. . . . He lay in his hammock utterly exhausted and with a confused feeling that he had been beyond the confines of life, somewhere near a star, and that it was very quiet there.

Soon afterwards, Renouard commits suicide by swimming "with a steady stroke—his eyes fixed on a star." That Conrad had accepted this attitude and expected as much of the reader is indicated by the sentimentalism of the last sentence of the story:

> A black cloud hung listlessly over the high rock on the middle hill; and under the mysterious silence of that shadow Malata lay mournful, with an air of anguish in the wild sunset, as if remembering the heart that was broken there.

Clearly then, the later Conrad has a new attitude toward the world, though hardly an affirmative one; he now considers evil to be external to his heroes and heroines and sees man's greatest good as complete repose, usually achieved through love. Such an extreme shift in attitude almost necessarily results in a drastic reorientation of Conrad's artistry. Perhaps the best way to see the effect of the later Conrad's attitude upon his early moral hierarchy of characters and upon his complex handling of structure and language is to compare *The Rescue* of 1920 with those portions of its first version, "The Rescuer," which were written in the nineties.

"The Rescuer" displays all of the important, early types of character . . . except one; it contains no perceptive hero like Marlow. . . . Tom Lingard of "The Rescuer" seems to be a first attempt at Lord Jim, the simple vulnerable hero. Linares prefigures Decoud, the complex vulnerable hero. Carter belongs among the ranks of simple, faithful seamen like Singleton and MacWhirr. While Mr. Travers and Jörgenson do not precisely fit any of our categories, they resemble certain characters of the early period. Mr. Travers has much in common with Alvan Hervey of "The Return," and Jörgenson belongs in the gallery of caricatures who serve as doubles for Lord Jim.

The most significant alteration of "The Rescuer" is the simplification and emasculation of Lingard. Through certain crucial cuts from the original manuscript, the later Conrad obscures the most important and interesting facts of Lingard's psychology: the subtle difference between himself and other seamen, his egoistic longings for power, his lack of

self-knowledge, his moral isolation. As a result, he has none of the vitality
and intensity of Conrad's great self-destructive heroes.

In revising the manuscript, Conrad cut out two passages that tend to
cast doubt upon Lingard's qualifications for membership in the fraternity
of loyal seamen. As originally described, Lingard does not quite *look*
like a seaman, and his motivation is *not* a perfect love of the work itself.
"The Rescuer" portrays him as a man who holds "himself very straight
in a most unseamanlike manner." He has "also—for a seaman—the dis-
advantage of being tall above the average of men of that calling." Moreover, although the Lingard of "The Rescuer" is passionately devoted to
his ship, as any good sea captain ought to be, his devotion seems to be
the expression of something different from a perfect love of his calling.
The later Conrad obscures Lingard's questionable attitude toward his
craft by cutting out the following description of Lingard bringing his
brig to anchor:

> A sudden listlessness seemed to come over him. It was one of his peculi-
> arities that whenever he had to call upon his unerring knowledge of his
> craft upon his skill and readiness in matters of his calling that big body of
> his lost its alertness, seemed to sink as if some inward prop had been sud-
> denly withdrawn.

"The Rescuer" tells us further that Lingard expects his brig to answer
"without hesitation to every perverse demand of his desire."

That the later Conrad is acting to distort his original conception of
Lingard as motivated not by love of the craft but rather by love of self
becomes more evident in the account of Lingard's motives for interfer-
ing in the political affairs of the native state of Wajo. *The Rescue* follows
"The Rescuer" here:

> There was something to be done, and he felt he would have to do it. It
> was expected of him. The sea expected it; the land expected it. Men also.
> The story of war and of suffering; Jaffir's display of fidelity, the sight of
> Hassim and his sister, the night, the tempest, the coast under streams of
> fire—all this made one inspiring manifestation of a life calling to him dis-
> tinctly for interference.

The Rescue omits, however, the most important of Lingard's motives—
his egoism. "The Rescuer" continues the passage thus:

> But above all it was himself, it was his longing, his obscure longing to
> mould his own fate in accordance with the whispers of his imagination
> awakened by the sights and the sounds, by the loud appeal of that night.

As originally conceived, Lingard's apparently charitable assistance
to his native friends was to have been motivated by unlawful desires for
personal power and even violence. The later Conrad cannot tolerate the
implication that his hero contains any of the old Adam, and so he

eliminates this very damning passage about Lingard's response to the opportunity to make war and history:

> the islands, the shallow sea, the men of the islands and the sea seemed to press on him from all sides with subtle and irresistible solicitation, they surrounded him with a murmur of mysterious possibilities, with an atmosphere lawless and exciting, with a suggestion of power to be picked up by a strong hand. They enveloped him, they penetrated him, as does the significant silence of the forests and the bitter vastness of the sea. They possessed themselves of his thoughts, of his activity, of his hopes—in an inevitable and obscure way even of his affections.
>
> But if Lingard obeyed the complex motives of an impulse stealthy as a whisper and masterful as an inspiration, without reflecting on its origins, he knew well enough what he wanted even if he did not know exactly why. . . .

The absence of this passage from *The Rescue* deprives the reader of several of the early Conrad's most profound perceptions. The passage reminds us that the romantic's seemingly free act of will, his act of interference, immediately costs him his freedom and brings about slavery to the dark powers. (We recall how Kurtz belongs to the jungle and how Jim is possessed by Patusan.) This remnant of "The Rescuer" also reveals Lingard's lack of self-knowledge. He does not reflect upon the origins of his inspiration and does not know "exactly why" he is doing what he does.

A final, important insight into Lingard that the later Conrad finds of no use is the increasing isolation that results from his egoistic involvement in an unlawful adventure. In revising "The Rescuer," Conrad cut out the account of the change that takes place in the once hearty, bluff, and friendly Lingard, the change to a man isolated and guilt-ridden. Some of his friends try to draw him out by chaffing him but he repulses them:

> they grew distant and Lingard had a subtle sense of solitude, the inward loneliness of a man who is conscious of having a dark side to his life. It hurt him. He needed the good fellowship of men who understood his work his feelings and his cares. . . . Before he had been many months engaged in his secret enterprise he began to feel unreasonably like an outcast . . . he imagined himself, at times, to be the object of universal detestation.

Lingard's sense of isolation parallels Jim's in Patusan and, like Jim's, becomes even more intense when white visitors from the West appear to break into his adventurous Eastern dream.

For the later Conrad, Lingard has little in common with the romantic egoists of the early period. The second half of *The Rescue,* wholly written during 1918-19, carries the emasculation of Lingard further by absolving him of responsibility for the deaths of his best friends and by sanctioning his passive acceptance of repose as his greatest good.

In this later portion of *The Rescue* Conrad raises a clear-cut moral issue, presumably to make Lingard decide whether to follow his duty to his native friends or his sudden love for Mrs. Travers. By an unfortunate chance, however, Lingard is unaware that Hassim and Immada have been seized as hostages, and thus he never has a real choice. Moral responsibility for the disastrous outcome of *The Rescue* would seem to lie with Mrs. Travers, who conceals Jörgenson's message to Lingard, and perhaps more seriously with Lingard himself, for loving and trusting such an unworthy person. In fact, critics who admire *The Rescue* tend to interpret it this way. The truth is, however, that although the later Conrad sets up a clear moral problem, no one is really to blame for the evil outcome. Instead, Conrad excuses Mrs. Travers' actions and makes her a victim of chance, unaware of the content of the message, suspicious of Jörgenson's intentions toward Lingard, and convinced by d'Alcacer, the voice of reason, that for Lingard's own good this obscure message must be concealed. Mrs. Travers' dilemma reminds us of similar situations in the later novels, especially in *Victory*. Like Lena, Mrs. Travers deliberately deceives her lover, but with the best intentions in the world. Disaster comes through the agency of an external, implausible, evil figure resembling Mr. Jones: "By the mad scorn of Jörgenson flaming up against the life of men. . . ."

If Mrs. Travers is not guilty, then Lingard is utterly blameless. Bad luck, coincidence, the misunderstanding of good intentions, someone else's madness—all these are to blame, not the impeccable hero. Yet like the zealous young captain of *The Shadow Line*, Lingard nobly asserts his guilt. He says that even if Mrs. Travers had given him the message "it would have been to one that was dumb, deaf, and robbed of all courage." Later Mrs. Travers protests: ". . . why don't you throw me into the sea? . . . Am I to live on hating myself? . . . No, no! You are too generous. . . ." The reader surely understands the moral of *The Rescue*: responsibility lies not with hero and heroine, but somewhere else.

The later Conrad perverts his original characterization of Lingard in another way, by sapping him of his powerful, if unacknowledged, longings for self-destruction. Although the Lingard of the nineties is a worthy forerunner of the intense, guilt-haunted Jim and Razumov, the Lingard of the second half of *The Rescue* is utterly debilitated. The highest point of his experience seems to be sitting at his beloved's feet, his head upon her knee, telling her, "I care for nothing in the world but you. Let me be. Give me the rest that is in you." He looks upon her as a

waking dream of rest without end, in an infinity of happiness without sound and movement, without thought, without joy; but with an infinite ease of content, like a world-embracing reverie breathing the air of sadness and scented with love.

It must be emphasized that the later Conrad presents all this absolutely without irony. There is not a hint of judgment against Lingard's lapse into passivity.

The later Conrad's handling of the early Lingard shows simply that Conrad either no longer understands his original creation or chooses to ignore it. What had begun as a most promising portrait of a romantic, egoistic, meddlesome figure becomes in the published book the characterization of a conventional hero of popular fiction, a generous, brave, inherently good man brought low by bad luck, human misunderstanding, and the machinations of fate.

Conrad makes fewer interesting revisions in the other important male characters of "The Rescuer." Yet it is clear from the changes he does make and from the essentially new roles these men assume in the last half of *The Rescue* that he views them in a new light. Linares, converted into d'Alcacer, loses his ironic perceptiveness, Carter his stern, unsentimental rectitude; Jörgenson and Travers become less complicated and more villainous.

Because the early Conrad sketched in Linares much less fully than Lingard, the later Conrad could leave him much as he found him although he saw fit to change his name to d'Alcacer. As originally conceived, Linares prefigures Decoud: a cosmopolitan Spaniard, he is an ironic and skeptical observer of the human comedy. He is immediately attracted to the "picturesque" Lingard, just as Decoud responds to the incorruptible Nostromo. But, unhappily, in the second half of the novel, d'Alcacer becomes more of a Heyst than a Decoud, with his "cultivated voice" speaking "playfully." Although he seems to be the *raisonneur,* his analysis of Lingard is actually inept, stuffy, and pretentious:

> More of a European than of a Spaniard he had that truly aristocratic nature which is inclined to credit every honest man with something of its own nobility and in its judgment is altogether independent of class feeling. He believed Lingard to be an honest man and he never troubled his head to classify him, except in the sense that he found him an interesting character. . . . He was a specimen to be judged only by its own worth. With his natural gift of insight d'Alcacer told himself that many overseas adventurers of history were probably less worthy because obviously they must have been less simple. He didn't, however, impart those thoughts formally to Mrs. Travers. In fact he avoided discussing Lingard with Mrs. Travers who, he thought, was quite intelligent enough to appreciate the exact shade of his attitude. If that shade was fine, Mrs. Travers was fine, too. . . .

D'Alcacer's imperception results naturally from his creator's loss of understanding of Lingard. The early Conrad would never have seen Lingard as "simple" unless, like Jim, he was simple in a complicated way.

Carter suffers even more seriously from Lingard's emasculation. As originally conceived in "The Rescuer," he belongs in the company of Singleton and MacWhirr. He is the calmest person aboard Travers' yacht, but also the one most aware of its dangerous position. He approaches all problems practically and unemotionally. Although he is as young as Jukes and Jim, he differs from them in his readiness to meet unexpected disasters. As "The Rescuer" makes clear, Carter always maintains "the professionally wide-awake state of a man confronted by rapid changes of circumstance." In the later half of *The Rescue,* Conrad does not bother to make Carter's actions plausible; he does not tell us how Carter can accomplish the ten day job of rehabilitating the yacht in sixty-six hours. More important, the able and experienced ship's officer of "The Rescuer" has regressed and must go through a maturing experience. "His personality was being developed by new experience, and as he was very simple he received the initiation with shyness and self-mistrust." Although Conrad asserts that Carter has not yet matured, he makes him sound like an old retainer in his solicitous conversation with Lingard after the catastrophe: "Why not lie down a bit, sir? I can attend to anything that may turn up. You seem done up, sir."

A long expository passage on Travers in "The Rescuer" (cut completely from *The Rescue*) shows clearly that Conrad intends him to be of the type of Alvan Hervey, in "The Return." Travers is described as a too wealthy, egotistical bourgeois; unimaginative and conventional, he despises other men yet longs for reputation. Conrad's failure with Alvan Hervey makes it unlikely that Travers could ever have become a successful creation. Yet the early Conrad at least makes an effort to understand him and permits him to have a little human inconsistency and to be a somewhat sympathetic figure. For example, in "The Rescuer," Travers seems honestly suspicious of Lingard's motives; he believes that Lingard is lying about the danger from natives in order to trick Travers into letting him seize the yacht for salvage. In revising "The Rescuer," Conrad eliminates any explanation of why Travers is hostile to Lingard. He also makes him completely unsympathetic by deleting passages that show Travers hearing out Lingard and restraining his indignation against Carter, and by removing indications that Carter and Mrs. Travers have some respect for him. Although Travers appears frequently in the later half of the novel, he can hardly be said to exist. He spends almost all of the time in bed, occasionally making some petulant remark from between the sheets.

Jörgenson becomes rather a bore in the second half of *The Rescue.* Yet as originally conceived, he holds much interest. He is, perhaps, the first true double, prefiguring the gallery of caricatures in *Lord Jim,* all of whom, from the "old stager" to Gentleman Brown, serve to illuminate Jim's romantic psychology. As Jörgenson appears in "The Rescuer," he is obviously meant to foreshadow by his past the inevitable destruction of Lingard's hopes: "He demonstrated one way . . . in which prosaic fate deals with men who dream quickly and want to handle their dreams in broad daylight." Even though Jörgenson has been

virtually destroyed by his early adventure into native politics, nevertheless, by his act of joining with Lingard in a new adventure, he reveals
the power of those illusions that lure the ego into action and self-destruction: "at times the invincible belief in old illusions would come back, insidious and inspiring." In *The Rescue,* "old illusions" become "the
reality of existence." To the later Conrad, the adventures in which Jörgenson and Lingard engage are the essence of existence; he finds it difficult to distinguish between illusion and reality.

The early Conrad emphasizes the physical closeness of Jörgenson and
Lingard. As soon as Lingard begins to collect supplies for his adventure,
Jörgenson starts to shadow him, finally lengthening his stride to come
abreast and engage Lingard in conversation. They become partners, and
their doubleness is apparent to the other characters. So Belarab, recalling to Lingard Jörgenson's help in former days, says abruptly, "He
resembled you." Even Lingard recognizes the equation, in a conversation
with Edith. She asks,

> "And this—this—Jörgenson, you said? Who is he?"
> "A man," he answered, "a man like myself."
> "Like yourself?"
> "Just like myself," he said with strange reluctance, as if admitting a pain-
> ful truth. "More sense, perhaps, but less luck."

This technique of employing a subordinate character to illuminate the
psychology of the main character culminates in "The Secret Sharer." In
the later half of *The Rescue,* however, it is lost entirely.

The Jörgenson of "The Rescuer" combines with his symbolic function
a persuasively human quality. He may be a skeleton, but he is a "powerful skeleton"; he is a drifter who cadges drinks from the traders, but he
can also pilot a ship through the Straits of Rhio. Jörgenson is enough
of a human being to have inspired the devotion of a native "girl," with
a "wrinkled brown face, a lot of tangled grey hair, a few black stumps
of teeth." Jörgenson returns her affection, and even though he cannot
resist Lingard's enterprise, he still demands that the girl be looked after,
indicating a greater sense of responsibility than Lingard has. Jörgenson's
past is as if it had never been, in the second half of *The Rescue.* The
later Conrad easily convinces us of Jörgenson's "other-world aspect," but
this is all that Conrad has to say about him, and he says it many times.
The later Jörgenson, with a rather ungrateful disregard for the years he
has spent with his "girl," has now become an unassailable misogynist
who expresses his opinions in a childish vocabulary and manner:

> "Woman! That's what I say. That's just about the last touch—that you,
> Tom Lingard, red-eyed Tom, King Tom, and all those fine names, that you
> should . . . come along here with your mouth full of fight, bare-handed
> and with a woman in tow.—Well—well!"

We must agree with Mrs. Travers' analysis of the later Jörgenson: "He was invulnerable, unapproachable. . . . He was dead." Jörgenson and Travers take their places among the tedious and unbelievable caricature villains of the later novels. Although they occupy far more space than do the caricatures of the earlier novels, they are greatly inferior to them. The reader longs nostalgically for Jim's many doubles, or for the fine gallery of republicans, revolutionists, and counterrevolutionists in *Nostromo*.

The later Conrad's oversimplification of potentially interesting characters comes as no surprise. A view of the world which finds men not responsible for their actions will hardly reveal great complexity. The emasculation of Lingard is representative of the fate of other similar heroes. Only Captain Anthony of *Chance* can be said to partake at all of the qualities of the simple, excessively romantic, exaltedly egoistic Lord Jim. Yet Anthony has none of the intensity and vigor of Jim. Moreover, one does not feel that Conrad really senses any plague spots in him.

Again, Conrad's handling of d'Alcacer in the second half of *The Rescue* is of a piece with his treatment of the ironic, skeptical, vulnerable hero in the later period. Only Heyst seems even superficially to partake of this type. He is somewhat skeptical, somewhat ironic; he is detached from society, although he has in the past been twice tempted into action, first exploring in New Guinea, next managing a coal company in the tropics. The second venture comes about, like Decoud's intervention in Costaguana politics, through a personal involvement rather than through commitment to an ideal. Yet Heyst is really much less like Decoud than critics have suggested. In fact, Heyst partly resembles a character completely different from Decoud, Charles Gould. Heyst recalls Gould not only because of his mustache and the ironic equation with "portraits of Charles XII of adventurous memory," but also because he is called a "utopist." It would be an interesting departure, an exciting development, if the later Conrad were trying to combine the character of the skeptic with that of the man of action, if Conrad were revealing that the utopian and the unbeliever share an "infernal mistrust of all life," that romanticism and skepticism are sometimes two sides of the same coin. Yet the feeling persists that Conrad simply does not know what he wants to make of Heyst. This is amply borne out by the conclusion in which, as we have seen, Heyst emerges as neither a romantic nor a skeptic, but as a good man brought down by chance and "other people."

Conrad's revisions of Carter in *The Rescue* are of interest because they signify not only the end of the type of the simple, faithful seaman, but the emergence of a new type. (For the faithful seaman does disappear; Conrad may have intended Peyrol to be a descendant of Singleton but he is not. . . .) Carter's altered role as immature hero has several counterparts in the later period. We have already seen in *The Shadow Line* one example of this type of character—the character for whom Conrad posits a development from naïveté to self-awareness but who, in fact, acts effectively from the beginning and never attains true maturity. There are other examples: young Powell in *Chance,* George in *The Arrow of Gold,* and Cosmo in *Suspense.* . . .

The emergence, in the later period, of the boy-hero, reminds us that there is another type, a new one which we have not yet considered— the heroine. In the best Conrad of the early period there is no special category for women; the most effective heroine, Mrs. Gould, succeeds insofar as she partakes of the qualities of the complex, perceptive hero. Therefore we shall have difficulty in contrasting later with early heroines. Moreover, "The Rescuer" will not help us much here because Edith Travers is ill conceived from the first. . . . Nevertheless, the heroine as a character in the later novels is worth a digression because, surprisingly enough, in the cases of Flora and Lena, she is somewhat more successful than other characters. The later women tend to vacillate between two states: homeless waif and assertive heroine. An examination of Flora and Lena will help us to understand how Conrad succeeds with his women only so long as they remain objects of pity. An analysis of Marlow's comments on women and Mrs. Fyne's character in *Chance* may explain why the appealing waifs must always degenerate into aesthetically unconvincing heroines.

The passages in *Chance* which the common reader is likely to find most moving are close in spirit to the sympathetic descriptions of Winnie Verloc in *The Secret Agent.* Unhappily, these successful scenes represent a very small part of a very long book. In the lengthy account of Flora's childhood which Marlow elicits from the Fynes, there is, perhaps, only one touching incident. The Fynes are on watch in their room in the private hotel next to the big Brighton house de Barral rented for his daughter and her governess. First the odious young man strides out the door, then the governess. At last, out flies the deserted Flora,

> right out on the pavement, almost without touching the white steps, a little figure swathed in a holland pinafore up to the chin, its hair streaming back from its head, darting past a lamp-post, past the red pillar-box. . . .

Fyne bounds down the stairs of the hotel, scattering porters, page boys, white-breasted waiters, to catch Flora:

> What might have been their thoughts at the spectacle of a middle-aged man abducting headlong into the upper regions of a respectable hotel a terrified young girl obviously under age, I don't know.

This scene is quite effective. It may have been the inspiration for a fine scene in a novel better than *Chance,* the scene in Elizabeth Bowen's

Death of the Heart in which young Portia, learning of her sister-in-law's treachery, runs away to the retired Major Brutt's attic in the Karachi Hotel.

Another scene in *Chance* which depends for its effectiveness on the idea of Flora as a homeless waif also takes place outside of domestic security on the pavement. This is at the end of Marlow's conversation with her in London on East India Dock Road, outside a door marked "Hotel Entrance." After Flora has told Marlow the history of her affair with Anthony, Marlow remarks that her lover must be eager to see her, and Flora admits that she has arrived too early. But for once Conrad does not sentimentalize Flora, does *not* have her say that she came early because of her deep and abiding love for this man whom she does not even know. Instead, Flora says, "I had nothing to do. So I came out." And Marlow has an intuition: "I had the sudden vision of a shabby, lonely little room at the other end of town. It had grown intolerable to her restlessness." Here, for a moment, Flora de Barral is not Woman to Conrad, but a lonely and ignorant person, staying in a rented room in the biggest city in the world, willing to stand outside the hotel that contains the only person among the city's millions who would even recognize her face.

Conrad has, on occasion, the same kind of perception into Lena's character in *Victory*. Although Heyst's first meeting with Lena is told in undistinguished and overwritten prose, the reader cannot fail to respond to Lena's brief explanation of her inability to defend herself: "They are too many for me." On the island, Lena often evokes sympathy for her bewildered incomprehension of Heyst's peculiar reasoning and capricious changes in mood. Lena acts like a child entrusted to a parent or guardian whom it suspects of being inadequate protection. When she talks with Heyst, her tone betrays "always a shade of anxiety, as though she were never certain how a conversation with him would end." During their futile quest for shelter on the road to the native village, Lena alternately clasps and drops Heyst's hand as her faith waxes and wanes. Her attitude toward Heyst reminds us a little of Flora's embarrassment at the antics of her father after he is released from prison. Although Conrad's stereotyped rendition of the sexual situations in both books may distress us, we still sympathize with the homeless waif who dwells within the two heroines.

We seem to be involved in a contradiction here, since we have already found that Conrad's characterizations of women usually fail, particularly in the later period. If Flora and Lena arouse our sympathy, how can we say that they fail as characters? The answer seems to be that all the failures occur in the most important scenes, the scenes that ought fully to express the intended meaning of the novel: Flora capturing Captain Anthony in the last chapter, and Lena defeating the evil of the world. Conrad's failure in these crucial scenes and, as a matter of fact, in virtually the entire presentation of Rita, Mrs. Travers, Arlette, and Adèle, comes about from a combination of two basic conditions of Conrad's art: his moral view and his almost irrepressible misogyny.

While Conrad does sympathize with the homeless female waif, his sympathy is not as complete as Hardy's or Dreiser's. He will not believe with Hardy that man deserves better than he gets or with Dreiser that man is the pawn of heredity and environment. Conrad's temperament is not that of the naturalist. His characters' crises are moral crises; his characters must *act*, and their actions must be judged. Although Conrad relaxes his moral judgment in the later period, the later novels still move in the same pattern as the early ones. Now, however, Conrad asserts (but cannot show) that his characters are morally triumphant.

Conrad's moral sense, demanding that his characters act upon their own volition, conflicts with his misogyny. Woman in action, woman as the competitor of man, is insufferable. Thus, Conrad's sympathy for the homeless waif vanishes as soon as she makes a gesture of self-assertion. Marlow's comments on women and Conrad's characterization of Mrs. Fyne in *Chance* both seem to evolve from unconfessed misogynistic feelings. Conrad tries, early in the novel, to convince the reader of Marlow's impartiality: "A woman is not necessarily either a doll or an angel to me. She is a human being, very much like myself." As so often in the later work, Conrad's assertions do not match the evidence, and Marlow's prejudices about women soon become clear:

> As to honour—you know—it's a very fine mediaeval inheritance which women never got hold of. It wasn't theirs. Since it may be laid as a general principle that women always get what they want, we must suppose they didn't want it. In addition they are devoid of decency. I mean masculine decency. Cautiousness too is foreign to them. . . .

> They were all alike, with their supreme interest aroused only by fighting with each other about some man: a lover, a son, a brother.

> Women don't understand the force of a contemplative temperament.

> Compunction! Have you ever seen as much as its shadow?

> It is the man who can and generally does "see himself" pretty well inside and out. Women's self-possession is an outward thing; inwardly they flutter, perhaps because they are, or they feel themselves to be, encaged. All this speaking generally.

Speaking generally indeed! Marlow apparently expects us to believe that, in general, women are dishonorable, indecent, without caution, without compunction; that only a man can engage a woman's "supreme interest"; that most women lack true self-possession and true self-knowledge, but that most men do have these qualities.

In the early period the narrator's ironic generalizations are of vital interest—Marlow's observations upon Jim reveal the whole inner meaning of "heroism." But the veneer of irony does not disguise the flaws in the later Marlow's commentary. The voice that attacks feminine self-assertion in *Chance* has lost much of its power to persuade.

> As to women, they know that the clamour for opportunities for them to become something which they cannot be is as reasonable as if mankind at large started asking for opportunities of winning immortality in this world. . . .

Conrad attempts to dramatize his distrust of feminine self-assertion through the characterization of Mrs. Fyne. Primarily she is a caricature, with her two repeated poses of folded arms and seated immobility, suggesting strength and intransigence. Mrs. Fyne appears first of all as a kind of Carrie Nation, with what Marlow calls a "knock me down" feminist doctrine:

> that no consideration, no delicacy, no tenderness, no scruples should stand in the way of a woman (who by the mere fact of her sex was the predestined victim of conditions created by men's selfish passions, their vices and their abominable tyranny) from taking the shortest cut towards securing for herself the easiest possible existence.

Because of the cruelty of her selfish father, Mrs. Fyne has come to meet the world with a cold detached manner. She is "neutral" toward her children; she makes a slave and a dupe of her husband; and their marriage, of course, produces only daughters. The Fynes are a caricatured middle class family with the "usual unshaded crudity of average people" and the "semi-conscious egoism of all safe, established existences." Unlike most feminists, caricatured or not, Mrs. Fyne (whom Marlow calls "practical") seems to have no specific program, a lack that casts doubt on her authenticity.

Conrad seems particularly to lose control over Mrs. Fyne when he attempts to show her interactions with Flora. Although her major interest in life is caring for downtrodden women, she does not really like Flora. Moreover, although Mrs. Fyne usually favors the woman over the man, and although she has made herself personally responsible for Flora's future welfare, she violently opposes Flora's conquest of Captain Anthony. This is especially strange since Mrs. Fyne does not love her brother and, in fact, has "nothing in common with that sailor, that stranger." We can only guess that Conrad loses control because he has no feeling for Mrs. Fyne as a character and because his own impulse is to oppose the Flora—Anthony marriage, or any marriage. Thus, Mrs. Fyne, whose single-minded feministic attitude should have made her a convincing object of Conrad's irony, is rendered implausible by the very feelings that created her.

The later Conrad's hostility to feminine self-assertion results in the immediate destruction of his women as soon as they embark upon a plan of action. Virtually all the [unsuccessful] scenes with women . . .

are scenes in which the woman acts for herself. Since Rita, Mrs. Travers, and Adèle assert themselves from their first appearance, they are unsuccessful from the first.

The active woman in Conrad seems to move in one of two directions, toward Society or Sex. Conrad intends Rita and Mrs. Travers to be brilliant and sensitive leaders of salons. Presumably he would like them to approach the complex humanity of a Henry James heroine, but most of Conrad's society women seem rather to derive from books of the quality of Bulwer-Lytton's *Pelham*. (This is the novel that old Singleton reads, and the early Conrad calls its sentences "polished and so curiously insincere," its language "elegant verbiage.") Lena and Arlette are swiftly transformed into symbols of sexual power and the life force; Conrad seems to hope that they will achieve the complex humanity of Shakespeare's Cleopatra. But only in Amy Foster and Winnie Verloc does Conrad dramatize successfully sexual force, and in neither characterization does he attempt to be explicit. Rita de Lastaola apparently represents Sex as well as Society; Mills calls her "old Enchantress." The reader is not fooled, however, knowing that one reference to Shakespeare does not make a Cleopatra. Nor does it make a Desdemona. Although Captain Anthony is "swarthy as an African" and Flora "whiter than the lilies," Flora in action convinces us no more of her humanity than do the other Conradian heroines of the later period.

We have seen that the later Conrad's denial of individual guilt and his espousal of repose result in the almost total destruction of the early, profound hierarchy of characters. In the place of faithful seaman and vulnerable hero, we find the untried boy and the impeccable hero. The perceptive hero disappears; the popular-magazine heroine and the unremittingly black villain dominate the scene. The only bright spot in the later characterizations, the handling of Flora and Lena in certain scenes, seems rather the reflection of the early Conrad's sympathy for lonely figures than of any new perception into his characters.

Conrad on the Theory of Fiction

by Ford Madox Ford

Style

We agreed on this axiom:

> The first business of Style is to make work interesting: the second business of Style is to make work interesting: the third business of Style is to make work interesting: the fourth business of Style is to make work interesting: the fifth business of Style. . . .

Style, then, has no other business.

A style interests when it carries the reader along; it is then a good style. A style ceases to interest when by reason of disjointed sentences, over-used words, monotonous or jog-trot cadences, it fatigues the reader's mind. *Too* startling words, however apt, *too* just images, *too* great displays of cleverness are apt in the long run to be as fatiguing as the most over-used words or the most jog-trot cadences. That a face resembles a Dutch clock has been too often said; to say that it resembles a ham is inexact and conveys nothing; to say that it has the mournfulness of an old, squashed-in meat tin, cast away on a waste building lot, would be smart —but too much of that sort of thing would become a nuisance. To say that a face was cramoisy is undesirable; few people nowadays know what the word means. Its employment will make the reader marvel at the user's erudition; in thus marvelling he ceases to consider the story and an impression of vagueness or length is produced on his mind. A succession of impressions of vagueness and length render a book in the end unbearable.

There are, of course, pieces of writing intended to convey the sense of the author's cleverness, knowledge of obsolete words or power of inventing similes: with such exercises Conrad and the writer never concerned themselves.

We used to say, the first lesson that an author has to learn is that of humility. Blessed are the humble because they do not get between the reader's legs. Before everything the author must learn to suppress him-

"Conrad on the Theory of Fiction" (editor's title) by Ford Madox Ford. From *Joseph Conrad: A Personal Remembrance.* (Boston: Little Brown & Co., 1924). Copyright 1924 by Ford Madox Ford. Reprinted by permission of Miss Janice Biala.

self; he must learn that the first thing he has to consider is his story and the last thing that he has to consider is his story, and in between that he will consider his story.

We used to say that a passage of good style began with a fresh, usual word, and continued with fresh, usual words to the end; there was nothing more to it. When we felt that we had really got hold of the reader, with a great deal of caution we would introduce a word not common to a very limited vernacular, but that only very occasionally. Very occasionally indeed; practically never. Yet it is in that way that a language grows and keeps alive. People get tired of hearing the same words over and over again. . . . It is again a matter of compromise.

Our chief masters in style were Flaubert and Maupassant: Flaubert in the greater degree, Maupassant in the less. In about the proportion of a sensible man's whisky and soda. We stood as it were on those hills and thence regarded the world. We remembered long passages of Flaubert; elaborated long passages in his spirit and with his cadences and then translated them into passages of English as simple as the subject under treatment would bear. We remembered short, staccato passages of Maupassant; invented short, staccato passages in his spirit and then translated them into English as simple as the subject would bear. Differing subjects bear differing degrees of simplicity. To apply exactly the same timbre of language to a dreadful interview between a father and a daughter as to the description of a child's bedroom at night is impracticable because it is unnatural. In thinking of the frightful scene with your daughter Millicent which ruined your life, town councillor and parliamentary candidate though you had become, you will find that your mind employs a verbiage quite different from that which occurs when you remember Millicent asleep, her little mouth just slightly opened, her toys beside the shaded night-light.

Our vocabulary, then, was as simple as was practicable. But there are degrees of simplicity. We employed as a rule in writing the language that we employed in talking the one to the other. When we used French in speaking we tried mentally to render in English the least literary equivalent of the phrase. We were, however, apt to employ in our conversation words and periphrases that are not in use by, say, financiers. This was involuntary, we imagining that we talked simply enough. But later a body of younger men with whom the writer spent some years would say, after dinner, "Talk like a book, H. . . . Do talk like a book!" The writer would utter some speeches in the language that he employed when talking with Conrad; but he never could utter more than a sentence or two at a time. The whole mess would roar with laughter and, for some minutes, would render his voice inaudible.

If you will reflect on the language you then employed—and the writer—you will find that it was something like. "Cheerio, old bean. The beastly Adjutant's Parade is at five ack emma. Will you take **my**

Johnnie's and let me get a real good fug in my downy bug-walk? I'm
fair blind to the wide to-night." That was the current language then
and, in the earlier days of our conversations, some equivalent with which
we were unacquainted must normally have prevailed. That we could
hardly have used in our books, since within a very short time such languages become incomprehensible. Even to-day the locution "ack emma"
is no longer used and the expression "blind to the wide" is incomprehensible—the very state is unfamiliar—to more than half the English-
speaking populations of the globe.

So we talked and wrote a Middle-High English of as unaffected a sort
as would express our thoughts. And that was all that there really was
to our "style." Our greatest admiration for a stylist in any language was
given to W. H. Hudson of whom Conrad said that his writing was like
the grass that the good God made to grow and when it was there you
could not tell how it came.

Carefully examined, a good—an interesting—style will be found to
consist in a constant succession of tiny, unobservable surprises. If you
write—"His range of subject was very wide and his conversation very
varied and unusual; he could rouse you with his perorations or lull you
with his periods; therefore his conversation met with great appreciation
and he made several fast friends"—you will not find the world very apt
to be engrossed by what you have set down. The results will be different
if you put it, "He had the power to charm or frighten rudimentary souls
into an aggravated witch-dance; he could also fill the small souls of the
pilgrims with bitter misgivings; he had one devoted friend at least, and
he had conquered one soul in the world that was neither rudimentary
nor tainted with self-seeking."

Or, let us put the matter in another way. The catalogue of an iron-
monger's store is uninteresting as literature because things in it are all
classified and thus obvious; the catalogue of a farm sale is more interesting
because things in it are contrasted. No one would for long read: Nails,
drawn wire, ½ inch, per lb. . . . ; nails, do., ¾ inch, per lb. . . . ;
nails, do., inch, per lb. . . . But it is often not disagreeable to read
desultorily: "*Lot 267,* Pair rabbit gins. *Lot 268,* Antique powder flask.
Lot 269, Malay Kris. *Lot 270,* Set of six sporting prints by Herring.
Lot 271, Silver caudle cup . . ." for that, as far as it goes, has the quality
of surprise.

That is, perhaps, enough about Style. This is not a technical manual,
and at about this point we arrive at a region in which the writer's memory is not absolutely clear as to the points on which he and Conrad were
agreed. We made in addition an infinite number of experiments, together and separately, in points of style and cadence. The writer, as has
been said, wrote one immense book entirely in sentences of not more
than ten syllables. He read the book over. He found it read immensely
long. He went through it all again. He joined short sentences; he in-

troduced relative clauses; he wrote in long sentences that had a gentle sonority and ended with a dying fall. The book read less long. Much less long.

Conrad also made experiments, but not on such a great scale since he could always have the benefit of the writer's performances of that sort. The writer only remembers specifically one instance of an exercise on Conrad's part. He was interested in blank verse at the moment—though he took no interest in English verse as a rule—and the writer happening to observe that whole passages of *Heart of Darkness* were not very far off blank verse, Conrad tried for a short time to run a paragraph into decasyllabic lines. The writer remembers the paragraph quite well. It is the one which begins:

> She walked with measured steps, draped in striped and fringed cloths, treading the earth proudly with a slight jingle and flash of barbarous ornaments. . . .

But he cannot remember what Conrad added or took away. There come back vaguely to him a line or two like:

> She carried high her head, her hair was done
> In the shape of a helmet; she had greaves of brass
> To the knee; gauntlets of brass to th' elbow.
> A crimson spot. . . .

That, however, may just as well be the writer's contrivance as Conrad's: it happened too long ago for the memory to be sure. A little later, the writer occupying himself with writing French rhymed *vers libre,* Conrad tried his hand at that too. He produced:

> *Riez toujours! La vie n'est pas si gaie,*
> *Ces tristes jours quand à travers la haie*
> *Tombe le long rayon*
> *Dernier*
> *De mon soleil qui gagne*
> *Les sommets, la montagne,*
> *De l'horizon.* . . .

There was a line or two more that the writer has forgotten.

That was Conrad's solitary attempt to write verse.

We may as well put the rest of this matter under a separate heading:

Cadence

This was the one subject upon which we never came to any agreement. It was the writer's view that every one has a natural cadence of his own from which in the end he cannot escape. Conrad held that a habit of good cadence could be acquired by the study of models. His own he held

came to him from constant reading of Flaubert. He did himself probably
an injustice.

But questions of cadence and accentuation as of prosody in general
we were chary of discussing. They were matters as to which Conrad was
very touchy. His ear was singularly faulty for one who was a great
writer of elaborated prose so that at times the writer used to wonder
how the deuce he *did* produce his effects of polyphonic closings to paragraphs. In speaking English he had practically no idea of accentuation
whatever, and indeed no particular habits. He would talk of Mr. Cunninghame Graham's book *Success* alternately as "*Success*" and "*Success*"
half a dozen times in the course of a conversation about the works of
that very wonderful writer. Over French he was not much better. He
became quite enraged when told that if the first line of his verse quoted
above was to be regarded as decasyllabic—and it *must* by English people
be regarded as decasyllabic—then the word *vie* must be a monosyllable
in spite of its termination in e. He had in the second line quite correctly allowed for *tristes* as being two syllables, and *tombe* in the third.
In the clash of French verse-theories of those days he might be correct or
incorrect without committing a solecism, but he could not be incorrect
in the first line and formal in the others. Conrad's face would cloud over.
He would snatch up a volume of Racine and read half a dozen lines. He
would exclaim contemptuously, "Do you mean to say that each of those
verses *con*sists of ten syllables?" . . . Yet he would have read the verse
impeccably. . . . He would flush up to the eyes. He would cry, "Did
you ever hear a Frenchman say 'vee-yeh' when he meant 'vee?' You
never did! *Jamais de la vie!*" And with fury he would read his verse
aloud, making, with a slight stammer, *vie* a monosyllable and, with impetus, two syllables each out of *tristes* and *tombe*. He would begin to
gesticulate, his eyes flashing. . . .

One would change the subject of discussion to the unfailing topic of
the rottenness of French as a medium for poetry, finding perfect har-
mony again in the thought that French was as rotten for verse-poetry as
was English for any sort of prose. . . .

The curious thing was that when he read his prose aloud his accentuation was absolutely faultless. So that it always seemed to the writer that
Conrad's marvellous gift of language was, in the end, dramatic. When
he talked his sense of phonetics was dormant, but the moment it came
to any kind of performance the excitement would quicken the brain
centres that governed his articulation. It was, indeed, the same with his
French. When conversing desultorily with the writer, he had much of
the accent and the negligence of an aristocratic, meridional lounger of
the seventies. . . . But when at Lamb House, Rye, he addressed compli-
ments to Mr. Henry James, you could imagine, if you closed your eyes,
that it was the senior actor of the Théâtre Français, addressing an eulo-
gium to the bust of Molière. . . .

Probably the mere thought of reading aloud subconsciously aroused memories of once-heard orations of Mr. Gladstone or John Bright; so, in writing, even to himself he would accentuate and pronounce his words as had done those now long-defunct orators. . . . And it is to be remembered that during all those years the writer wrote every word that he wrote with the idea of reading aloud to Conrad, and that during all those years Conrad wrote what he wrote with the idea of reading it aloud to this writer.

Structure

That gets rid, as far as is necessary in order to give a pretty fair idea of Conrad's methods, of the questions that concern the texture of a book. More official or more learned writers who shall not be novelists shall treat of this author's prose with less lightness—but assuredly too with less love. . . . Questions then of vocabulary, selection of incident, style, cadence and the rest concern themselves with the colour and texture of prose and, since this writer, again, will leave to more suitable pens the profounder appraisements of Conrad's morality, philosophy and the rest, there remains only to say a word or two on the subject of form.

Conrad, then, never wrote a true short story, a matter of two or three pages of minutely considered words, ending with a smack . . . with what the French call a *coup de canon*. His stories were always what for lack of a better phrase one has to call "long-short" stories. For these the form is practically the same as that of the novel. Or, to avoid the implication of saying that there is only one form for the novel, it would be better to put it that the form of long-short stories may vary as much as may the form for novels. The short story of Maupassant, of Tchekhov or even of the late O. Henry is practically stereotyped—the introduction of a character in a word or two, a word or two for atmosphere, a few paragraphs for story, and then, click! a sharp sentence that flashes the illumination of the idea over the whole.

This Conrad—and for the matter of that, the writer—never so much as attempted, either apart or in collaboration. The reason for this lies in all that is behind the mystic word "justification." Before everything a story must convey a sense of inevitability: that which happens in it must seem to be the only thing that could have happened. Of course a character may cry, "If I had then acted differently how different everything would now be." The problem of the author is to make his then action the only action that character could have taken. It must be inevitable, because of his character, because of his ancestry, because of past illness or on account of the gradual coming together of the thousand small circumstances by which Destiny, who is inscrutable and august, will push us into one certain predicament. Let us illustrate:

In rendering your long friendship with, and ultimate bitter hostility towards, your neighbour Mr. Slack, who had a greenhouse painted with Cox's aluminum paint, you will, if you wish to get yourself in with the scrupulousness of a Conrad, have to provide yourself, in the first place, with an ancestry at least as far back as your grandparents. To account for your own stability of character and physical robustness you will have to give yourself two dear old grandparents in a lodge at the gates of a great nobleman: if necessary you will have to give them a brightly polished copper kettle simmering on a spotless hob, with silhouettes on each side of the mantel: in order to account for the lamentable procedure of your daughter Millicent you must provide yourself with an actress or gipsy-grandmother. Or at least with a French one. This grandmother will have lived, unfortunately unmarried, with some one of eloquence— possibly with the great Earl-Prime Minister at whose gates is situated the humble abode of your other grandparents—at any rate she will have lived with some one from whom you will have inherited your eloquence. From her will have descended the artistic gifts to which the reader will owe your admirable autobiographic novel.

If you have any physical weakness, to counterbalance the robustness of your other grandparents, you will provide your mother, shortly before your birth, with an attack of typhoid fever, due to a visit to Venice in company with your father, who was a gentleman's courier in the family in which your mother was a lady's maid. Your father, in order to be a courier, will have had, owing to his illegitimacy, to live abroad in very poor circumstances. The very poor circumstances will illustrate the avarice of his statesman father—an avarice which will have descended to you in the shape of that carefulness in money matters that, reacting on the detrimental tendencies inherited by Millicent from her actress-grand- mother, so lamentably influences your daughter's destiny.

And of course there will have to be a great deal more than that, always supposing you to be as scrupulous as was Conrad in this matter of justifi- cation. For Conrad—and for the matter of that the writer—was never satisfied that he had really and sufficiently got his characters in; he was never convinced that he had convinced the reader; this accounting for the great lengths of some of his books. He never introduced a character, how- ever subsidiary, without providing that character with ancestry and hereditary characteristics, or at least with home surroundings—always supposing that character had any influence on the inevitability of the story. Any policeman who arrested any character must be "justified," because the manner in which he effected the arrest, his mannerisms, his vocabulary and his voice, might have a permanent effect on the psychology of the prisoner. The writer remembers Conrad using almost those very words during the discussion of the plot of *The Secret Agent*.

This method, unless it is very carefully handled, is apt to have the grave defect of holding a story back very considerably. You must as a rule bring the biography of a character in only after you have introduced the character; yet, if you introduce a policeman to make an arrest the rendering of his biography might well retard the action of an exciting point in the story . . . It becomes then your job to arrange that the very arresting of the action is an incitement of interest in the reader, just as, if you serialise a novel, you take care to let the words *"to be continued in our next"* come in at as harrowing a moment as you can contrive.

And of course the introducing of the biography of a character may have the great use of giving contrast to the tone of the rest of the book. . . . Supposing that in your history of your affair with Mr. Slack you think that the note of your orderly middle-class home is growing a little monotonous, it would be very handy if you could discover that Mr. Slack had a secret, dipsomaniacal wife, confined in a country cottage under the care of a rather criminal old couple; with a few pages of biography of that old couple you could give a very pleasant relief to the sameness of your narrative. In that way the sense of reality is procured.

Philosophy, etc.

We agreed that the novel is absolutely the only vehicle for the thought of our day. With the novel you can do anything: you can inquire into every department of life, you can explore every department of the world of thought. The one thing that you can not do is to propagandise, as author, for any cause. You must not, as author, utter any views; above all, you must not fake any events. You must not, however humanitarian you may be, over-elaborate the fear felt by a coursed rabbit.

It is obviously best if you can contrive to be without views at all; your business with the world is rendering, not alteration. You have to render life with such exactitude that more specialised beings than you, learning from you what are the secret needs of humanity, may judge how many white-tiled bathrooms are, or to what extent parliamentary representation is, necessary for the happiness of men and women. If, however, your yearning to amend the human race is so great that you cannot possibly keep your fingers out of the watch-springs there is a device that you can adopt.

Let us suppose that you feel tremendously strong views as to sexual immorality or temperance. You feel that you must express these, yet you know that like, say, M. Anatole France, who is also a propagandist, you are a supreme novelist. You must then invent, justify and set going in your novel a character who can convincingly express your views. If you are a gentleman you will also invent, justify and set going characters to express views opposite to those you hold. . . .

You have reached the climax of your long relationship with Mr. Slack; you are just going to address a deputation that has come to invite you to represent your native city in the legislature of your country. The deputation is just due. Five minutes before it arrives to present you with the proudest emotion of your life, you learn that your daughter Millicent is going to have a child by Mr. Slack. (Him, of course, you will have already "justified" as the likely seducer of a young lady whose cupidity in the matter of bangles and shoes you, by your pecuniary carefulness, have kept perpetually on the stretch.) Mr. Slack has a dipsomaniac wife so there is no chance of his making the mater good. . . .

You thus have an admirable opportunity of expressing with emphasis quite a number of views through the mouth of the character whom you have so carefully "justified" as yourself. Quite a number of views!

That then was, cursorily stated, the technique that we evolved at the Pent. It will be found to be nowadays pretty generally accepted as the normal way of handling the novel. It is founded on common sense and some of its maxims may therefore stand permanently. Or they may not.

Progression d'Effet

There is just one other point. In writing a novel we agreed that every word set on paper—*every* word set on paper—must carry the story forward and that, as the story progressed, the story must be carried forward faster and faster and with more and more intensity. That is called *progression d'effet,* words for which there is no English equivalent.

One might go on to further technicalities, such as how to squeeze the last drop out of a subject. . . . To go deeper into the matter would be to be too technical. Besides enough has been said in this chapter to show you what was the character, the scrupulousness and the common sense of our hero.

There remains to add once more:

But these two writers were not unaware—were not unaware—*that there are other methods of writing novels. They were not rigid even in their own methods. They were sensible to the fact that compromise is at all times necessary to the execution of a work of art.*

The lay reader will be astonished at this repetition and at these italics. They are inserted for the benefit of gentlemen and ladies who comment on books in the Press.

Language

It would be disingenuous to avoid the subject of language. This is the only matter on which the writer ever differed fundamentally from Conrad. It was one upon which the writer felt so deeply that, for several years, he avoided his friend's society. The pain of approaching the question is thus very great.

Conrad's dislike for the English language, then, was, during all the years of our association, extreme, his contempt for his medium unrivalled. Again and again during the writing of, say, "Nostromo" he expressed passionate regret that it was then too late to hope to make a living by writing in French, and as late as 1916 he expressed to the writer an almost equally passionate envy of the writer who was in a position to write in French, propaganda for the government of the French Republic. . . . And Conrad's contempt for English as a prose language was not, as in the writer's case, mitigated by love for English as the language for verse-poetry. For, to the writer, English is as much superior to French in the one particular as French to English in the other.

Conrad, however, knew nothing of, and cared less.for, English verse— and his hatred for English as a prose medium reached such terrible heights that during the writing of *Nostromo* the continual weight of Conrad's depression broke the writer down. We had then published *Romance* and Conrad, breaking, in the interests of that work, his eremitic habits, decided that we ought to show ourselves in Town. The writer therefore took a very large, absurd house on Campden Hill and proceeded to "entertain." Conrad had lodgings also on Campden Hill. At this time *Nostromo* had begun to run as a serial in a very popular journal, and on the placards of that journal Conrad's name appeared on every hoarding in London. This publicity caused Conrad an unbelievable agony, he conceiving himself for ever dishonoured by such vicarious pandering to popularity.

It was the most terrible period of Conrad's life and of the writer's. Conrad at that time considered himself completely unsuccessful; ignored by the public; ill-treated by the critics (he was certainly at that date being treated with unusual stupidity by the critics); he was convinced that he would never make a decent living. And he was convinced that he would never master English. He used to declare that English was a language in which it was impossible to write a direct statement. That was true enough. He used to declare that to make a direct statement in English is like trying to kill a mosquito with a forty-foot stock whip when you have never before handled a stock whip. . . .

The writer was at the time very much harassed. The expense of keeping up a rather portentous establishment made it absolutely necessary that he should add considerably to his income with his pen—a predicament with which he had not yet been faced. There was nothing in that except that it was almost impossible to find time to write. An epidemic of influenza running through the house crippled its domestic staff so that all sorts of household tasks had of necessity to be performed by the writer: there were, in addition, social duties—and the absolute necessity of carrying Conrad every afternoon through a certain quantum of work without which he must miss his weekly instalments in the popular journal. . . .

At an At Home there, amongst eminently decorous people, a well-meaning but unfortunate gentleman congratulated Conrad on the fact that his name appeared on all the hoardings and Conrad considered that these congratulations were ironical gibes at him because his desperate circumstances had forced him to agree to the dishonour of serialisation in a popular journal. . . .

Conrad's indictment of the English language was this, that no English word is a word; that all English words are instruments for exciting blurred emotions. "Oaken" in French means "made of oak wood"—nothing more. "Oaken" in English connotes innumerable moral attributes: it will connote stolidity, resolution, honesty, blond features, relative unbreakableness, absolute unbendableness—also, made of oak. . . . The consequence is that no English word has clean edges: a reader is always, for a fraction of a second, uncertain as to which meaning of the word the writer intends. Thus, all English prose is blurred. Conrad desired to write prose of extreme limpidity. . . .

We may let it go at that. In later years Conrad achieved a certain fluency and a great limpidity of language. He then regretted that for him all the romance of writing was gone—the result being *The Rover,* which strikes the writer as being a very serene and beautiful work. . . . In between the two he made tributes to the glory of the English language, by implication contemning the tongue that Flaubert used. This struck the writer, at that time in a state of exhausted depression, as unforgivable— as the very betrayal of Dain by Tom Lingard. . . . Perhaps it was. If it were Conrad faced the fact in that book. There are predicaments that beset great Adventurers, in dark hours, in the shallows: the overtired nerve will fail. . . . We may well let it go at that. . . .

> *For it would be delightful to catch the echo of the desperate and funny quarrels that enlivened these old days. The pity of it is that there comes a time when* all *the fun of one's life must be looked for in the past.* . . .

Those were Conrad's last words on all the matters of our collaborations here treated of. They were, too, almost his last words. . . . For those who can catch them here, then, are the echoes. . . .

Chronology of Important Dates

1857	Joseph Conrad (Józef Teodor Konrad Naleçz Korzeniowski), only child of Apollo Korzeniowski and Ewelina (Bobrowska) Korzeniowska, born December 3 on an estate managed by his father near Berdichev in the Ukraine.
1861	Father imprisoned by Russian authorities for Polish patriotic activities.
1862	Father, accompanied by wife and 4-year-old son, exiled to northern Russia.
1865	Mother dies.
1869	Father dies. Conrad in care of his maternal uncle, Tadeusz Bobrowski.
1874	Leaves Poland for Marseilles, where he joins French merchant marine.
1877-1878	Involved in smuggling, a love affair, and gambling debts. Attempts suicide February or March 1878.
1878-1894	In British merchant marine. Receives master's certificate 1886. Numerous voyages, chiefly to Far East.
1886	First story, "The Black Mate."
1889	Begins *Almayer's Folly*, completed 1894.
1890	Voyage to the Congo.
1896	Married to Jessie George. "An Outpost of Progress."
1897	*The Nigger of the "Narcissus."*
1899	*Heart of Darkness.*
1900	*Lord Jim.*
1902	*Typhoon*
1904	*Nostromo.*
1906	*The Secret Agent.*
1910	*Under Western Eyes.*
1912	*Chance.*
1914	*Victory.*
1915	*The Shadow Line.*
1922	*The Rover.*
1923	Visit to the United States.
1924	Dies August 3 at Oswalds, Bishopsbourne, near Canterbury. Buried at Canterbury.

Notes on the Editor and Authors

MARVIN MUDRICK (b. 1921), Professor of English at the University of California, Santa Barbara, is the author of *Jane Austen: Irony as Defense and Discovery*.

JOCELYN BAINES (b. 1924), Managing Director of Thomas Nelson & Sons Ltd., Publishers (London), is the author of *Joseph Conrad: A Critical Biography*.

MAX BEERBOHM (1872-1956), essayist, parodist, caricaturist, and wit, is the comic historian of the English 'Nineties.

DANIEL CURLEY (b. 1918), Professor of English at the University of Illinois, is the author of two novels, *How Many Angels?* and *A Stone Man, Yes*, and a collection of stories.

FORD MADOX FORD (1873-1939) is one of the distinguished men of letters of the century: novelist, memoirist, editor of *The English Review*, collaborator with Conrad on two novels, senior associate of the new generation of writers whose publicist was Ezra Pound.

ALBERT GUERARD (b. 1914), Professor of English at Stanford University, is the author of six novels and of critical books on Bridges, Conrad, Hardy, and Gide.

DOUGLAS HEWITT (b. 1920) is the author of *Joseph Conrad: A Reassessment*.

THOMAS MOSER (b. 1923), Professor of English at Stanford University, is the author of *Joseph Conrad: Achievement and Decline*.

STEPHEN A. REID (b. 1925), Assistant Professor of English at San Fernando Valley State College, has published articles on Conrad, Hemingway, and James.

E. M. W. TILLYARD (1889-1962) is the author of *The Epic Strain in the English Novel*, and of books on Milton, Shakespeare, and the English epic.

PAUL L. WILEY (b. 1914), Professor of English at the University of Wisconsin, is the author of *Conrad's Measure of Man* and *Novelist of Three Worlds: Ford Madox Ford*.

MORTON DAUWEN ZABEL (1901-1964), critic and teacher, is the author of *Craft and Character*, and the editor of the Viking *Portable Conrad*.

Selected Bibliography

By Joseph Conrad

WORKS

Uniform Edition of the Works of Joseph Conrad. 22 volumes. London, J. M. Dent and Sons Ltd., 1923-1928.

LETTERS

Curle, Richard, ed., *Conrad to a Friend, 150 Selected Letters from Joseph Conrad to Richard Curle.* New York, 1928.

Garnett, Edward, ed., *Letters from Joseph Conrad, 1895-1924.* Indianapolis, 1928.

Gee, John A. and Sturm, Paul J., trans. and eds., *Letters of Joseph Conrad to Marguerite Poradowska.* New Haven, 1940.

Jean-Aubry, G., ed., *Lettres françaises.* Paris, 1929.

On Joseph Conrad

BIOGRAPHY

Baines, Jocelyn, *Joseph Conrad: A Critical Biography.* New York, McGraw-Hill, 1960.

Conrad, Jessie, *Joseph Conrad and His Circle.* New York, 1935.

Jean-Aubry, G., *Joseph Conrad: Life and Letters.* 2 volumes. New York, 1927.

CRITICISM

In addition to the studies reprinted here *in toto* or in part, the following are of particular interest:

Books

Hay, Eloise Knapp, *The Political Novels of Joseph Conrad.* Chicago, The University of Chicago Press, 1963.

Morf, Gustav, *The Polish Heritage of Joseph Conrad.* London, 1930.

Articles

Leavis, F. R., "Joseph Conrad," in *The Great Tradition*. New York, Anchor Books, 1954.

Milosz, Czeslaw, "Joseph Conrad in Polish Eyes," in *Atlantic Monthly*, CC, No. 5 (1957).

Warren, Robert Penn, "Introduction" to *Nostromo*. New York, Modern Library, 1951.

BIBLIOGRAPHY

Beebe, Maurice, "Criticism of Joseph Conrad: A Selected Checklist with an Index to Studies of Separate Works," *Modern Fiction Studies*, I, No. 1 (February 1955), 30-44.